VICTORIAN
NORTHAMPTONSHIRE:
THE EARLY YEARS

Scene on Daventry Reservoir, February 1838

VICTORIAN NORTHAMPTONSHIRE: THE EARLY YEARS

Eric Jenkins

CORDELIA

Published by and obtainable from
Cordelia
60 Newton Road, Rushden
Northamptonshire NN10 0HQ

ISBN 0 9522 481 07

Typeset, printed and bound by
Stanley L. Hunt (Printers) Ltd
Midland Road, Rushden

Explanation

During over thirty years of teaching history in Northampton-shire, a vast accumulation of source material has grown in my files. It is straining to get out and tell stories. Some of the most important – and the most entertaining – parts of this collection are Victorian.

It was not difficult – though it was time-devouring – to collate and edit the sources, throw out those that were neither enlightening nor entertaining, add explanation to the abstruse and the obscure; and ransack every Northampton newspaper of the period for additional illumination.

The order of presentation is chronological, so that there is a global narrative, but readers seeking special topics such as railways, crime, Chartists or workhouses for example, will find them easily enough.

Newspapers are identified in the text. The other sources are acknowledged in one numerical sequence at the end of the text. Sources not so listed are in my files in original form.

My gratitude is offered to the librarians and archivists who are the guardians of the public collections of source material; and to the many enthusiasts who have sampled my stories, discussed them with me, and shared my enjoyment.

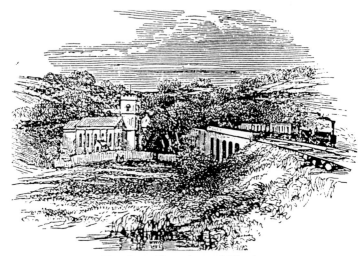

Weedon Church and Viaduct

Northampton Infirmary (1793)

A WEDDING

Drayton is one of the grand mansions of Northamptonshire. In 1837 it belonged to the Duke of Dorset, but he seldom lived there. The estate was managed by his younger brother, George Sackville Germain. George had a twenty-two-year-old daughter, Caroline, and it was her wedding day. She married William Bruce Stopford at the parish church, a mile away at Lowick. Her uncle, the Duke, did not share the pleasure of the other guests. After the ceremony, as they emerged from the church, he put his feelings into words: "I am ashamed, Caroline, at your marrying on the day that his Majesty the King has died."[1]

This was the first day of Victoria's reign.

Blisworth Excavation

St. Edmund's Hospital, Northampton –
(Union Workhouse 1837 by Giles Gilbert Scott)

INTRODUCTION

The Condition of Northamptonshire in 1837

The Victorian period began at 2.12 a.m. on Tuesday, 20th June, 1837. It was a time when Britain was adjusting to many dramatic changes, constitutional, economic and social. Northamptonshire had its own adjustments to make, being greatly affected by change and innovation, not all of it welcomed by the natives as beneficial.

The purpose-built workhouses, required by the amended Poor Law, were nearing completion, and the boards of guardians were considering the staffing, equipping and provisioning of them. The legislation of 1834 had brought to an end the parish relief system. Parishes were now grouped into "unions", each with an elected board of guardians in charge. One of the main intentions was to end the payment of benefits to the poor while they lived at home. Those on the poverty line now awaited with apprehension, the opening of the workhouses.

The landscape in many parts of the county had been transformed beyond recognition by the enclosure of the open fields. This process was well-advanced, ending the old system of agriculture. More than half of the total area of Northamptonshire had already been enclosed by private acts of Parliament.[2] Several landowners had enthusiastically seized this opportunity for using new farming methods. The most influential was the former Whig cabinet minister, Earl Spencer, whose own philosophy of farming could be summed up in his own words, "Practice with Science", which became the motto of the Royal Agricultural Society, of which he was to become foremost among its founders.[3]

On a smaller scale, another experimenter was the Reverend Samuel Smith, Vicar of Lois Weedon, with his land in long, narrow, equal strips of wheat and fallow, side by side, dug by hand, no manure, no fertiliser, but a yield the equal of any of his neighbours.[4]

The condition of labourers on the enclosed land was miserable. Thomas Wallis, interviewed on his 86th birthday

1

in 1904, recalled the work at Rothwell Lodge in 1837. "We used to employ a number of men on my father's farm. They walked four miles to their work before six o'clock in the morning, and that distance back again after six o'clock at night. They were paid about eight or nine shillings per week, and boys were paid threepence or fourpence per day. They used to bring their day's food with them, very often only bread, sometimes bread and an onion. Occasionally a little bit of cheese; but a bit of meat I scarcely saw ever. I used to get up about five o'clock in the morning and boil a kettle of skimmed milk for these men, so that they might have a comfortable bowl of bread and milk before they started work. That was entirely a favour given them by my father. . . ."[5]

Another matter of visual impact upon the landscape was the London and Birmingham Railway Company, literally gouging its pathway through the county. At the areas of major construction, around Kilsby, Blisworth and Roade, the work force was a source of trouble, adding to the local crime rate, and easily aroused into riotous disorder. Frequent accidents at the workings put a strain on medical resources. There were hopes of great benefits to travel and trade; but the inevitable effects on some key aspects of the economy, not least the canal, the turnpike roads, carriers, and the operators of coach services, were easy to foresee.

The great cutting between Roade and Blisworth was a mile and a half long, and the depths up to 54 feet. A million cubic yards of earth, clay and rock were being hacked and blasted out of it. Under it all were beds of loose shale, bearing water that needed constant pumping by steam engines. Eight hundred men and boys were at work there.[6]

Further north, the Kilsby tunnel project was in great trouble. The initial trial borings had failed to detect a vast hidden area of quick-sand. Once the tunnelling had started, the water in the quicksand became a major problem. On one occasion after snow, the works were inundated. At this site, two successive contractors-in-charge had suffered fatal heart attacks, and Robert Stephenson himself had taken over the superintendence of the operation. 1,250 men, 200 horses and thirteen steam engines were at work there. Night and day, 1,800 gallons of water per minute were being steam-pumped out of the quicksand.[7]

The first uniformed policemen in Northamptonshire had gone on duty in the county town in 1836. The first police station was in Derngate, nearly opposite Hazelwood Road. The Superintendent, Joseph Ball, had living accommodation on the ground floor, a few feet away from the room used for the retention of prisoners. "A tenant" lived on the upper floor. Ball was paid thirty shillings a week [£1.50] plus coal and candle allowance. The other officers were described as night constables. They received fifteen shillings a week for six months, and twelve shillings a week for the other six months when the nights were shorter. They did no day-time duty, even though twenty-four hour policing had been requested of the Watch Committee by the Borough Council. In 1837 day-time duty commenced, but only on Market days and Fair days.[8]

There was no county police force. Parishes continued to appoint their own constables, as they had done for centuries.

At this time when public services and utilities were being developed, the name of James Sharp came to the fore. He was a Northampton watchmaker, of Mercer's Row, and while retaining that trade, he had become assistant manager to his namesake Thomas Sharp at the Northampton Gas-light Company. The number of street lamps was rapidly increasing, and house-holders were being encouraged to use domestic gas-lighting equipment designed by James Sharp at his shop.[9] In 1836, having successfully experimented with gas-cooking, he had begun to manufacture his own design of cooker – the world's first.[9]

Northampton was about to have the benefits of mains water. The Water Company had a steam engine on a plot between the Infirmary and St. Andrew's Asylum, which would force water to a reservoir constructed on an elevated site on the Mounts.[10]

The same James Sharp was advising, and providing the labour for the laying of the mains pipes under the town's streets. Public baths were under construction at Albion Place.

Hospital accommodation was expanding at the County Infirmary. The number of beds was now over a hundred.[11]

The remarkable James Sharp was involved in this service, too, advising on, and manufacturing surgical and optical instruments, and an adjustable bed for spinal cases.[9] The treatment of mental patients would soon be started at a newly-built asylum.

It is likely that the trades followed by most individuals in Northamptonshire were those contributing to the production of textiles. Hundreds of females made lace. A glance into contemporary directories would show that the number of shoe manufacturers in Northampton exceeded those of butchers, and of bakers, but only just.

The longest-lasting shoe firm (no pun intended) was newly-established (1836). This was Thomas Bostock's Northampton concern, which became the Lotus Company in 1919.[12] Mechanisation was two decades in the future. Outworkers collected the leather and returned the handsewn shoes. Thomas Wright describes Bostock's shoemakers bringing in their boots in boxes on wheels drawn by dogs, six in hand, racing the stage coaches with their dog carts downhill on the London Road.[12]

Peterborough and the Soke were part of the County of Northampton, as was the St. Martin's parish of the town of Stamford, with Burghley House and park. Events in these places are part of Northamptonshire history, and this will be recognised in the following pages.

It is not easy to imagine the county's administration without a County Council and District Councils, but there were no state schools, no health laws to enforce, and no council housing. Northampton had an elected Borough Council (1836). The affairs of the rest of the county were governed by justices of the peace sitting in Quarter Sessions. Vestry meetings determined minor matters in the villages.

Two rival weekly newspapers recorded and commented on events in the county. They were printed within a few feet of each other on the Market Square in Northampton. The *Northampton Mercury* was owned by T. E. Dicey, and edited by George James de Wilde. It presented the prominent news from Northamptonshire and adjoining counties. It carried London news and notable items from the rest of Britain, extracted from other papers. Parliament was well covered, and there was foreign and imperial news. Meetings of professional, religious and political organisations were reported, sometimes verbatim. Letters to the editor were printed uncut. The births, marriages and deaths of gentlefolk were listed; and so were stock market prices. There were advertisements of property, patent medicines, publications, horses to cover, private education (between term), businesses, livestock and timber.

The *Northampton Herald* had been brought into existence in 1831 by a syndicate of county Tories "to counteract the democratical and licentious principles which are industriously propagated in certain metropolitan and provincial journals and tend to subvert the order of society and bring ruin on the most ancient and valuable institutions of this kingdom".[13] Although he was not the editor, the rector of Farthinghoe, the Reverend Francis Litchfield, was the voice of the *Herald*, eloquent, hard-hitting, obsessive, manipulative of the facts.

Let us now travel through Northamptonshire and take a chronological selection of the stories of 1837 from a variety of sources. We shall uncover many different topics – events, problems, controversies, crimes, accidents, and quirks of human behaviour. There is no pattern other than the order of time. It would be possible, by selection, to produce several other different books: *The Coming of the Railway to Northamptonshire; Victorian Crime; Early Victorian Northampton; Curiosities of Victorian Northamptonshire.* This is all of them in one. In compilation the intention has been to inform and entertain, with faithful observance of the self-imposed criteria: "This item may be included if it is important; or if it exemplifies contemporary trends or attitudes; or if it is funny, horrific, surprising, or otherwise stirs the emotions."

Most of the people in the stories are not ordinary inhabitants of the county. The decent, law-abiding, industrious people of any period are rarely noticed by history. We must remember that they were there, but give our attention to the untypical and surprising characters who entertain us with their colourful activities. Do not resist them, because they tell us more than the silent majority of what was happening in 1837.

District Council Offices, Thrapston (1836 Workhouse)

Isebrook Hospital, Wellingborough —
1837 Union Workhouse block

6th January 1837

RUSHDEN

At the Baptist Sunday School, Samuel Summerly, who was both a tailor and a dairyman, was relinquishing his appointment as Superintendent. Some of the hundred and forty children called him "The Foreman". He was a figure of awe "on account of the freedom with which he wielded his pointer".[14] Two of Mr. Summerly's habits were recalled by former scholars. "He was wont to hold up his own boyhood as a pattern worthy of all imitation, and this lapse into egotism, too frequently repeated, excited feelings of revolt amongst the boys. They regarded their Superintendent as a prejudiced witness in the case...."[14] It was also his practice to add misleading false endings to the closing prayer, and some of the boys, hearing "henceforth and for ever, world without end" assumed that the final "Amen" was imminent, and made a dash for the door. They were always brought back to their seats, "the end far out of sight".[15]

Two Superintendents were appointed at the teachers' meeting on Friday 6th January, Alfred Manning and John Corby; and two brothers, William and John Radburne were appointed Secretary and Treasurer respectively.[16] William Radburne had invented a method of punishment for unruly boys and girls. A card bearing the words "BAD BEHAVIOUR" printed in large capitals was hung round the offender's neck, and "the wearer of it was compelled to mount the table in front of the pulpit, and thus in all likelihood face the adult congregation who were assembling for the public service to follow". At least one boy is known to have buttoned his jacket over it.[16]

The two Radburnes were the sons of a Rushden draper and lace dealer. On transferring his business to new premises further along the same street, he announced to his customers that he was "removing nearer to London".[17]

6th January 1837

THE SAME DAY AT THE KILSBY TUNNEL

A second village has sprung up at Kilsby. It was a shanty town, standing on the ridge over the tunnel workings, housing hundreds of labourers and camp followers. The real village of Kilsby itself housed many of the workers. In several houses there were sixteen lodgers *per room*. "There were four beds in each apartment, two navvies were constantly in each; the two squads of eight men as alternately changing places with each other in their beds as in their work."[7] The two settlements housed not only the workers, but also "suttlers and victuallers", a good number of wives and children, and also "tally-wives" (the description of a relationship difficult to explain in 1837). Many of the navvies also kept dogs, some of which were bought and sold within the camp for any price up to £10 each.[7]

The engineer in charge, and assistant to Robert Stephenson himself, was Charles Lean. During the previous month, December 1836, he had reported a lowering of seven inches in the water level of the quicksand. On 6th January, he sat writing his first report of 1837. It was addressed to Captain Moorsom at the railway's main office at St. John's Wood, London.

"Dear Sir,
I am glad to be able to report that the first length under the quicksand in No. 1 shaft was keyed this morning at 5 o'clock. As this is a very important length, I write in purpose to let you know it is completed.
Chas. Lean."[18]

An unforeseen inconvenience resulted from this engineering success. The wells of Kilsby, within four years, ran dry. Domestic brewing came to a halt. A maltster went out of business, and there was great fear of the consequences of any outbreak of fire. Appeals to the railway company for help were ignored.[19]

10th January 1837

IN DEENETHORPE WOOD

Late on Monday 9th January, fifteen of the Earl of Cardigan's keepers went into the wood, a mile from Deene Park, and prepared an ambush for a gang of poachers from Sudborough. What happened was reported in the *Lincolnshire Chronicle* on 14th January. Sudborough was described as "a notorious harbour" for poachers. The keepers "discovered a strong gang of poachers laying snares ...". They counted twenty-five men thus engaged. The instant the "ruffians" saw they were discovered they commenced a ferocious attack on the keepers, with bludgeons, long poles, and other weapons, "beating them dreadfully". The keepers defended themselves with spirit, according to this account which obviously came from one of them. "At length the keepers got the better of their ruffianly assailants, securing three of them, together with 18 dozen of snared rabbits, and 600 yards of netting, used by the poachers to take partridges and pheasants. On Tuesday morning the body of one of the poachers was found lying dead in a field, about 80 yards from the scene of the conflict. On the examination of the corpse, no wound or contusion was discovered that would account for this fatal result."

The same paragraph reported the inquest on the dead poacher. He was identified as William Mays, of Sudborough, whose brother worked for the landowner, Lord Cardigan, as a "carrier to London". The surgeon who carried out the post mortem examination gave "over-exertion" as the cause of death, and the verdict was "Found Dead". The inquest was held on the following day, Wednesday, and on the same day, the three prisoners went before magistrates at Kettering, and were committed to the county gaol for trial at the next assizes. The *Lincolnshire Chronicle* account (actually printed in Northamptonshire at Stamford Baron) concludes with more from the keepers, "who used the greatest forbearance in this unequal conflict". They were "dreadfully injured". One of them had his hand "crushed to pieces" needing instant amputation.

The case was heard on the second day of Northampton-shire Lent Assizes, 1st March. John Newton, 40, Samuel Swann, 25, and Robert Lee, 40, pleaded not guilty to the charge of having entered certain lands in the parish of Deene Thorpe, for the destruction of game and rabbits. Compare the press account above with the evidence given by Charles Bushnell:

"I am a gamekeeper on Lord Cardigan's property, at Deene Thorpe. On the night of the 9th of January last, I went with fourteen assistants to Burnt Coppice, and stationed them in three different positions, two men on one side, two on the other, and the remainder in the middle of the cover. About one o'clock in the morning, we went into a field called the Home Close, and there we saw Lee and Swann standing beside some nets. I went up to them with James Sanders. Swann immediately struck Sanders with a long staff. Lee also struck at Sanders, but Sanders parried the blow. Sanders drove Lee into the hedge dividing the Home Close from a field called the Slade, and secured him. Meantime, a keeper named Barrett had come up and secured Swann. I got over the stile into the Slade, and saw a number of men there, standing together. I waited for my party and then we advanced towards the men. One of them struck me violently across the shoulder and knocked me down. The fight lasted about half an hour, and ended with all the men running away. I had previously called on them to surrender, but they answered that they would not. Nor would they leave a man or a net on the ground. We followed, and a keeper named James Wells overtook Newton and secured him. We returned to the Slade and found 600 yards of rabbit netting. There were about three dozen rabbits in the nets. Altogether there were fifteen dozen rabbits and one hare."

The judge: What weapons did they use to fight with?

Bushnell: They fought with bludgeons.

The three poachers were found guilty, and sentenced to one year in prison, with hard labour.

The well-known ballad *Sudborough Heroes* gives a third version of this incident, from the point of view of the poachers. The dead man, Mays, is named as Sam not William, and described as "a poacher by day and night".

Well-refreshed with "nut brown ale", the poachers marched along with a strong net. One of the keepers, called "Shiner", had a gun with a bayonet. "John Millow" was seen there. (This was Milley, the Earl of Winchelsea's gamekeeper from the Kirby Hall estate. In the following December he was the instigator of another concerted action against poachers at Corby.) The song says that Mays was stabbed through the heart, that no one answered his cry for help, and as he lay there "till break of day" the dogs licked his blood. Lee, Swann and Newton "nobly stood their ground", and Lee "received a dreadful wound" from the staves and spears carried by the keepers.[20]

In 1982, F. J. Mayes commented on the same sources, inferring that the poachers believed that the keepers were armed with spears or similar weapons, and that despite the inquest verdict, Mays had been killed by a keeper.[21]

8th February 1837

ON THE RAILWAY

George Abbey, the County Coroner, was no stranger to Kilsby. On this Wednesday morning he arrived there to conduct an inquest on view of the body of Joseph Deacon, aged 21 years, who had been killed at the bottom of one of the shafts in the tunnel, when a brick fell on him from a skip which was being lowered. The brick penetrated the soft hat of the deceased, and fractured his skull. The verdict was death by accident.

On the afternoon of the same day, the Coroner travelled southwards up the line, using the Watling Street, parallel to the railway to Flore. There he presided over another inquest, on another railway labourer. William Rogers was 34. He had been employed in undermining earth at the other tunnel working, at Stow. Suddenly a great quantity of the overburden gave way and fell on him, killing him instantly. The verdict was accidental death.[22]

11th February 1837

COURT OF KING'S BENCH, LONDON

George Payne, of Sulby Hall, was the Master of the Pytchley Hunt. "He was Northamptonshire born and bred, young, handsome, and still rich . . . and he possessed above most that greatest of gifts, charm."[23]

"The very handsomest man I ever saw . . ." wrote Uncle Scribbler, in the *Huntsman*.[24] "His dress was perfection; utterly free from the smallest taint of dandyism. . . . His well curled black side whiskers matched his short curled hair. . . . From top to toe, he was . . . the perfect model of an English gentleman. His face was clear and open, his eyes were grey, with dark lashes, expressive . . . of excitement [or] of purest good nature. . . ." He was popular with "all sorts and conditions of men, and women, and children – by his genial bearing – his generous spirit – his refined gaiety – his quaint sayings – the twinkle of his eye – his imperturbable countenance – his black and white linen cravat (the Payne tartan) . . .".[25]

George Payne was also an inveterate gambler. After an argument among the members of Graham's Club, Lord de Ros received a letter from George Payne, J. Cumming, Brook Greville and Lord Henry Bentinck, dated 2nd December 1836, inviting him to take action against one of them. He did that. The action for libel, De Ros v Cumming was heard in February 1837. On the first day, a succession of witnesses for the prosecution appeared to absolve De Ros of "unfair play". On the second day, Saturday 11th February, George Payne was a witness for the defence.

The evidence of one of the waiters describes the part played by Payne in the events that brought him to Court.

James Turner: I am a waiter at Graham's Club. On the 2nd of July last year, Mr. Payne, Lord Bentinck and Lord De Ros were playing whist, but I have no recollection of the name of the fourth gentleman. Mr. Payne called for fresh cards. He selected a card from out of the pack which had been played with, and held it up to the candle. It was the ace of clubs. . . . Mr. Payne appeared angry, and threw the card down on the table violently. I removed the packs, including the ace of clubs. Mr. Payne told me to take care of the cards – he would have them saved. I afterwards examined the cards. . . . Several of them were marked. Mr. Payne afterwards gave directions at the bar to have the cards tied up. . . .

Attorney General (for the plaintiff): Did you see any one throw down the cards and say "Bring on fresh cards?"

Turner: I did not see that.

It was now George Payne's turn to enter the witness box.

George Payne: I live at Sulby Hall, in Northamptonshire. I was a member of Graham's last year. I received a communication from Mr. Greville, about the 21st of June, respecting Lord De Ros. I continued to play with his Lordship after that, and observed a particular mode of dealing the cards. On one occasion, I observed the under card come to me, instead of the top one. When they were cut, he would draw the cards into his lap, and I have seen the card which was at the bottom when they were given to me to cut, turned up. He generally used to cough when dealing, but not at other times. I have seen him turn up the ace of clubs and king of diamonds. I communicated what I had seen to Colonel Anson and Mr. Greville. I played afterwards with Colonel Anson for a partner, and observed the same movement. We had no ace in our hands. I selected two aces from the pack, threw them down, with some violence on the table, said "Damn the cards" and ordered some fresh ones. I went to the bar, and gave directions for the old ones to be kept. I afterwards received the cards from one of the waiters. Some of the cards were slightly marked. I did not mark them.

Payne cross-examined: I have not engaged to contribute to the expense of the action, and I have not interfered with the defence. Mr. Cumming is to bear the whole expense, as far as I know. In the early part of my career, I was unfortunate at play, and lost a considerable sum of money. My ill luck has continued throughout. During the last two years it has not been so bad. I have been a good deal connected with the racecourse. I have played several times with Lord De Ros since witnessing what I stated. I may have betted with him, but not unless it was a standing bet. After the cards were removed, I played two rubbers with Lord De Ros as my partner, and lost them. I did not win a rubber with him. I cannot swear that I have not betted with Lord Bentinck or Lord De Ros. I have kept a private bank at hazard.

The verdict went to the defendant, Mr. Cumming.

21st February 1837

HOUSE OF LORDS, WESTMINSTER

Church rates, chargeable by the Anglican Church, caused much resentment in Northamptonshire where there were many Baptist and Methodist communities. Churchwardens had the right to request a vestry meeting to authorise the financing of any project by imposing a rate. These Church rates were not repealed for another twelve years.

On Tuesday 21st February, in the House of Lords, Earl Fitzwilliam presented petitions against Church rates, from Northampton and other places. The noble Earl stated that he did not entirely concur in the prayer of the petitioners. It was not unnatural that those who dissented from the Church should conceive that they ought to be relieved from the payment of these rates. . . . "If there is any place where the Dissenters outnumber the members of the Church of England, it is a certain town in the county of Northampton. . . ."

An account of these proceedings is given in the *Northampton Mercury* of 25th February 1837, on page 2. Those who speculate as to which town Earl Fitzwilliam was alluding to will realise that more than one would fit. On the next day, the Earl presented another petition from Peterborough, for the total and unconditional abolition of Church rates.

26th February 1837

GUILSBOROUGH CHURCHYARD

The burials register tells us that William Cave of Nortoft, aged 24, was buried at midnight, having died of virulent smallpox.

1st March 1837

AT THE INFIRMARY

On this Wednesday morning, a labourer, Thomas Amos, from the Kilsby tunnel, died of a compound fracture of the skull. He had been brought in the previous day. Some bricks had fallen on his head. Another labourer, Samuel Thompson, was brought in from the tunnel with a fractured leg. A third man, James Ringrose, from the railway workings at Roade, was also brought to the Infirmary, this day, with a fracture of the leg.[26]

Later in the month, the Infirmary Management Committee convened a Special Court to take into consideration the question of dealing with railway accidents. This Court ordered "That the contractors or managers of the Railroad within reach of Northampton be informed, that in consequence of the great number of patients in the Infirmary, it is impossible that any more cases of simple fracture can be received into the House. Compound fracture, or such other cases only as are attended with danger can be admitted."[27 and 28]

THE SAME DAY AT NORTHAMPTONSHIRE LENT ASSIZES

On the day that the Sudborough poachers were before the Court, a Raunds shoemaker's case was heard. George Morris, 27, was charged with breaking into the dwelling-house of William Finedon, at Raunds, and stealing therefrom one pair of button boots, made up; and the tops of one other pair, and one pair of low shoes.

William Finedon: I live at Raunds, and work for Mr. William Nicholls, a shoemaker. I went to bed about nine o'clock, on the 26th of August last. During the night, I heard a noise, and I went downstairs. I found that a pane of glass had been taken out, and some unfinished boots had been stolen. I saw some tops afterwards at Morris's house.

Mr. Miller (defending): Are you sure you fastened the windows before retiring?

Finedon: The window was fastened by a man named Hazeldine, who works at my house. John Hazeldine went with me to the prisoner's house, and found the boot-tops in a seat drawer.

The jury found George Morris not guilty of this charge, but he was not free to go. He was again put to the bar, charged with stealing men's and boys' shoes, and other items from the shop of *John* Finedon at Raunds.

John Finedon: I am a shoemaker . . . I locked up my workshop on the 8th of July last year, about nine o'clock at night. On going to my shop the next morning, I found that the door had been broken open, and several men's and boys' shoes had been stolen. They were the property of Mr. Owen Parker. I went with Hazeldine and William Finedon to the house of the prisoner, Morris, on the 5th of September, and found several of the shoes I had lost.

R. Marchant: I am the parish constable. I searched for the prisoner, and advertised for him. The warrant was issued on the 14th of September, and an active search was made for him, but he was not taken until the 25th. A reward of £10 was offered for his apprehension.

Charles Coleman: I saw Morris running away when the constable and the Finedons were going to search the house.

The jury found Morris guilty of this charge, and he was sentenced to be transported for life.

2nd March 1837

WELLINGBOROUGH

"PUBLIC HOUSE AND LAND
In WELLINGBOROUGH
TO BE LET BY AUCTION,

BY MR. CLEAVER

At the Town Hall, in Wellingborough . . . on Thursday the second day of March, 1837, precisely at Ten o'Clock in the Morning in one lot. The following part of the TOWN LANDS and TENEMENTS belonging to and situate in the Parish of WELLINGBOROUGH aforesaid, viz:

ALL that old-established and good-accustomed PUBLIC HOUSE, now in full Trade, known by the Sign of the SOW AND PIGS, in the East End, in the occupation of Mrs. Lucy Palmer, with the Butcher's Shop, Pig Yard, Styes, Barn,

Stables, Yard, Garden and Appurtenances to the same belonging; and A CLOSE of Remarkably rich old Pasture Land, being the East Part of the Close called Rowledge's Close, containing by Statute Measure (exclusive of the Fences), 4A, 3R, 20P, also in the occupation of the said Lucy Palmer.

Possession may be had at Lady Day next. . . ."

(*Northampton Mercury* 18th February 1837, page 1. The area measurements are Acres, Rods and Perches.)

More of the Town property was to be offered for sale or rent in July and October. There was a reason for this. The Poor Law Union had been given a substantial loan from the Exchequer to finance the building and establishment of the new workhouse. The constituent parishes, including Wellingborough itself, were required to contribute towards the repayment.

We have descriptions of the appearance of parts of Wellingborough at this time, in John Cole's *History and Antiquities of Wellingborough*, which was published in the town, this year, by C. M. Darby. A familiar feature of modern Wellingborough is considerably less familiar in Cole's 1837 description of the Swanspool brook. From Croyland grounds "it pursues its deviously wild meandering course along the meadows, in the most picturesque and grotesque windings that can possibly be imagined, and is occasionally overhung by varieties of trees and shrubs. . . . In some places appears the nest of the eel, who, as occasion serves, peeps forth from his retreat in search of food. In an elevated field, not far from Croyland, one of the finest little natural cascades that can be imagined, rolls down the hill with its gurgling, harmonious tones, pleasing the eye with the silvery effect of its water, and the ear with its bubbling melody, until it falls into the rivulet at its foot, near the roots of the flourishing ash. . .".[29]

John Cole also described a piece of Wellingborough landscape which by 1870 had been completely transformed. This was the land adjoining Swanspool House. Cole does not use this name: he calls it simply the residence of Charles Hill.[30] "The house is completely screened from the town by trees and walled enclosures, which form a compact and secluded domain; possessing, within its boundaries, many trees of luxuriant growth.... The ground of the park, too, is agreeably diversified by different undulations on its surface sloping to glades of verdure. . . . On the boundary of the principal portions of the park are several inviting gravelled walks, shaded by venerable trees. . . . These walks are shaded by trees of a general admixture and of varied foliage. . . . A peculiar charm is thrown over this little demesne, through the facility with which every portion of the gardens and out-buildings may be approached, without wandering many yards from the house, or out of the regular gravelled path which surrounds the chief part of the grounds; the pinery, the green-house, the flower and the kitchen-gardens form, as it were, a border to the lawn, and mingle and contrast their own cultivated beauties with those of the more exuberant and wildly-spreading productions of the park."

Inside the house, Cole admired the pictures and books, and was particularly intrigued by a skull, bearing the inscription: "Head, picked up by the owner on the field of Waterloo, on the left of the French position. August 1818."

4th March 1837

NORTHAMPTON

The *Northampton Mercury* of 4th March carried two curiosities from the county town. A net-maker had his advertisement on page 3.

> "CHARLES AGER
> (son of the late John Ager)
> HAIR CUTTER & NET MANUFACTURER
> NEXT DOOR TO THE PEACOCK INN.
> Market Square, Northampton.

RESPECTFULLY returns thanks to his friends for the very extensive patronage shown to his late father in the net trade, and begs to assure them that nothing shall be wanting on his part to maintain the superior character of the nets hitherto manufactured on his premises.

C. AGER, having advantages possessed by few other persons, is determined not to be undersold by any in the trade, and invites public inspection to his Cast Nets, Trammels, Flews, Minnow Nets, Thief Nets, Hay Nets, Purse Nets, and every other kind of Net manufactured.

DRAGS made on the shortest notice, and all descriptions of Nets made to order.

FOR READY MONEY ONLY."

The other curious item was an equine tracheotomy. "This very interesting operation was successfully performed, a few days since by Mr. Waters, veterinary surgeon, of this town, on a valuable grey horse, the property of Mr. F. Mulliner. The animal was afflicted with an abscess in the throat, which obstructed the respiration, and threatened suffocation. The trachea was divided below the abscess, and a metal tube inserted, through which the animal breathed for several days. Meantime, the irritation being thus removed from the diseased part, the abscess suppurated and discharged, and the animal is now in a state of recovery. It was evident that the only means of saving the horse's life was by cutting his throat."

11th March 1837

A MILL TO LET AT TOWCESTER

"TO BE LET
And entered upon at Lady Day,
A very superior WATER-CORN MILL, working four pair of stones, situate at TOWCESTER . . . now in full trade, and most eligibly situated for markets. For further particulars, apply . . . to Mr Perkins, Towcester, or Mr. Tatam, the present tenant."

(*Northampton Mercury* 11th March 1837, page 2.)

14th March 1837

ESCAPE FROM CUSTODY AT PIDDINGTON

There are echoes of Hue and Cry in this case, heard at Quarter Sessions on Friday the 5th of January 1838. It was medieaval common law that anyone within earshot of the scene of a crime was required to assist in detaining the culprit.

The parish constables of Piddington, having arrested a dangerous criminal, would need a warrant from the nearest magistrate to lodge him in the County Gaol to await trial. The most convenient magistrate was Mr. Bouverie at Delapre, on their direct route into Northampton. The constables were greatly displeased with a bystander named Campion, who failed to help them when their prisoner escaped. Campion was indicted for refusing to assist Daniel Westley, a constable, in the execution of his duty. The Court heard the constable's version of the event.

> Westley: I am the constable at Piddington. On the 14th of March last year, I and another man were bringing a prisoner named Ash down to Mr. Bouverie's when the prisoner tried to escape. I called upon Campion to assist. Another man was present, named Weston, and another constable named Whiting. Ash was very violent, and got upon a stone heap, and pelted us. Weston had his teeth knocked out. Ash also drew a knife, and ripped up my waistcoat. Campion stood by, smoking his pipe, with his hands in his pockets.

> Benjamin Whiting: I am a constable at Piddington . . . I gave Campion Ash's arm, while I got out the handcuffs. He took the arm, but while my head was turned, he let go the arm, and Ash got his knife out and struck at Westley. Ash then got away, and Campion did not attempt to stop him. After Ash had gone, he offered to help.

Campion denied that he had refused to help. "I did help to the utmost of my power." He called a witness. This was a labourer who had been at work on the road, nearby, who said that Campion had done his best. The jury's verdict: not guilty.

17th March 1837

BOOTS FROM NORTHAMPTON FOR
QUEEN ADELAIDE

"REMARKABLY CHEAP
LADIES' & GENTLEMEN'S BOOTS & SHOES
AT
W. DUCKETT'S SHOE WAREHOUSE,
MARKET-SQUARE, NORTHAMPTON

W.D. returns his sincerest thanks to his Friends and the Public in general, for the very liberal support he has hitherto received and begs to inform them that he has REMOVED to more eligible Premises, FIVE DOORS HIGHER UP, and that he has, Manufactured, a large and fashionable ASSORTMENT of SHOES and BOOTS, of every description, superior in shape and quality, and well suited to the approaching season, which he is determined to sell for READY MONEY, at such low prices as must ensure him general patronage and support.

W. D. likewise begs to call their attention to a newly-invented Boot, called
"THE QUEEN BOOT".

It has lately been presented to her Majesty, and has received her particular sanction. It is made without a seam, and combines ease and elegance, surpassing any other boot ever invented.

Market Square, Northampton, March 17th, 1837."

(*Northampton Mercury* 25th March 1837, page 3.)

27th March 1837

EASTER MONDAY AT PETERBOROUGH

Andrew Percival was the son of a Northampton doctor. He had come to Peterborough in 1833. Writing in 1905,[31] he recalled two large breweries that stood where Queen Street and North Street were later built. By the end of the century, Buckle's Brewery and Squires' Brewery had completely disappeared, which surprised him because of their great size. "Buckle's Brewery was certainly a remarkable one, and carried on with great energy and spirit." On Easter Monday the partners and their friends assembled to spend the afternoon playing at marbles. The party was refreshed from two large containers of beer. Percival was not sure whether they were tuns or barrels. One was called "Mrs. Clarke" and the other "The Duke of York". This application of names was to perpetuate a scandal of the time of the construction of those vessels. (Earlier in the century, the Duke had relinquished command of the Army over his relationship with Mary Anne Clarke.)

Percival described other features of the Peterborough of the 1830s. The old Town Bridge over the Nene was made of timber, and "there was always a fear that it would fall, and everybody thought it ought to fall, but it did not . . .". The river was "very necessary to the comfort of the town". Grain and timber and other goods were carried in lighters from Wisbech. "We derived our whole coal supply from the river." Passengers and light goods travelled on Simpson's Packet and another vessel belonging to James and Thomas Hill. The captain of the former was a "wooden legged" retired admiral of the Royal Navy.

"Peterborough was one of the last places in which sedan chairs flourished. They went on until some time after the railways were established."

Another peculiarity was the pavement toll. "The town . . . was confined by toll-bars." There were the usual toll-gates on the turnpike roads out of the city, but within the city were several other smaller gates and bars where a toll was charged for using the pavement. Outsiders paid, but inhabitants paid only on Sundays, or if they used a hired vehicle. "If you were an inhabitant of the place, and had the luck to keep your own carriage or gig or waggon . . . you might use the pavement as much as you pleased, and pay nothing. But if you were a poor person, or could only treat yourself occasionally with the luxury of a gig, or were obliged to hire a trap for business, you were immediately taken toll of. . . ." By pavement, of course,

Percival meant the paved streets, as distinct from those streets which were still "mud".

1st April 1837

A LETTER FROM OHIO

It cost £50 to send James Tagg of Kettering, with his wife and eight children, to America. A subscription raised by George Gill and Robert Wallis brought in £25, and the Board of Guardians paid the other £25 out of the Poor's Rate. This family could have cost the ratepayers much more than that over the years, if they had remained in Kettering.

> "Roots Town, Ohio.
> 1st April 1837.

"To Messrs. Wallis & Gill.
Kind Gentlemen,
   According to your request when I left England, I write to inform you of my journey and prospects in this country.
   We set sail from Liverpool on the 13th August last, we had a fine morning, and went out very majestic we had a safe passage, and should have enjoyed it much, only we were very sea sick, and afterwards very unwell, but I believe the voyage has done us all good, as we have had good health since we arrived.
   We were six weeks and three days on our voyage to New York, we staid but two days, determining to persevere up the country, but we should never have accomplished the distance of near eight hundred miles, had we not have met with friends. My brother (whom I had not seen for twenty eight years) lent me 20 dollars, and William Norwich [sent out by subscription in 1835] 10 dollars, there is a combination of the Canal Companies, that I could not have got here without their assistance. . . . We came near six hundred miles up the canals, and then crossed Lake Erie. . . .

My eldest son [17] is at his trade as a blacksmith, and can get from six to eight dollars per week, and his board.

I have let my two youngest sons, John and Joseph [11 and 10] for twelve months, for 15 dollars, clothing, lodging and washing. They are to have three to four months schooling in the year, their employers are steady, serious, pious men – methodists.

My twins [14] are at New York with my brother, he would make me leave some of my children with him, they earn already two dollars each per week, with which they pay for their board and lodging . . . but I shall be obliged to send for one of them this spring, as I have no one to assist me. . . . I have now such a prospect for my children which I never could have had in England, though I love her still. . . .

I am

Yours in due respect

J. TAGG."

George Gill sent this letter in to the *Northampton Mercury*, and it was published on 10th June (page 4).

? April 1837

KETTERING'S FIRST TEMPERANCE MEETING

Thomas Whittaker, of Scarborough, a pioneer of temperance campaigning, was invited by Thomas Cook (famous later as a tourist promoter) to visit Leicestershire and Northampton-shire. He described his experience at Kettering in his auto-biography, half a century later.[32] The Sunday before my arrival [at Kettering] two of the Nonconformist ministers took occasion to preach to their people with special reference to my intended visit. One of them took for his text, 'Be not righteous overmuch'; the other, 'Beware of false prophets'."

One of those ministers was put into the chair for the temperance meeting, in the British School. This was the Rev. John Jenkinson, who said that he hoped that the audience would listen to the speaker and ask questions at the end – but if they had no questions he should take him in hand himself. He added that he hoped the day would come when every working man would have at least "two pints of ale a day". Whittaker wrote that the schoolroom had been hired by the Society of Friends, but that it had been "taken possession of by the rowdies of the town, and they had the meeting conducted after their own fashion". Several men were flourishing bottles, and were already asking questions before he could begin. "The interruption was continuous, but I spoke for an hour, and I think I made some impression. . . . At length someone set fire to some loose shavings lying on the floor. (Some benches had been undergoing repairs during the day.)" At the cry of "Fire!" there was general excitement. "The roughs made a rush at me, and jammed me against the wall. . . . I think they were more hurt than myself."

The meeting broke up in disorder. The banker, John Cooper Gotch arrived, a man commanding so much respect that Whittaker incorrectly assumed that he was a magistrate. He had with him one parish constable. A Quaker wine-merchant named Wright had overheard a plot to throw Whittaker into one of the town ponds. He said, "Thomas, wilt thou take my arm? Those men mean mischief." Another Quaker, Wallis, farmer and maltster offered his arm on the other side; and with Gotch leading, and the constable at the rear, they escaped to Wright's house, where the temperance man was lodged for the night. Whittaker explained that he did have some success. "The wine merchant . . . in his little parlour, before retiring for the night, signed the pledge and kept it to his death, and never sold another bottle of wine. The maltster also signed, and never made another grain of barley into malt; and his partner, good James Wells also signed. . . . The reverend gentleman [Jenkinson] who opposed me at my first meeting, within two years of that time became a teetotaller, and built a temperance hall."

At Wellingborough, he was pelted with testaments and hymn-books during his speech, and had to be protected after the meeting.

6th April 1837

THE STRANGE STORY OF A STOLEN WILL

On Thursday morning, William Ralph Cartwright, M.P. arrived at the Sessions House in Northampton from his home at Aynho, to take the chair at Quarter Sessions. One of the criminal cases was to have bewildering repercussive effects.

William Smith stood indicted for the theft of a will. The Prosecutor, Waddington, addressed the jury: "The facts are novel, and it has never fallen to my lot to be engaged in a similar case. in the 7th and 8th years of George IV, there was an Act passed regulated this particular offence, and declaring it to be a misdemeanour. All you will have to consider is whether this will was the property of another person, and if so, whether it was dishonestly taken away by the prisoner. . . ." He called his first witness.

Hannah Green: I live at Ringstead. The prisoner at the bar is the son of the late William Smith, a lace-dealer, of Ringstead. There are three other sons, a daughter, and a grandson named Patrick. Mr. Smith died last February. About three months before that, he gave me his will to take care of. I was a subscribing witness to it. On the day of Mr. Smith's funeral, I gave the will to my husband.

She was cross-examined by Mr. Miller for the defence: Did you read the will?

Hannah Green: No.

Miller: Did you hear it read at the time you signed your name to it?

H.G.: No.

Waddington: Did you hear Mr. Smith declare the paper which you and other witnesses signed, to be his last will and testament?

H.G.: I did.

John Green: I am the husband of the last witness. I received the will from her. After the funeral, I took it to Mr.

27

Williamson at the house of William Smith, the deceased, and delivered it to him in the presence of John Smith, James Smith, William Smith and the prisoner, and Mrs. Patrick the daughter, and some relatives. Mr. Williamson read the will aloud. When he came to that part which left the house, garden, orchard, and all that pertained to it, to Mrs. Patrick's son, the prisoner, William Smith, snatched the will out of Mr. Williamson's hand, and put it into his pocket. I begged him not to destroy it, but he replied that I should see nothing more of it. I never saw it after that. When he was before the magistrate, he said, in my presence that it was destroyed, but that he did not destroy it.

John Williamson: I am a farmer at Ringstead. I received the will of the deceased Mr. Smith in the evening of the day of the funeral. The cottage and garden was left to the grandson. After I read it over to myself, I began to read it aloud. When I came to the part relating to the cottage, the prisoner snatched it from my hand and put it in his pocket. I cautioned him not to destroy it, because of the consequences, and endeavoured to persuade him to give it up, as I believed there was something for all. We all went before the magistrate, Mr. Wilkins, and the prisoner said there, that the will was destroyed, but not by him; nor did he see the destruction.

Miller now stated the case for the defence, telling the jury that they should acquit William Smith because there had been no theft. He had snatched the will and destroyed it "in a fit of indignation" with no possibility of personal gain. "In the present case, the father dies, and leaves four sons and a daughter. The eldest son, John, is a married man with several children, but the father wills the real property to the son of his daughter. . . . The prisoner is the third son. By no probability whatever could he have benefitted from the destruction of the will. He was actuated by a feeling of indignation that this little property should have been taken from its natural successor, his brother John, and delivered over to one who, although a relation, did not bear their name."

One witness gave evidence for the defence, Edmund French, who had known the prisoner for twenty years. All that time he had borne an excellent character.

The Chairman addressed the jury: "In my opinion . . . the taking away of the will in those circumstances did constitute stealing. . . . It is impossible for us to know what private arrangements might exist between himself and the eldest brother." The jurymen were not obliged to act on these remarks; and some of them might have regarded them as improper. It was for the prosecution to produce evidence to show that the accused would gain from the destruction of the will. Nevertheless, the verdict was "Guilty".

The magistrates conferred, and then the Chairman addressed the prisoner: "William Smith, the Court is of the opinion that the offence was one of a serious and aggravated nature. You will be transported for seven years."

After Smith had been taken down, Miller began some words of protest: "Perhaps the Court will consider that the offence, being of rare occurrence, the law is not generally known −" He was cut short by the Chairman: "The Court were unanimous in awarding sentence." Waddington, the Prosecutor, added his satisfaction: "The offence is a very heinous one. I am astonished that the legislature should have made it a misdemeanour only."

The Quarter Sessions hearing and sentence did not put an end to the matter. Early in September, Thomas Wilkins, the magistrate who had originally committed William Smith, wrote to the Chairman, Cartwright, stating that he had just heard that Smith's sentence had been commuted to three months' imprisonment in the Milbank Penitentiary. Cartwright wrote to the Home Office to inquire, and received a reply from Mr. Fox-Maule confirming that Smith's sentence had been commuted. Enclosed was "an extract from the representation of a Dr. Watson" which had persuaded the Home Secretary, Lord John Russell to order the commutation. Dr. Watson had written:

"The prisoner in the tortured heat of the moment snatched the will from the hands of the party making it, before he had finished, and destroyed it. Such an act, of course, led to his apprehension, in which, for example's sake, I joined consent and approbation with the executor. Fully sensible of the impropriety of the act, and having declared his contrition in ample terms, the prosecutor, with others interested therein, feeling with myself that the [needs] of justice had been answered by teaching him, and through him, all others, that the laws are not to be violated with impunity, and having received a good character from his masters, &c. that under the circumstances, they beg leave to recommend him &c. I understand that the prisoner is suffering considerably in constitution as well as mind, having become emaciated and desponding."

Cartwright thought this so extraordinary that he placed it on the agenda of the October Quarter Sessions. The magistrates were unable to understand why they had not been informed of the Home Secretary's decision, and Thomas Wilkins, who lived at Ringstead, and was more closely involved than his colleagues, returned home to obtain information. He wrote to Cartwright the next day:

"Ringstead House,
October 19, 1837.

My dear Sir,

William Smith's prosecution at the last spring Quarter Sessions. . . . He is now at large, a cause of regret and surprise to many. I must observe upon the representation made by Dr. Watson to the Secretary of State for the Home Department, that it by no means meets the case. It is incorrect in some instances, and altogether false in others. Dr. Watson's statement that the act was committed 'in the tortured heat of the moment' is not true, for I could readily establish by undoubted proof, that the convict and his two brothers had previously agreed to obtain and destroy the will. Dr. Watson goes on to say that 'for example's sake he joined consent and approbation with the executor' in the proceedings against Smith. To this I can only say that Smith was apprehended under my warrant late at night, and without any communication with Dr. Watson. Nor have I any reason to suppose that he knew that such an act had been committed, till Smith was in the custody of the constable and on his way to gaol. Dr. Watson adds that the prosecutor (John Green) 'feeling with him that the ends of justice have been satisfied, recommends', &c. This is so far from true that the prosecutor denies having ever had any communication with Dr. Watson on the subject, and I now send you enclosed, his disclaimer. What can have led Dr. Watson to take such a step? I am quite at a loss to imagine, and more particularly that he should have moved in the business without first consulting me, the committing magistrate, living as I do within 200 yards of his home. Smith is not a parishioner of Dr. Watson, and I think I may venture to say, was never known to, or even seen by Dr. Watson till his return from imprisonment. I will only add that the destruction of the will has led to the most painful circumstances.

I am, my dear Sir,
Your faithful servant,
THOS. WILKINS."

John Green's disclaimer, enclosed with Wilkins' letter said:

"I prosecuted William Smith at the last Spring Quarter Sessions for stealing and destroying his father's will. He was found guilty and sentenced to be transported for seven years. Soon afterwards James Smith (the brother of William Smith), brought a paper to me, which he said was a petition in favor [sic] of his brother, and asked me to sign it, but which I at once declined. I have never at any time given Dr. Watson authority to use my name in the business, nor have I ever thought that the sentence passed upon William Smith was more severe than was due to the crime he had committed. William Smith has been at home about three weeks or a month. Ringstead, Oct. 19, 1837

JOHN GREEN."

On receiving the above information, the Court unanimously resolved "that Mr. Cartwright be requested to transmit a copy of these minutes, and of Mr. Wilkins' letter, to Lord John Russell, and to express their strong feelings of surprise that such an application as that of Dr. Watson should have been attended to without any further enquiry into the case, or any communication with the Chairman, the committing magistrate, or any of the magistrates. . .".

The case, and sentence, are dealt with in both the

Northampton Mercury and *Northampton Herald* of 8th April 1837. The indignation of the magistrates at the treatment of the matter by the Home Office is described in the *Herald* of 11th November (p. 3, col. 3). Editorial comment suggested that the explanation was political: the action of a Whig Government against Cartwright, who was a Tory M.P. It is tempting to substitute an alternative explanation: the Government, so soon after the Tolpuddle scandal, was more than willing to quash a sentence of transportation for a "misdemeanour".

In the House of Commons on Wednesday 29th November, another Northamptonshire Tory M.P. confronted the Home Secretary.

Sir Charles Knightley: . . . At the last Lent quarter sessions for the county of Northampton, a man named William Smith was convicted of destroying his father's will, by which means his nephew was supposed to have been deprived of considerable property. There was not the slightest doubt as to his guilt, and the Court were unanimously agreed as to the justice of the sentence. He was condemned to transportation for seven years. Shortly afterwards, Mr. Wilkins, the committing magistrate, obtained information that this man had been commuted from . . . transportation to three months' imprisonment. . . . The Chairman of the quarter sessions wrote to the Secretary of State to inquire on what grounds the commutation had taken place. . . . He received no reply to his letter. It was generally reported that a Doctor Watson was the person who had mediated for the prisoner, and had got up a petition in his own parish in his favour; and that it was in consequence of this petition that the commutation had taken place. With reference to the gentlemen in question, Doctor Watson, I do not know whether he styled himself Doctor of Divinity, of Law, or of Physic, but I am assured that Doctor Watson has taken his degree neither in the University of Oxford, nor of Cambridge. The only information I possess . . . is that it is a very short time since he was an inmate of Northampton Gaol. . . . Her Majesty's ministers have offered the grossest insult to the magistrates of the county which I have the honour to represent, and have scandalously abused that prerogative which, though nominally exercised by the Crown, it is well understood the ministers of the Crown wield in whatever manner might to them seem most meet.

Lord John Russell: The motion of the Honourable baronet is of a most unusual nature, and I trust that the House will not accede to it. The reasons why the punishment of this convict was commuted are shortly these: a memorial was sent to me by Doctor Watson, who stated himself to be clergyman of the parish where the convict lived, and it was signed by that gentleman and by several other respectable persons in the parish. It stated that the man had undoubtedly been guilty of destroying his father's will, but it had been done under feelings of great excitement on his part, and that he appeared to repent sincerely . . . and it also added that he was in such a bad state of health that the carrying into effect of the sentence would most probably occasion his death. This petition came under the consideration of the Under Secretary for the Home Department, who recommended that the convict should be pardoned. I, however, thought it advisable that the sentence should be commuted in the way in which it has been, namely, after the man had been imprisoned three months in the penitentiary. If I had entertained any doubt as to the guilt of the man, I should have sent to the Chairman of the Quarter Sessions of Northamptonshire; but in cases where there is doubt of guilt, and where reason might appear to arise for the remission of any portion of the punishment, it is not usual to make application to the judge who tried the prisoner. Hundreds of cases of the kind have occurred at the Home Office in which no application has been made to the judge. Above all, in cases where . . . the sentence is likely to be attended with danger to the life of the prisoner, the judge is not questioned on the subject. The honourable baronet, however, seems to think that the prerogative of mercy lies in the Chairman of the Quarter Sessions, and not in the Crown. . . .

The motion was negatived without a division.

8th April 1837

THE FIRST GAS COOKERS

The involvement of James Sharp in the early development of Northampton's public utilities has already been described in the introduction. At his own home, in 1826, he had begun to experiment with cooking by gas. In 1834 the Angel Hotel at Northampton had acquired from him one of the two first commercially-produced models. As a publicity stunt, he had provided a gas-cooked lunch for Earl Spencer, at his, Sharp's, house in the Drapery. This paved the way for the opening of his factory in 1836, in Bradshaw Street, Northampton, employing thirty-five workmen.[33] The next year, in the *Northampton Mercury* of 8th April (p. 3, col. 2) he announced a change in his personal circumstances:

"JAMES SHARP
BEGS to inform the Inhabitants of NORTHAMPTON and its vicinity, that having disposed of the Clock and Watch Making Business lately carried on by him in the Drapery to Mr. William Kirk, he has REMOVED into BRADSHAW STREET, where he is carrying on the Manufacture of Patent GAS COOKING APPARATUS and GAS STOVES, with every variety of Gas Fittings, &c., Orders for which he shall now be able to execute with dispatch.

"J. S. having devoted an immense amount of time and attention to the subject of the application of Coal Gas to the various purposes of light and heat, can with confidence state that the result is so satisfactory as to render Gas available to an almost universal extent.

"GAS COOKING APPARATUS
The really beautiful, simple, cleanly and economical Invention is calculated for Families of every grade, from the Palace to the Cottage. . . .

First – for boiling water. This may be accomplished for Breakfast or Tea in Ten to 15 minutes . . .

Secondly – For Roasting Meat, poultry, Game, &c. . . .

Thirdly – For Boiling, Steaming, and Baking . . .

Fourthly – For Broiling and Frying . . .

Where also may be had, the Patent GAS HOT-AIR STOVES, for warming buildings.

***The keys of the Northampton Fire Engines are now kept in Bradshaw-Street."

These first gas cookers were iron upright cuboid containers, with a circle of burners on the base, and hooks inside the top from which to hang meat. One of them lay rusting at Wellingborough Gasworks from 1884 to 1953.[34] In a picture frame was a bill for 2,200 feet of gas for this cooker in 1840, and an explanation: "The cooking apparatus referred to in this account consisted of a roaster and boiler fitted with connections for cooking by steam and also some boiling burners. The roasting portion continued in use until 1884 when it was replaced by a more modern gas cooker."[34]

It is to be hoped that this survivor found a place in a suitable museum.

15th April 1837

A DEN OF THIEVES IN NORTHAMPTON

Young Elizabeth Foster stood before the Recorder, N. R. Clarke, at the Northampton Town Sessions on 16th June 1837, indicted for stealing £125, the property of Nicholas Marsh on the 15th of April. The prosecutor told the Court what happened:

"I am Nicholas Marsh. I am a farmer at Hannington. On the 15th of April I was at Northampton Market. I met the prisoner at the top of Bridge Street, about eight o'clock in the evening. I had a hundred-and-twenty-five pounds in my pocket at the time, in notes of the Northampton Union Bank. She asked me to walk with her. I refused and walked on, but she followed me, and passed one of her arms round me. When we got to Whitworth's Bank, she suddenly left and ran off. I suspected I was robbed, and I was about to run after her, when I was stopped by two men who laid hold of my arm. After she ran away she was joined by another woman, and they both ran off together. . . ."

The story continued in police evidence, given by Constable Samuel Pack:

". . . I accompanied Mr. Marsh to a lodging house of the town, on the night he was robbed. The prisoner was in bed, and was identified immediately by Mr. Marsh. There were three other women in the same room, and a man was with the prisoner. There was also a coffin, with the corpse of a man in it, in the same room. I searched the clothes of the woman, but found none of the money."

Elizabeth Foster was asked if she wished to give evidence on her own behalf, or call witnesses. She said:

"I did not commit the robbery. Mr. Marsh told the police that the person who robbed him wore a cloak and a white straw bonnet. I have no such articles."

Marsh was re-called, and questioned about this. He replied:

"I did state that the woman who robbed me was so dressed; but I can speak positively to the identity of the prisoner. I was quite sober when I met her, and had full opportunity of observing her."

The verdict was "Guilty, but recommended to mercy on account of her youth."

The Recorder passed sentence:

"Elizabeth Foster . . . I shall best carry into effect the merciful recommendation of the jury by separating you from the scenes of horrible depravity to which you have hitherto been accustomed. You will be transported for seven years."

24th April 1837

RAILWAYMEN ON THE RAMPAGE AT KILSBY

"On Monday . . . the village of Kilsby . . . was the scene of great disturbance among the labourers employed upon the line of railway. . . . Two excavators had determined to fight out a quarrel on the village green. The Rev. C. Gillbee interposed and endeavoured to prevent the disgusting exhibition. He was unsuccessful, and the men, surrounded by a large [crowd] began the contest. Two of the London police at length interfered, and one of the pugilists was taken into custody to the Devon Ox Inn. His comrades proceeded to his rescue, which they affected by making a forcible entry into the house by the liberal use of stones and brickbats. The policeman, however, seized three or four of the ringleaders and secured him in the lock-up house. Upon this a body of the men went to the railway and insisted that the labourers who were pursuing their work should accompany them to the village and release the prisoners. They threatened that unless they complied they would throw them down the shafts. . . . Probably two hundred in number accordingly proceeded to the lock-up house upon which they made a ferocious attack. Ultimately they gained admittance, released their comrades and took off their handcuffs. The two policemen stood alone against the infuriated men, defending themselves [with] their pistols and cutlasses. . . . The mob afterwards attacked another house, where one of the constables was supposed to be concealed, and smashed a large number of windows. . . . The policemen made their way over to Weedon, and about two o'clock on Tuesday returned with a detachment of the military. Four or five of the rioters were taken at their lodgings, and seven or eight more as they were going to their work in the morning. They were brought to our county gaol under military escort at ten o'clock on Tuesday night. . . . At least a hundred of the railwaymen have absconded from a dread of apprehension. Many have been met with in different parts of the surrounding country without shoes, hat or coat."

(*Northampton Mercury* 29th April 1837, p. 3, col. 5.)

2nd May 1837

AN INQUEST AT ROADE

"On Tuesday last . . . an inquest was held before George Abbey, Esq., coroner, at Roade, . . . on a view of the body of James Vennimore, a stone-mason, aged 46 years. . . . As the deceased was employed on the railway in dressing stones, a triangle, consisting of three poles, used for the purpose of raising large stones . . . suddenly gave way, and falling with considerable force on the back of the deceased, killed him instantly. Verdict: Accident."

(*Northampton Mercury* 6th May 1837, p. 3, col. 6.)

9th May 1837

A RAILWAY ACCIDENT AT BLISWORTH

"On Tuesday last a labourer on the London and Birmingham Railway . . . was thrown from one of the waggons, and had one of his legs broken in a frightful manner. The accident was occasioned by a stone which lay on the rail. . . ."

(*Northampton Mercury* 13th May 1837, p. 3, col. 5.)

11th May 1837

ANOTHER RAILWAY ACCIDENT AT ROADE

"On Thursday evening another labourer on the railway at Roade . . ., in consequence of his foot slipping, fell, and the axle-tree of the waggon crushed his back so shockingly as to leave little hope of recovery. He lies at the Infirmary."

(Ibid.)

1-?th May 1837

A STRANGE DISINTERMENT AT ARMSTON

Armston is a hamlet within the parish of Polebrook. It has been listed as a depleted village, but tax and population records show that it has never had many inhabitants.[35] More extensive human activity in earlier times is suggested by the interesting earthworks, but they are difficult to interpret.[36]

In mid-May 1837 "as some men were employed . . . in digging in the garden of Mr. Chew . . . they discovered, within three feet of the surface of the ground, six human skeletons of gigantic stature. One of them was in nearly an erect posture in a most beautiful state of preservation; and evidently the remains of a young person. The jaw bones of all are of an immense size, and the teeth in admirable order and quite sound and white. Some portion of a Roman pavement was also discovered near the same spot."[37]

This discovery has been overlooked by modern archaeologists. There is no mention of it in the inventories of the Royal Commission on Historical Monuments, nor in the addenda published in the later volumes.[38] The Northamptonshire Archaeology Unit does not have it on the computerised Monument Record. Three Roman sites are known in Polebrook, all of them some distance from Armston. "Roman" often denotes the finders' assumptions about nineteenth century archaeological discoveries, but the pavement portion may well have been identifiable. A thirteenth century religious house is believed to have stood in Armston, possibly with a graveyard, but the upright position of one of the skeletons tells us that this was not a Christian burial.

24th and 29th May 1837

TWO MORE FATAL ACCIDENTS ON THE RAILWAY AT ROADE

The *Northampton Mercury* of 3rd June 1837 (p. 3, cols. 3-4) reported two inquests. The first had been held in Northampton on the previous Saturday, on the body of Thomas Blunt, a boy of thirteen years. "While in the act of unhooking a horse attached to a railway waggon, at Roade, on 24th May, his foot slipped, and the waggon passed over his thigh, and occasioned a severe compound fracture. He died at the Infirmary on Saturday last." The verdict was "Accidental Death."

The other inquest had been held at Roade on the following Tuesday "on the body of George Henman, a labourer employed on the London and Birmingham Railway. He was engaged the preceding day with some other men in undermining, when the earth suddenly gave way, and upwards of two tons weight falling on him, he was so much injured that he died after enduring the most excruciating pain, within three hours. . . . Two other men were partially buried, but they were dug out and not seriously injured. The deceased left a widow and five children." A similar verdict was recorded.

2nd June 1837

THE DEATHS OF TWO MORE RAILWAY NAVVIES, AT WHILTON AND ASHTON

The inquest on the body of John Leeson, aged 47, took place at the Infirmary at Northampton on Tuesday 6th June. John Baker was the first witness called:

"I am a labourer on the railroad at Whilton. The deceased was also a labourer there. On the second of this month, about a quarter past six in the evening, we was employed in filling waggons with earth from a sand bank, when the sand parted at the top and toppled over. The bank was about six feet high, and about ten ton fell. I saw it coming and I cried out 'Ware', but as he was looking up, it fell on him, and covered him entirely, except for a small portion of the upper part of his head. Me and other labourers released him as quick as possible. His head was bleeding, and he seemed very much hurt. Mr. Dix, of Buckby, was sent for, and his assistant came. By his advice we got a cart, and brought him here. The earth was not undermined. The cause of the fall was a sand vein giving way, from wet. Instead of falling in a sloping direction as it usually does, it toppled over. I do not think the accident was caused by anyone's negligence. He has left a wife and three children. He lived at Ravenstone."

There is a possibility that the witness meant Ravensthorpe which is only two parishes away from the scene of the accident at Whilton. On the other hand, Ravenstone is a village south west of Northampton, convenient for the railway at Roade, and the deceased may well have been employed by the Company before the railway progressed north-west to Whilton.

The medical witness was James Mash:

"I am house surgeon here at the Infirmary. The deceased was brought here about twelve on Friday night. His nose was fractured, and the lower part of the body much injured. He was exhausted, and complained of great pain. He died on Sunday morning about ten o'clock. I afterwards examined the body externally, and found extensive fracture of the pelvis, severe laceration, and extravasation of blood in the cavity of the abdomen. The injury was so extensive that I can scarcely think it possible for him to survive as long as he did."

Another labourer, Robert Hensby, had, at the time of the accident, been working about two yards from the deceased. He corroborated Baker's evidence completely. The verdict was "Accidental Death".

41

On the same day that Leeson was injured, twenty-nine-year-old John Addington was crushed by falling earth at Ashton. He died on Tuesday, leaving a widow and two young children at Grafton Regis. His inquest took place on Wednesday 7th June.

John Mills: I am an excavator on the London and Birmingham Railway at Ashton. On Friday, the second of June, about half past seven in the morning, the deceased . . . was filling his waggon, when about two or three tons of earth, which had been undermined, gave way, and fell on him. I saw it falling, and called to him, but he had no time to get clear, and he was nearly covered with it. We got him out in about ten minutes or a quarter of an hour. We thought he was dead. His legs were bleeding, and he was hurt about the head and neck. A surgeon of Roade was sent for. He examined him, and he was brought to the Infirmary directly. The earth was about fourteen feet above where the deceased was standing, and it was undermined to a depth of about two and a half feet. It was not propped up at all. It is not the practice to prop up the earth when it is undermined. I have been an excavator twelve years, and I have never seen propping up. The earth was very loose and full of joints. Several persons were working on a remove about nine feet above, and when the earth gave way, one of the men narrowly escaped being carried with it.

James Mash: I am house surgeon at the Northampton Infirmary. The deceased was brought into the Infirmary between ten and eleven on the second of this month. The left leg was fractured, and he had sustained concussion of the brain. He was quite insensible, and died about four o'clock on Tuesday morning.

Duncan Camp: I live in Ashton. I am employed on the railway as an excavator. I saw the accident [This witness corroborated the evidence by Mills] I do not believe there was carelessness on the part of anyone.

After the expected verdict of "Accidental Death" had been announced, the foreman of the jury himself offered an expert's observation:

"I have seen a good deal of this kind of work, and I am of the opinion that it is impossible to guard against accidents where the earth is so jointy and loose."

The *Northampton Mercury's* account of these two inquests appeared on Saturday 17th June 1837 (p. 2, col. 1).

4th June 1837

BURGLARY AT LITCHBOROUGH

William Wise, the victim of a "daring burglary" placed an advertisement in the *Northampton Mercury* of 10th June 1837 (p. 2, col. 5) offering a reward of ten pounds:

WHEREAS in the night of Sunday the 4th of JUNE inst. the DWELLING HOUSE of Mr. WILLIAM WISE, in the parish of Litchborough, Northamptonshire, was forcibly entered by three Ruffians, who proceeded to the bed-rooms of the family, threatened their lives if they made any resistance. Whoever will give such information as will lead to the detection of the offenders, shall receive the above reward."

7th June 1837

A RISING CRIME RATE BLAMED ON THE RAILWAY

There were times when some among the multitude of railway labourers became unruly, especially after the consumption of alcoholic refreshment. Undoubtedly, quite a few of those men had criminal tendencies. The county police force would not be formed until long after the railway had been completed. Only the magistracy and the traditional

43

parish constables stood against an alarming rise in the rate of crime. It has been noted how the Army was called upon to restore order after a major disturbance at Kilsby. The burglary of 4th June was quite likely related to this problem. Litchborough was only a short distance from the railway, and the crime occurred on a Sunday, when the work-force had not been required to use up their energy in a day's work.

A meeting was convened by the Rev. W. M. Butlin, senior, by "public notice", and took place at the Cock Inn at Roade, on Wednesday 7th June. There was a large male attendance of "gentlemen" from Roade and its neighbouring villages. Three resolutions were unanimously passed. The first stated "That this Meeting, through their Chairman [Butlin], do represent to the Directors of the London and Birmingham Railway Company, that in consequence of the works now being carried on at Roade, and the neighbouring villages, crime has increased to a very great extent, and that it has become absolutely necessary to take some measures to prevent it, and that they hope the Directors will establish some kind of Police to protect the persons and property of individuals living in the parishes bordering on the line between Ashton and Blisworth." The second resolution was to adjourn the meeting to the 22nd June to consider the response of the railway company. We have no record of the adjourned meeting, nor of any answer from the railway directors. More tragic occurrences not related to crime soon occupied the attention of those near the railway workings.

The third resolution was to insert a report in the three Northampton newspapers, *Mercury, Herald* and *Chronicle*. It appeared in the *Mercury* of 10th June (p. 3, col. 1).

11th June 1837

HORROR ON THE RAILWAY AT ROADE

"On Sunday a young girl named Mary Ann Hodges, was walking on the railroad at Roade, when the engine caught her dress, and her arm was so shockingly mutilated that it was found necessary to take it out at the socket, and to amputate a large portion of the breast. The operation was successfully performed by Mr. Nott, of Blisworth, and Mr. Elston, of Bugbrook. The poor creature's foot was also severely injured, and fears were entertained on Thursday morning that mortification had taken place."

(*Northampton Mercury* 17th June 1837, p. 3, col. 6.)

The most sickeningly horrific aspect of this incident was the fact that all the medical attentions described were carried out without the benefit of anaesthetic.

13th June 1837

"I SHALL DIE IN FIVE MINUTES"

A brief report of the inquest at the Guildhall in Northampton, on view of the body of George Baldwin, was given in the *Northampton Mercury* of 24th June (p. 3, col. 5). He was a thirteen-year-old boy, and had been at work on the railway, at Blisworth, driving a waggon laden with earth. He stumbled over a sleeper, and fell across the rails. The two rear wheels of the waggon passed over his body, causing external and internal injuries. "A Surgeon of Blisworth [Mr. Nott, probably] was immediately sent for, but he was absent, and the deceased was brought to the Infirmary, and died before he was removed from the cart." It is pleasing to note that he "did not suffer much". As the cart passed through the gates of the Infirmary, George said to his companion: "Bill, I shall die in five minutes."

There was a curious relic of medieval law in the verdict of the inquest jury, delivered as "Accident. Deodand, one shilling". When death was caused by an item of someone's property, it was possible to confiscate that object and give it to God. Deodand means something given to God. In effect the railway sleeper that had tripped George Baldwin and caused his death was deemed to be worth a shilling, so the London and Birmingham Railway Company was required to pay that shilling to the Church. Deodands were not abolished until 1846.

21st June 1837

A WINDMILL: AND A STEAM MILL DISMANTLED AT OLD STRATFORD

At eleven o'clock on the morning of Wednesday, June 21st, Edward Johnson, of Old Stratford Wharf, offered for sale by auction, various parts of his mills, which the auctioneer, W. Day, described as follows:[39]

"Lot 1. Iron Wind Shaft.
      2. Break wheel wallow, &c.
      3. The roof of the windmill, fan-tail, & patent sails.
      4. Iron upright shaft, with brass carriages, &c.
      5. Spur-wheel, pinions, and spindles.
      6. A governor.
      7. Pair of 4-feet French stones, with cases, &c.
      8. Ditto . . . ditto
      9. Ditto . . . ditto
    10. Ditto . . . ditto
    11. Meal-trough.
    12. Capital steam-engine, of 12-horse power, complete.
    13. Iron pit-wheel and wallower.
    14. Wood upright shaft, with fixtures.
    15. Spur-wheel, and two pinions.
    16. Crown wheel, and ditto.
    17. Sack tackle.
    18. 4-feet dressing machine, with joggle screen, &c.
    19. Bolting screen, complete.
    20. Smut ditto.
    21. Three large dressing straps, and 3 smaller ditto.

22. Large meal trough.
23. Corn screens, &c.
24. Large iron beam, scales, and weights.
25. Smaller ditto.
26. Screw-jack.
27. Mill bills.
28. Oak timber."

24th June 1837

BOUGHTON GREEN FAIR

For several days, traders had been arriving in Northampton and the villages on the north of the town, with carts and waggons of all sizes. On 24th June, the largest annual fair of the Midlands was in full operation, on Boughton Green. The produce of many counties and towns was on sale. Agricultural implements, conveyances, ladders, tools, rope and string, hurdles, timber, besoms, and many other commodities all had an allotted portion of standing room.[40] Horses, cattle, sheep and pigs, each had a special day of sale. There was entertainment in the form of sideshows, swings, stalls, dancing and fortune-telling.

Thieves, cheats and tricksters were, of course, attracted to the Fair, but this year a warning had been placed in the *Northampton Mercury* on 17th June:

"BOUGHTON GREEN FAIR
THE Public are respectfully informed that BOW STREET OFFICERS are engaged to attend. Thimble Ring [sic], Dice, Garter Tables, &c. will not be allowed during the Fair."

The first of those forbidden activities was a misprint of Thimble Rig, a game in which money was taken from innocents who were unable to guess which thimble concealed a pea.

24th June 1837

THE SAME DAY AT THE UNION WORKHOUSE IN WELLINGBOROUGH

The Poor Law Amendment Act of 1834 had reorganised the relief of the poor, taking it out of the hands of the parishes. Groups of parishes became "unions", and each union had a board of elected guardians. A workhouse had to be built by every union, large enough to house the paupers of all the constituent parishes.

The Wellingborough Union had inherited workhouse accommodation, in Wellingborough and in most of the villages, and this had continued in use while the big new union workhouse was being built on the south of town. This was now complete, standing on the road soon to become Union Lane. (Now this is Irthlingborough Road, and the gaunt red-brick workhouse blocks still form the nucleus of the Isebrook Hospital complex.)

During May, advertisements had been placed in the Northampton newspapers for a porter and a nurse, and for a chaplain at £30 per annum. The latter appointment, going to an Anglican clergyman, was certain to generate opposition from the nonconformist communities in the area. When it was known that the doors would open on 24th June, an advertisement invited tenders for provisions:[41]

"BREAD, of good Seconds' Flour . . . at to weigh Four pounds	per loaf,
Best SECONDS' FLOUR . . . at	per stone
ROUNDS AND RANDS of good FAT BEEF at	per pound
BUTTOCKS, CLODS, & STICKINGS of Ditto (free from Bone) at	per pound
Fore quarters of good MUTTON . . . at	per pound
Good Butter . . . at	per lb.
Good thin Cheese . . . at	per cwt.
Good hard Yellow Soap . . . at	per cwt.
Good moist Sugar . . . at	per cwt.
Soda . . . at	per cwt.
Good White Peas . . . at	per bush.

New Milk . . . at	per gallon
Candles . . . at	per 12 lbs.
Coals . . . at	per ton."

Henry Hodson, the Wellingborough solicitor who was the clerk to the Board of Guardians, and over whose name the advertisement had been printed, also invited tenders for the supply of bread and flour of similar quality to the "Out Poor". This meant the people claiming relief without going into the Workhouse. The 1834 Act intended all paupers to become inmates, thus ending out-door relief, but that was hardly realistic. There were many circumstances that could make it desirable if not essential for a pauper to remain at home. The twenty-seven parishes that made up the Wellingborough Union are listed in the advertisement. Three of them were in Bedfordshire. All the villages within a radius of five miles of Wellingborough were included, and the civic pride of Higham Ferrers had been hurt by its peripheral position, no more prominent than the hamlet of Strixton.

26th June 1837

PROCLAIMING THE QUEEN AT NOON

The first Victorian *Northampton Mercury*, on 24th June, had broad black borders to every page and every column, of both editorial and advertising matter. Succeeding issues had similar mourning borders on the front pages. King William IV had died on the morning of 20th June, and in that *Mercury*, in the first column of the third page was the following:

"NORTHAMPTONSHIRE, TO WIT
WHEREAS WILLIAM WILLES, Esquire, the High Sheriff of the said County, hath received a precept commanding him to PROCLAIM The High and Mighty Princess ALEXANDRINA VICTORIA, QUEEN of the United Kingdom of Great Britain and Ireland, Defender of the

49

Faith, saving the rights of any issue of his late Majesty King William the Fourth, which may be born of his late Majesty's Consort.

"These are therefore to give notice, that the said Sheriff hath issued his precept to the High Bailiff of the reverend Dean and Chapter of the Cathedral Church of Saint Peter, otherwise Peterborough, the Mayors of the several Towns and Boroughs of Northampton, Daventry, Brackley, and Higham Ferers, all in the said county, directing such Proclamation to be by them forthwith made, within their respective jurisdictions.

"And the said Sheriff doth hereby give notice, that he shall proceed to make such Proclamation at the following places, on the respective days, and at the times hereinafter mentioned (that is to say):-

"At Northampton, on Monday next, the 26th day of June instant, at twelve o'clock at noon.

"At Towcester, on the same day, at Three o'clock in the afternoon.

"At Wellingborough, on Wednesday, the 28th day of June instant, at Twelve o'clock at noon.

"At Thrapston, on the same day, at Three o'clock in the afternoon.

"At Oundle, on Thursday, the 29th day of June instant, at Ten o'clock in the forenoon – and

"At Kettering, on the same day at Two o'clock in the afternoon. Sheriff's Office, Northampton 23rd June 1837."

When Sheriff Willes had read out the Proclamation in Northampton, the bells of the churches rang out. The ringers of St. Giles' were paid eight shillings.[42]

Christopher Gibson kept the Windmill Tavern on the Market Square. In successive poll books he had called himself "Professor of Music", "Teacher of Music", "Fiddler", and "Musician", so there is no doubt about the nature of the entertainment in that house on this day. He decided that the name of his tavern should be changed. Henceforth it would be "The Queen's Arms".[43]

Early summer 1837

A CONVERSATION WITH A POET

Since the publication of his last book of verse in 1835, the mental condition of John Clare had deteriorated beyond mere eccentricity. In 1837 he became a resident at High Beech, in Essex, an experimental private asylum, under the care of Matthew Allen. He was visited by Cyrus Redding, a writer who specialised in descriptions of unusual people. Redding published several accounts of his conversation with Clare. This one is in a letter quoted by Edmund Blunden.[44] "I found Clare in a field cutting up thistles, a small man and slender rather than stout. He was pleased to see me." They began at once to discuss poetry, Clare speaking in simple terms as in his poems. "He had nothing of the clown about him but his dress. He leaned upon the tool he was using, and spoke of Byron and his poetry in perfectly good taste. . . ." Suddenly, Clare changed the topic from poetry to boxing, but this slight confusion was the only mild characterisation of mental illness that Redding noticed.

An experienced farmer of the present day has suggested late June or early July as the time of year when John Clare would have been "cutting up thistles".

3rd July 1837

A BENEFIT OF THE EXTENDING WATER SUPPLY IN NORTHAMPTON

"NORTHAMPTON PUBLIC BATHS
PATRONIZED BY
DR. ROBERTSON, DR. KERR,
And the Medical Gentlemen of Northampton.

THE DIRECTORS respectfully announce to the Ladies and Gentlemen of NORTHAMPTON, and its neighbourhood, that the above BATHS will be ready for the accommodation of the public on MONDAY, the 3rd of JULY.

In addition to Hot, Cold, and Plunging Baths, a large SWIMMING BATH has been commenced, and will be got ready with the least possible delay.

Prospectuses of the Establishment, and Terms of Bathing, may be had of Mr. Alderman Freeman, the Treasurer, on the Market-square, and at the Baths.

June 23rd, 1837."

(*Northampton Mercury* 24th June 1837, p. 3, col. 3.)

7th July 1837

TREASURE IN THE WORKHOUSE AT MOULTON

The parish of Moulton became part of the Brixworth Union when it was formed in 1835. The Moulton workhouse continued in use until the new Union workhouse had been built at Brixworth, and the Board of Guardians paid rent for it. The fittings and property in it were taken at a valuation. This included possessions brought into the old workhouse by the paupers. There was, for example, an old bedstead and a trunk which had been the property of an old woman who had died an inmate. Her nearest of kin had been invited to contribute towards the cost of her interment, but had declined, so she was buried at the cost of the parish, and her humble possessions remained in store.

On Friday 7th July 1837, the Brixworth Union sold by public auction all the furniture from the redundant Moulton workhouse, including the old lady's bedstead and trunk, which now parted company. The trunk was knocked down for two shillings, but two bidders claimed it, so it was put up again. This time it went for two shillings and ninepence to the wife of a Moulton labourer. The husband immediately began to examine his wife's acquisition with great curiosity. He had heard of secret drawers in antique trunks, and he began to peel off the old paper with which it was covered. His wife became annoyed: he was spoiling her trunk. But he persisted, and eventually uncovered a drawer hidden in the side.

It was closely packed with over a hundred pieces of gold coin, of the reigns of James I, Charles II, James II, William and Mary, and William III. The *Northampton Mercury* reported this occurrence on 15th July (p. 3, col. 6) but wisely, without giving any names.

8th July 1837

BURGLARY AT FERMYN WOODS

Henry Goddard was a Bow Street Runner. He was 37 years old, five feet nine inches tall, and had thirteen years' service as a law officer in London. Three years later, after the Bow Street Runners had been disbanded, he became the first Chief Constable of the County of Northampton. On 10th July 1837 he was assigned by Sir Frederick Roe, the Chief Magistrate at Bow Street, to a case in Northamptonshire. It was quite common for the London officers to be called on to deal with cases in all parts of the kingdom, and their expenses were met from public funds. Henry Goddard wrote his memoirs during the late 1870s, and they are now in the possession of the Metropolitan Police. They were edited by Patrick Pringle and published in 1956.[45]

Goddard says that he was in the office when the messenger arrived from Northamptonshire. He heard what was said, and was directed to go on the night mail to investigate. The messenger was Wade, the house-steward to the Ladies Fitzpatrick of Fermyn Woods. Goddard's spelling of names is not reliable, nor was his memory of smaller details, as will be seen if comparison is made of his account with the evidence given in court. "Farming Woods" had been burgled on the night of 8th July. In the bailiff's room, a bureau had been broken open and money stolen from it.

Goddard was at the scene on the morning of 11th July. He found that a crow bar had been used to break open the outer back door, and the bureau. He was told that all the local criminals would be attending Weedon Fair, and decided to consult a doctor, Chard, at Brigstock, and a baker at Oundle, both of whom were reputed to know all the bad characters of the district.

On the day of the fair, he disguised himself as a "country-man" in a barn at Fermyn Woods, with the assistance of the bailiff. He arrived at the fair at 2 p.m. and had a meal of salt beef, potatoes and carrots. He was astonished to find the doctor and the baker staking their money with the "Pea and Thimble Riggers" and losing. As the three toured the fair, the baker drew their attention to two brothers named "Clair". Only a few days previously they had been poverty-stricken, but now they were challenging the crowd at pitch and toss, ostentatiously displaying pockets full of sovereigns. One of them announced that he was passing them from one hand to the other "to prevent them getting mouldy".

Goddard apparently considered the evidence of new and unexplained wealth sufficient to make the "Clair" brothers suspects, and he obtained warrants for their arrest from the Reverend Mr. Hogg, the magistrate at Kettering. He apprehended Samuel "Clair" at Oundle, and found ten sovereigns and a jemmy in his possession. They went in a hired conveyance to Kettering, where the magistrate remanded him to Northampton County Gaol. Then on to Stamford, where the other "Clair" was arrested, with, on his person, a purse stolen from the bureau at Fermyn Woods. It contained a few sovereigns.

Goddard says that he next arrested a loose character, Richard Knight on suspicion of sheep-stealing. In custody, Knight gave Goddard the names of several local sheep and deer stealers, and also confirmed that the "Clair" brothers were guilty of the Fermyn Woods burglary.

Now let us see what happened when the "Clair" case came to court. Some discrepancies will be noticed between Goddard's account written forty years later, and the evidence given before the magistrates at Quarter Sessions on Thursday 19th October 1837. James Clare was indicted for stealing from a bureau, thirty-five sovereigns, the property of William

Hight, and three pounds in silver, the property of the Ladies
Fitzpatrick. Samuel Clare was indicted as an accessory before
the fact. A third Clare, John, no relation to the poet, was the
father of the other two, and indicted as accessory after the
fact.

William Hight: I am bailiff to the Ladies Fitzpatrick at
Fermyn Woods. On the 7th of July last, I had thirty-five
sovereigns in a bag, and three pounds and ten shillings in
silver, in a bureau in a saddle-room. In that night the house
was broken open, and the money was stolen. There was a
ticket in the bag, with my name upon it.

Richard Knight: I was in the House of Correction in
Northampton from February to April. Samuel Clare was
there also. He asked me whether I had ever seen much
money at the Ladies Fitzpatrick's stable. I said I had, as I had
received my wages there during the previous six years.
Clare asked whether I thought I could get it. I said I did not
know. I left prison about the twenty-fifth of April; and in
June, shortly before the robbery, the Clares came to me at
Brigstock. James Clare asked me whether I would go with
them to break open the stables. I refused. I saw Samuel
again at Weedon Fair, and went up and asked him if he had
broken into the stable. He said, "No". I said I thought it must
be him, and Clare told me to go away lest people should
notice him. He said if I wanted money he would give me
some. A little time after that, he gave me a shilling. About a
fortnight or three weeks after me and Clare left prison I was
passing the stable with James Clare, and he asked me which
was the front stable. I was taken up on suspicion of the
robbery, and taken to Kettering. While I was in the lock-up
house, Clare was brought to me, and I asked him if he had
broken into the stable. He said, "No". I asked him what he
had done with the money he had at Fotheringhay. He said
that he had put his uncle up to the rigs, and had given him
the money. He could dress his dog so that when he sent him
into the other dogs, they would make no noise.

George Trossill: I live at Market Deeping. On Sunday the
ninth of July last, two days after the robbery was

committed, I saw James Clare at Fotheringhay. I sat against him, and he showed me a great lot of sovereigns and silver in a canvas purse. He said there was thirty-five pounds. He had a chisel.

Henry Goddard: I am a London police officer. I came from London to inquire into this affair. I went to the house where Samuel Clare lodged. John Clare was there. There was a box in the room which I desired John to open. He opened it, and Oddy, a constable, searched it and found a quantity of sovereigns. I asked Clare if he knew how many there were, and he answered: "Ten". I then asked whether anybody knew that he had this money, and he said, "No". He said he did not tell anybody about what money he had. He said he had saved it up, and it was his own. On the Saturday following, I went to Stamford, and found Samuel Clare there, in custody. Ashby Mayes, a constable, searched him and took from him a dark lantern, a canvas bag, and four or five half-crowns. I asked him where he had been staying, and he said with his uncle at Barston [Baston, Lincs.], about eight miles from Stamford. I searched the bedroom which Clare had occupied, but found nothing. I went again with Ashby Mayes on the twenty-fourth, and searched a bureau, and found a canvas bag, and three sovereigns, and a bundle of lucifers.

[Ashby Mayes produced the purse found in the bureau, and William Hight identified it as the one he had lost containing the sovereigns.]

James Clare: The money they found on me was my own property. I had been saving it up for two years and a half, to pay a fine for catching a few hares. I am a machine-maker by trade, and can earn from a pound to five-and-twenty shillings a week.

Samuel Clare: The money they found was my own.

John Clare: I wish to call Robert Berridge to be my witness.

Robert Berridge: I live at Oundle North Bridge. John Clare has worked for me since March 1836. I found him steady and industrious. At the time he was apprehended, I was paying him seventeen shillings and sixpence a week, and board and lodging.

James and Samuel Clare were found guilty. John Clare was found not guilty. James Clare had previously been convicted of felony, and had been confined for a month and privately whipped in the House of Correction [that means not publicly whipped].

T. P. Maunsell, M.P., in the chair: There is another indictment against James and Samuel Clare, for stealing a ham, but it is needless to offer any evidence, as they have been convicted of the heavier offence. James Clare, you will be transported for fourteen years. Samuel Clare, you will be transported for seven years.

Henry Goddard tells us in his memoirs what happened to the witness Richard Knight after the trial. Having given evidence for the prosecution it was considered too dangerous for him to return to Brigstock. The Ladies Fitzpatrick offered to pay his passage to America, and provide money for him to live on when he arrived there. He was taken to London by Goddard, and lived for three weeks at his house, before being put on board a ship bound for New York. All his living expenses were paid, and he was given a sovereign to spend. The captain was given twenty pounds to give him on his arrival in New York. When the ship returned to London, the captain gave Goddard Knight's signed receipt for the money, and told him that during the outward voyage Knight had decided to go to Canada with a fellow passenger.

The very last thing that Goddard says in his account of the case is about the clock in the stable-yard at Fermyn Woods. It was always kept one hour fast.

16th July 1837

AN ATTACK ON THE PARISH CONSTABLE
OF COGENHOE

On the same day at Quarter Sessions that the Clare brothers were sentenced, eleven Cogenhoe men were also before the Court, indicted for assaulting John Pell, a constable in the execution of his duty. Pell described himself as "the chief constable of Cooknoe". This simply means that he had an assistant to share his duties with him. We have encountered these plain-clothed guardians of the law on earlier pages. There was a common opinion that good order in the villages was safe in their hands. The episode described below by those who participated in it might be regarded as a strong argument in favour of an organised county police force.

John Pell: I am the chief constable of Cooknoe. On Sunday evening, the 16th of July, a great number of persons were assembled in a close near the town, to see a fight. I told them to disperse. They refused at first, but they then went into the lane, where the fight was continued. I followed, and threatened to take them into custody. I was pushed about and struck; and Harlot struck me so violently on the mouth as to cause a great bleeding. Tipler and Britten, who were the parties fighting, also struck me, but not so severely. Barker said he would take the men where I had no authority, and they all went to a place called the Mere Ground. I followed, and again ordered them to disperse. They then threatened to kill me if I did not leave them alone, and about five of them fell upon me and collared me, and I was struck and kicked till my legs ran with blood, and were swollen the size of my body. They then threw me into a ditch, and at least ten of them trampled upon me, and threatened to stab me. I have a very bad leg at this moment, and I have never had a boot on that leg since.

Robert Bilson: I am a cordwainer.* I live at Brafield. I was at Cooknoe on the evening of the 16th of July. There was a

---

*Shoemaker.

fight. Mr. Sharman, the constable, ordered them off his premises, and they then went into Mr. Pell's premises. He also ordered them off, and they went into the lane. Mr. Pell followed them, and they began to knock him about. John Battison was one. David Harlot was another. Clark also put his fist up. I saw Mr. Pell afterwards, knocked in the ditch. Harlot was one of the men who were upon him in the ditch.

At this point, the accused men were given the opportunity to question the witness about his evidence. As commonly happens in court, there was a tendency to begin statements rather than put questions.

Thomas Fitzhugh: I was hit by the blacksmith, because I tripped his heels up. The blacksmith, in falling, pulled Mr. Pell with him into the ditch.

Did you see that?

Bilson: He was knocked down. Mumford said, "Knock him down."

John Coles (witness): . . . I saw the affray. Several persons struck at Mr. Pell but I could swear to only one, William Bingham.

James Langley: . . . I heard Thomas Fitzhugh say he tripped Mr. Pell's heels up, and gave him a "nope in the neckhole".

At the conclusion of the prosecution evidence, the accused, all unrepresented, had their turn to give their own evidence. Thomas Fitzhugh said that he went to assist Mr. Pell; Mumford said that he was looking on, and merely went to advise Mr. Pell to go away, lest the mob should murder him. Mr. Pell had told him to go about his business, which he did. The others denied using any violence towards Mr. Pell. Several said that they went to assist him, but that he kicked and cuffed them, upon which they "gave a swing" and went away.

They were all found guilty. Harlot was sentenced to six months imprisonment with hard labour; six others to four months with hard labour; and four others, including Fitzhugh, to one month with hard labour.

25th July 1837

THE GENERAL ELECTION

Parliament was dissolved on the accession of the new sovereign, and a general election took place. Voting in elections was "open". The ballot was not introduced until 1872. Voters had to approach the hustings, the covered wooden platform on which the poll clerk sat with the book of registered electors, and publicly name the candidate or candidates for whom they wished to vote. Landowners had the right to vote, and since 1832, men who paid ten pounds a year rent if they lived in a borough (Northampton or Peterborough); or fifty pounds in rent per year, if they lived in the county area. The voting went on for several days, and ended on 25th July.

In Northampton, the Whigs took both seats (Vernon Smith and Currie); and the same in Peterborough (Fitzwilliam and Heron). The Tories took all four county seats (Cartwright and Knightley in the south, and Maunsell and Maidstone in the north). Straddling the border of Northamptonshire and Lincolnshire was the "pocket borough" of Stamford. It was in the pocket of the Marquis of Exeter, and he controlled it utterly for the Tory party. He lived at Burghley House, then in Northamptonshire, and owned a great part of the town. Local officials, church livings, the magistrates: all were appointees of the Cecil family of Burghley. Within the system of open voting described above, the tenants and employees of the Marquis were unlikely to elect members of Parliament who were not his nominees.[46]

We have an eye-witness account of some of the campaigning in Northampton by Sir Charles Knightley.[47] He was a county M.P., so you may well ask why he thought it worth while to brave a political crowd in the borough. The explanation is plural voting. Many landowners had votes in more than one constituency by the qualification of owning land in them. H. O. Nethercote says that Knightley "was not greatly blessed with the gift of eloquence, and with a slight difficulty of utterance, his attempts to address the great 'unwashed' in the County Hall, or from the balcony of the

George Hotel at Northampton, were generally provocative of much amusement". Knightley also lacked the gift of memory, and could not speak without the assistance of notes, which he kept inside his top-hat. "Either from not being clearly written, or from not being held at an angle suiting the vision, the 'hatograph' occasionally refused to yield up its written treasure without coaxing and manipulation. This excited the mirth of the 'paid unruly' attached to the opposition, and gave rise to cries of, 'Put your hat on Charley'; and 'What 'a you got a-looking at inside of that 'at?' and other irreverent remarks begotten of beer and bribery and electioneering manners."

When Knightley had finished speaking, says Nethercote, his agent, the Reverend Francis Litchfield, the rector of Farthinghoe, took over, "and the mob fairly settled down into quietude". All were content to listen "to the glib and energetic utterances of this bulwark of the Tory faith".

Litchfield was responsible for most of the political columns in the Tory-owned *Northampton Herald*. Some of his more outrageous pronouncements and accusations, though anonymous, on account of their style are readily attributable to that controversial cleric. The following item in the *Northampton Herald* of 15th July 1837 (p. 4, col. 1) purports to be a letter from an ordinary correspondent with fears of unfair treatment in the run-up to the election:

"To the operative shoemakers of N-ton.
  'Light Shoeman Wanted.'
  Brother Shoemakers. − The Whig Masters having displayed bills with the above welcome news to us poor fellows out of work and half-starved, although many of us felt surprise, after the croaking we have heard from them, for many weeks as to heavy stock, and the like, at such an announcement so suddenly made; still, anxious to obtain the means of honestly supporting ourselves outside the walls of the Whig prison workhouses, we lost no time in making application. To my dismay and astonishment, instead of inquiries as to my workmanship, I was questioned as follows:- − Good morning, Sir, I believe you want hands?' 'Eh, Sir, (eyeing me from head to foot) why let me

see, we do want a few', — a pause — 'What's your name?' 'John ─────'. 'Oh, ah, let's see, have you got a vote?' 'No, Sir, not at present, but I SOON SHALL HAVE.' 'Oh, no vote, hem! Let me see' — a pause again — 'No, I am sorry to say you are not one of the light shoemen we want at present.' 'I hope you will give me a little, Sir, if it is only enough to keep me from starving.' — 'Eh, no, Sir, no, not now, but I'll tell you want you may do, as I know you are a steady workman, you may call again in a few weeks, when we can get rid of a few of the old devils and give you work if we have any.' 'If it's ever so little, Sir, I can assure you ───' 'Eh, no, Sir, no. The fact is, as you know, we want votes just at present, and not men. You may call in a few weeks after the election, — Good day!' The door was opened to me, and I returned to my own dwelling with almost a broken spirit. Brother Shoemakers, voters! — Are you the things these men make ye appear? — Will you stand for ever lowest in the scale of trades for want of independence and spirit? Can ye not see how completely ye are now the tools of men who except at the hour your votes are wanted for their dirty purposes, despise you as loathsome carcases? Will you play their game at the coming election, which is to secure their Whig poor starving placeman, and reject your candidate the Radical Currie? Will you, I ask, not only be yourselves the despised slaves of such men, but seeks also to put the fetter on your fellow craftsmen. If so, then are ye unworthy of your manhood, and fit only to be scoffed at, and spit upon as beings having all the powers, but not a grain of courage to be independent.

Brother shoemakers, look to yourselves,

Believe me, your sincere friend,

A JOURNEYMAN SHOEMAKER."

This is a clumsy but amusing piece of propaganda. We must suppose that the writer believed that workmen spoke to each other in the same way that they would speak to an Anglican clergyman. In any case, unemployed shoe-stitchers would be unlikely to read the *Herald*. The real message was a warning to Tories that the Whig employers were likely to pressurise their employees into voting Whig. We do know how the shoemakers cast their votes. The poll book for Northampton is preserved in Northampton Public Library, and V. A. Hatley has analysed the voting pattern.[48] Of the 1,927 men who voted, 487 were journeymen-shoemakers. 373 of them voted for Whigs only; 22 voted for a Whig and a Tory; and only 92 voted for Tories only.

27th July 1837

PATTISHALL: THE COMPONENTS OF THE WATER MILL

"To MILLERS, MILLWRIGHTS, & OTHERS.
TO BE SOLD BY AUCTION
BY JOHN MARTIN.
On Thursday, the 27th day of July, 1837, on the premises at PATTISHALL MILL, Northamptonshire,
THE whole of the machinery, consisting of a large water wheel and shaft, pit wheel and upright shaft, one pair of four feet French stones, one pair 4ft. 10in. Peake stones, dressing machine, cylinder, sack tackle, large cast-iron cistern, three-step ladder, scales, beams and weights, tools, an excellent grindstone, and a number of other articles.
A patent Iron Work for an Oven.
The Sale to commence at Two o'clock.
May be viewed by applying on the premises.
Towcester, 13th July, 1837."

(*Northampton Mercury* 15th July 1837, p. 2, col. 3.)

29th July 1837

A WINDMILL FOR SALE AT ROADE

"TO MILLERS and OTHERS
TO BE SOLD BY PRIVATE CONTRACT,
A WINDMILL, to be SOLD OR LET, standing in the parish of
ROADE, in the county of Northampton, the property of
WILLIAM STURGESS, Roade.

(*Northampton Mercury* 29th July 1837, p. 1, col. 1.)

11th August 1837

THE BRETHREN OF THE POMFRET LODGE

The original medieval Freemasons specialised in the building
of churches. There was an opportunity for the Northampton
Freemasons to return briefly to that interest, when the
foundation stone of St. Katherine's Church was laid on 11th
August.

The Pomfret Lodge, number 463, had been inaugurated at
the Ram Inn in Sheep Street in 1819; and after trying the
hospitality at other inns during succeeding years, it became
re-established at the Ram in 1837.[49] The Brethren paraded to
attend the ceremony in the clothing normally hidden from
the public. "The dresses and paraphernalia of the Masonic
Brethren were of the most splendid description, and called
forth the unbounded admiration of the spectators. . . . We
particularly noticed three superb candlesticks of the Doric,
Ionic and Corinthian Orders. . . . The manufacturing of these
reflects the greatest possible credit on Bro. Downs, the highly
respected superintendent of Mr. Brettell's Foundry of this
town."[50] Before the Marquis of Northampton laid the foundation stone, the appropriate Masonic checks with square, level
and plumb rule were carried out.[49]

Following the ceremony, the Brethren returned to the Ram, where the landlord, Thomas Cox, provided dinner for over forty. The Ram was demolished during the 1970s.

14th August 1837

DEENE, AND THE EARLDOM OF CARDIGAN INHERITED BY A CONTROVERSIAL ARMY OFFICER

When Robert Brudenell, 6th Earl of Cardigan, died in London, on August 14th, at his town house in Portman Square, his son, James Thomas Brudenell was in India, serving with his regiment, the 11th Light Dragoons (soon to be converted into Hussars).

The new Earl had been removed from command of his regiment in 1834. "Upon the event of my trying a captain by court-martial . . ." he wrote, thirty years later, "He was acquitted and the court fell upon me, the prosecutor."[51] In 1836, in the face of fierce political opposition, he was reinstated, and accompanied by his wife, went off to India. He received the news of his father's death while visiting the camp of the Commander-in-Chief, Sir Henry Fane.[52] The Earldom brought with it the Deene estate and other lands in Northamptonshire, the mansion and stables in London, lands in Leicestershire, Yorkshire coal mines, and an income of £40,000 a year.[53]

There were to be many other controversies in the military career of the 7th Earl. During the following two decades, he would earn widespread admiration for his bravery, and widespread detestation for his arrogance.

22nd August 1837

A PRIZE FIGHT WITH BARE KNUCKLES
AT COLLYWESTON

"On Tuesday [22nd August] a brutal fight took place for five pounds between a baker named Hibbins, a Conservative, and Ashley, the landlord of the O'Brien Arms public-house, Stamford, a Radical, who had a political quarrel a few days before. The parties went into the county of Rutland, where a ring was formed, when they were compelled by the Magistrates to leave that county. The fight took place at Colly-Weston-Wood . . . and lasted for upwards of an hour, when Hibbins was declared the victor, after having burst both of the eyes of his antagonist, Ashley, who is thus rendered blind for life."

(*Stamford Mercury*, 26th August 1837.)

25th August 1837

THE ROAD TO KINGSTHORPE

Thomas Cox, the landlord of the Ram Inn, host to the Northampton Freemasons (see 11th August above), was very angry indeed. He wrote a brief, furious note, and submitted it to the *Northampton Mercury* for publication the next day (26th August 1837, p. 3, col. 1):

"TO THE PUBLIC

I, THOMAS COX, of the RAM INN, having had my property on GORDON PARADE, KINGSTHORPE ROAD, maliciously injured several times, do hereby caution all persons, that I will keep a nightly watch, and that I will SHOOT the FIRST PARTY I see committing any depredation."

Let us take that road to Kingsthorpe as it was in the 1830s. "There is not a prettier village near Northampton . . . than

Kingsthorpe. Half an hour's leisurely stroll will conduct you thither. . . ."[54] From the Ram we follow Sheep Street northwards on to the "London road" (the main road from Leicester to London). A row of houses faces the race course (Adelaide Terrace, built in 1832), and just beyond is a gate. "Push open the gate, and continue along the delightfully pleasant and picturesque lane, and you will find yourself again in the high London road, and after proceeding a few yards along the road, step over a low stile on the left into a path running parallel with the road, but separated from it by a row of fine elms. On the left is a prospect . . . lovely as an inland county can possibly present. Crossing a stile or two, which are annoyingly numerous hereabouts, you will enter the Park and catch a pretty view of a stone mansion . . . embowered in some of the finest forest trees. . . . By a stile at the end of this path, you are once more in the high road, but at a very picturesque portion of it. On the east side is a cluster of primitive-looking cottages, built of stone, and thatched. Upon an attentive inspection they appear to have been formed from the remains of some ancient ruin, probably of an hospital founded here about the year 1200. . . ." There is a toll-gate, "modern and very ill-assorted with its antique and lowly neighbours. It has an impertinent, perkish look, which disconcerts the eye. Pass it, and taking the first turning on the left, pursue a lane formed on one side by the low stone wall and noble trees of the park . . . and on the other by closes and the stabling belonging to an antique-looking farmhouse. This lane will bring you to . . . Kingsthorpe."[54]

31st August 1837

A PICK-POCKET AT THE RACES

At the Northampton Town Sessions, before N. R. Clarke, Recorder, on Monday 11th September, Eliza Jackson and Joseph Tomlinson pleaded not guilty to the charge of stealing a shilling and a purse from the person of Mary Chandler.

Mary Chandler: I live in Chapel Place. On the 31st of August I was at the races in Northampton, and I was looking at some jugglers, when I felt a hand go into my pocket. I turned round, and saw the woman, Eliza Jackson; and I said, "You've stolen my purse." She denied that she had it, and was very abusive. I saw her go into a booth, and give the purse to the male prisoner. I am positive the prisoners are the same persons. They were taken up immediately. When the policeman took the male prisoner, he dropped the purse, and I picked it up and gave it to the policeman.

Joseph Webber: I was at the last Northampton races with Mary Chandler. I saw Eliza Jackson give Tomlinson a purse. I charged Tomlinson with having it, and when the policeman came up, he dropped it.

John Collier: I am one of the police of this town. I apprehended the prisoners. I saw Tomlinson draw his hand from his pocket and drop the purse.

Recorder: You have heard the cause against you. Do you have anything to say in your defence?

Tomlinson: The whole story is untrue.

Recorder: Do you have any witnesses to produce?

Tomlinson: No. We are strangers.

The verdict was guilty; and both the accused were sentenced to seven years' transportation.

1st September 1837

A GREY FRIARS BURIAL DISCOVERED, IN NORTHAMPTON

"Yesterday, as the workmen were digging foundations near the new line of buildings in Newland, they discovered, about four feet below the surface, a stone coffin. On removing the lid which was fastened down with iron cramps, a skeleton was discovered, wrapped in a kind of coarse but close net work. Of the skull, little remained but a mass of dark dust, but the bones of the arms and legs, and the ribs were tolerably perfect. The hands and feet were wholly decayed. One arm lay by the side, but the other had apparently been placed on the bosom. The small size of the bones indicate that the skeleton is that either of a female or a youth. The coffin is very thick and heavy, and the stone is hewn semi-circularly for the reception of the head."

(*Northampton Mercury*, 2nd September 1837, p. 3, col. 4.)

This must have been the first of the Grey Friars interments to be discovered, but if anyone in 1837 Northampton realised the monastic significance of the discovery, he did not publish his comments. Newland was a street leading north-wards from the Market Square, and its site now lies beneath the Grosvenor Centre and the Grey Friars 'Bus Station. The site of the medieval friary lay to east of Newland. In 1887, when a temperance hall was built on that side of Newland, many graves were discovered as the area was prepared. Some contained stone coffins similar to the one found in 1837.[55] So exactly fifty years later, this patch was confirmed to be the burial ground of the Grey Friars from the twelfth to the fifteenth centuries.

13th September 1837

TRAGEDY AT HOLLOWELL

The death of a small boy at Hollowell could be seen as an indirect consequence of one of the many accidents on the railway construction. The disturbed behaviour of the boy's father, following a head injury, led to the mysterious accident in which a violent, fatal injury was inflicted. To approach as near as possible to the truth of what happened, we shall be aided by the evidence given by witnesses at the trial of the father for murder.

William Lantsbury stood in the dock before Sir James Allen Park, at Northampton Lent Assizes on Tuesday 27th February 1838, charged with the wilful murder of his own son, Henry Lantsbury, at Hollowell, on 13th September 1837. Mr. Miller, prosecuting, called —

Thomas Good: I live at Hollowell. I have known the prisoner, William Lantsbury, a long time. He has lived for some years past at Hollowell. He rents an acre of land, and has a wife and two children. I knew the little boy who died. He was about seven years old. William always seemed to have great affection for the child. On September the 13th, he came to me about ten o'clock in the day, to ask me to thatch his little corn stack. The child was with him. I went to the stack directly, taking my scythe with me for cutting the stubble. I was employed about an hour at the stack. William Lantsbury and the boy were picking up ears of corn which I had cut off. I went away for about twenty minutes, leaving the scythe behind. When I returned, William had gone. I found the child lying dead near the place I left him. He was cut on the back of the head. One of his ears was cut off, and the back of his neck was also cut. The scythe was lying about four yards away from him. It was bloody half way along the blade, and there was human hair on it. I gave the alarm to two men, Cryer and Johnson, who were mowing in the field about two hundred yards from the stack. I met the child's mother coming in at the gate of the close. William Lantsbury was formerly in the army. About a year ago, when he was working on the railroad, some earth fell on him — on his head — and he was laid up in consequence. I recollect that he had a paralytic stroke after that.

The Judge: Did you see any signs of violence on the part of the prisoner whilst you were at work on the stack?

Good: No, your Honour.

Judge: Where did you leave the scythe? Could the child have done the injury itself?

Good: The scythe was on the ground. The child could not have injured itself by playing with it.

Judge: How long after the accident on the railroad did the prisoner suffer a stroke?

Good: About a month after.

Judge: How often did you see the prisoner?

Good: About twice a week.

Judge: Did you say anything about the prisoner's state of mind to the Coroner at the inqeust?

Good: I believe I told the Coroner that my impression was that his mind was unsound.

Judge: Did you see any symptom of aberration of mind on the day that the child was destroyed? Did the other two men notice any sign?

Good: I did not, and neither Cryer nor Johnson had seen or heard anything until I called them.

Judge: Are you able to say anything more about the incident?

Good: I sent Mary Cleaver for the child's mother. I did not see William Lantsbury touch the scythe before I left. The boy's cap was lying at his feet when I returned. I saw no blood on it.

Thomas Cryer: I live at Hollowell. I am a labourer. I was mowing stubble with Johnson on the thirteenth of September. I saw Good, and Lantsbury, and the little boy, near the stack. Whilst Good was away, I heard the noise of laughter and playing. That was the prisoner and his boy. I remember Good coming back. . . . He instantly gave the alarm, and I went to the child. . . . [Cryer's description of the scene was similar to that of Good.] I went in search of the prisoner, accompanied by Haychurch. I met him in custody of Charles Litchfield, and I was placed on guard over him for two days and nights. His stockings were on all that time. When he took them off, one stocking was found marked with blood, just above the boot. He was very ill the first night, but afterwards revived, and was better. He was not violent when under my care. A strait waistcoat was put on him, because Mr. Williams, the doctor, desired it. This was about an hour after I had him in my charge.

[Joseph Johnson corroborated Cryer's evidence.]

Charles Litchfield: I am a labourer. I was with Samuel Cole, searching for the prisoner. We found him about seven o'clock on the evening of the 13th of September. He was standing beside a hedge, with a stick in his hand, and made no attempt to run away. I told him he must go home. He answered, "I have done nothing – I have done nothing. What should I go home for?" He accompanied me and Cole quietly. Cole asked him what he had done with his little boy, and he seemed not to understand.

Owen McMain: I am a boot and shoemaker at Hollowell. I live in the same yard as the prisoner. I have known him four or five years. He was often at my shop. Before the accident on the railroad, he was steady and sober, and a rational man. The accident was a few months before the death of the child. It was a severe injury on the head, and he complained that his memory was bad, afterwards. About ten days after the accident, he had a paralytic stroke which kept him in bed. At frequent intervals he was unsettled in his mind, and his left side was completely paralysed. He used to talk incoherently, fancying himself in the army, or on the railroad; and when he could move neither hand nor foot, he wanted to go to his work. He never recovered in his mind. On the Wednesday before the death of the child, he brought the boy's shoes to me, asking me to mend them, as the boy had not a bit of shoe to his feet. At the very moment, the child was at my window in a pair of shoes which I had made only a week ago.

James White: I am a farmer at Hollowell. I have known the prisoner for fifteen years. Ten and a half years of that I employed him. About the middle of last harvest, after the accident on the railroad, his conversation was less rational than before. His ideas were confused and wandering, and he passed wildly from one subject to another. His mind seemed to get worse daily, and his memory seemed about gone. I cautioned his wife to be on her guard against his violence.

William Williams: I am a surgeon, at Guilsborough. I am the medical officer at the Brixworth Union. At five o'clock on the thirteenth of September, I examined the body of the deceased boy, Henry Lantsbury. There was a very extensive wound on the side of the head, nearly two inches deep in the brain. This was inflicted by a large and sharp instrument. I have known the prisoner about ten years, and I remember his having an attack of paralysis from which he only partially recovered. Going to work before he was fully recovered from the injury on the head would be likely to bring on paralysis. Paralysis will, of itself, frequently affect the intellect, and when induced by injury of the head, it is much more likely to do so. I saw the prisoner shortly after the death of the boy – within an hour of the event. I observed that the pupil of the eye was dilated. Dilation of the eye is often evidence of insanity. I believe that on that day the prisoner was incapable of judging between right and wrong.

Sir James Park's summing up took the form of a brief recapitulation. The verdict was "Not guilty, on the grounds of insanity".

Sir James: William Lanstbury, I desire that you be kept in custody until the pleasure of Her Majesty be known.

16th September 1837

A WILLING SERVANT SEEKING A NEW PLACE

"WANTS a Situation, a Young Man, aged 25, as UNDER GARDENER. Is capable of driving and taking care of a pair of horses, and has waited at table occasionally, and wishes to make himself useful.

Address, A.B. Post Office, Welford. Has lived five years in his last place and can have a character."

(*Northampton Mercury* 16th September 1837, p. 3, col. 1.)

18th September 1837

VIOLENT RAILWAY LABOURERS AT BLISWORTH

There is evidence of much sub-contracting for the construction of the London and Birmingham Railway. At Blisworth, the railway engineer, Martin Farrell, had a contract with John Brown, who put work out to Thomas Richardson. Pay-day was Saturday. On Saturday 16th September, Richardson failed to pay his men, so they went into Blisworth on Sunday and demanded that John Brown pay their wages. Brown insisted that he had not only paid all Richardson's claims upon him, but that Richardson had overdrawn his account by over £50. The engineer, Farrell, saw the importance of pacifying the men, and advanced Richardson another £70. Some time before work resumed on Monday morning, Brown set another sub-contractor on, to replace Richardson.

At lunch-time on Monday 18th September, Richardson and his men went to the Royal Oak public-house at Blisworth, where Brown was eating. Because he had broken his contract with them, they insisted that another payment was due. They would have Brown's money "or Brown's liver".[56] This pressure was sufficient to induce Brown to go again to the engineer's office. Farrell agreed to a further advance of money, but when Brown emerged from the office he was grabbed by some of the men before he could announce that a further payment had been arranged. His hands were forced from his pocket, and they took from him £8 15s., a couple of purses and a pocket book. The labourers shared the money and then dispersed. One who had been more active than the

74

others was followed, and taken into custody and locked in a room at the Royal Oak. His comrades gathered in a strong body and made an attack on the public house to rescue him. A messenger had been sent to the Northampton Police, and six officers hastened to Blisworth, where, together with two local constables, they stood alone against over a hundred rioters.

The police managed to arrest ten, including the escapee, and Thomas Richardson. The next day, before the magistrates, nine of them were committed for trial at the next Quarter Sessions.

The account of this incident in the *Northampton Mercury* is very muddled. Richardson's name changed to Robinson towards the end, probably because the journalist writing it caught a glimpse of the list of prisoners committed to gaol on remand, where it was given as Robinson. Martin Farrell, the railway engineer, wrote in to the *Mercury* to correct several points. His letter was published on 30th September (page 2, col. 3). The original version reported "every window within reach" broken.[56] Farrell wrote:

> "One window in the lower part of the house where the railway office is, having been accidentally pushed in by the people who crowded about Brown, the sub-contractor, on his imprudently commencing to pay some of them in front of the house . . . and at the Royal Oak, one window (that of the room where the prisoner was) alone suffered. . . ." He said that he wished to encourage the complaints of the workmen when they were under-paid. "I could not look upon their coming in a body to make such a complaint in the light of a riot, when they . . . received their money and dispersed." He added that the scuffle to rescue the man who stole Brown's money was short because of the resolute conduct of the police, and also because most of the men were not inclined to join in.

At the Quarter Sessions on 19th October, Robinson had become Richardson again. He and the other eight on remand were sent forward to the Assizes. They appeared before the same court as poor William Lantsberry of Hollowell, on 27th February 1838. Richardson and two of the others were acquitted on the instructions of Judge Sir James Park. John Brown, in his evidence, said that Richardson had given back the purse and money within minutes of the incident, so there had been no intention to steal.

One final comment is needed. It concerns the attitude of the company engineer at Blisworth, Farrell. Why did he go to so much trouble to minimise the seriousness of the incident on 18th September? One reason was probably the concern, expressed in his letter, that the men should be properly paid and fairly treated by the sub-contractors. All jobs are carried out better if there is good will. Another is almost certainly the anxiety of local residents, described in previous pages, about the behaviour of the railway labourers. Reports of this latest incident would certainly reach the London offices of the company. It would be better for the engineer on the spot if their gravity could be shown to be exaggerated.

26th September 1837

THE DEATH OF A WELL-LOVED ECCENTRIC

Sir John English Dolben died at Finedon Hall, at the age of 87. Since he gave up his Oxfordshire seat in Parliament, he had become popular for his charming eccentricities. He sought out the company of young children, "saying he was the youngest among them", having begun to count his years afresh from the age of seventy.[57] He carried so many small books about with him in his numerous and capacious pockets, that "he appeared like a walking library". Lodged in his memory was a rich store of classical quotations. His visiting cards were printed in black gothic script, and when asked why they were in old English, his reply was that he actually *was* "old English Dolben".

In a letter written, by coincidence, on the anniversary of Sir English's death, on 26th September, 1884, the Rev. Arthur Isham recalled a morning in Northampton spent with him. The writer was born in 1832, so this must have been a day very shortly before the last illness. "Sir English came to our house at Kingsthorpe with a confidential servant. His big pockets, the Squire's dress of the day, were filled with classic lore, Virgil and Horace. After breakfast Sir English and I set off to walk to Northampton, the servant attending. He handed a gold cane to me, saying . . . 'You shall have the honour of walking with Sir Gilbert's cane!' [Sir Gilbert Dolben was an ancestor.] So we trudged along. He took me to an inn in Gold Street on the left a little below Marshall's the shoe-maker. There he gave me some coffee, to the best of my remembrance. And I have an indistinct vision of a soldier in the inn to whom he addressed a few words. . . ."[58]

Sir John English Dolben lies in the Dolben vault, open to the outside air, at the east end of Finedon church. At the other end of the village is the obelisk he erected in 1789 to celebrate the recovery of George III from "illness".

26th September 1837

THE SAME DAY, A WEDDING IN NORTHAMPTON

A change in the law allowed weddings to take place officially in nonconformist churches. An inscription in a family Bible records the first such ceremony in the county town:

"September 26, 1837, Tuesday morning, at Castle Hill Meeting, married by Rev. Wm. Gray, Rev. John Bennett, pastor of that place, to Miss Taylor; the first wedding in Northampton in a dissenting place of worship."[59]

Register Office weddings had begun in August 1837. The first couple to be married at Northampton Register Office were Richard Hopkins, a tailor, of George Row, and Millicent Hewitt. The fifth man to be married by the Registrar was also a George Row tailor, Joseph Gurney, later to be Mayor of Northampton.

28th September 1837

UNUSUAL AUCTION SALES AT ROADE AND WELLINGBOROUGH

"IMPORTANT SALE OF HORSES
CART HORSE GEARING, ALDERNEY COW, SHEEP, &c. &c.
TO BE SOLD BY AUCTION
By B. CAPELL,

On Thursday, September 28th, 1837, at the NEW INN, ROADE, Northamptonshire, THE remaining part of the Stock of HORSES and GEARING, the property of Mr. BECKETT, who has declined HORSEING the works on the Railway, on Blisworth Bridge, consisting of upwards of 20 valuable strong horses and mares, 20 sets of cart horse gearing, nearly new, with extra weight of chains, several sets of gearing for Barrows, Chaff cutting machine, chaff boxes, and bean mill, all nearly new; portable mangers, rack and mangers, 40 feet long; excellent broad-wheel waggon, ditto broad-wheel cart, narrow wheel ditto, one light Scotch cart, with frame; one one-corner box for stable, handsome Alderney cow, in full profit; upwards of 20 ewe and wether lambs, valuable brown cob horse, five years old, 15 hands high, and quiet in harness; neat gig and harness, nearly new; one three-year-old horse pony, one four-year-old ditto, quiet in harness. Several lots of useful HOUSEHOLD FURNITURE. . . . The Sale to commence at Eleven precisely.

The New Inn is situate one mile from Roade, and five miles from Northampton, near the great cutting where steam engines are daily at work."

Although it is possible to speculate on possible reasons why Beckett might be giving up this seemingly vital element of the railway construction at Blisworth, it certainly had nothing to do with the violent episode of 18th September, described on a previous page. His advertisement appeared on 16th September, in the *Northampton Mercury* of that date (p. 3, col. 1). The same newspaper carried the following (p. 2, col. 6):

"NAVIGATION HORSE PUMP,
MATERIALS, STONES, IRON, &c.
TO BE SOLD BY AUCTION
By Mr. CLEAVER.

The property of the Commissioners of the Nen Navigation, at their WHARF, in the parish of WELLINGBOROUGH, in the County of Northampton, on Thursday, the 28th day of September, 1837 at one o'clock in the afternoon, consisting of a two-horse pumping engine with frame complete, chain pump, two single lifting ditto, oak and elm beams, sills and scantlings of large dimensions, a large quantity of old materials, old piles and implements, large quantity of fire-wood, six cast iron paddles, two feet square; a quantity of old wrought-iron plates, bolts, &c. a quantity of free-stone, and wrought lime-stones, with various other articles."

The pumping engine was not an engine at all. In another part of the country it would have been called a winding gin. The two horses would have been harnessed to an overhead revolving circular frame which could provide the power for a number of pulling, lifting or pumping actions.

At this time landing places for river boats were situated off the north bank of the Nene, both sides of the London Road, near the river bridge at Wellingborough.

2nd October 1837

DEATH OF A PIOUS WOMAN AT KETTERING

Betsey Wright lived a righteous life, utterly devoted to the Christian God. Her diary was published in Kettering shortly after her death. It is filled with remarks of extreme piety. Practically everything she did was in the interest of her religious belief. Phrases like "going to glory" abound, and she did not disguise her desire to die virtuous and pure, to be sure of her place in heaven. She did that.

Her last diary entry, on Wednesday September 13th, concluded:

> ". . . my mind [has been] exercised in various ways. Most deeply I lament that brotherly love does not more abound in our society. God is my refuge and strength, a very present help in trouble."

W. B. Browne described her last two days.[60]

> "On Saturday the 30th of September . . . her Mother remarks, 'I heard my dear Betsey, lifting up her heart to God. . . . She beckoned me to her bedside, and with an affectionate look said, Mother ought we not to rejoice together that the Lord has not cut us off as he might have done. This affliction is sent for some good end. . . .'
>
> "On the Sunday she lay calm and tranquil. Her intimate friend Mrs. Abbott called to see her. Looking upon her she faintly articulated 'Ann is it you?' During the following night she appeared to enjoy peaceful slumbers, and a trembling hope was entertained she would wake refreshed, but alas! The next morning a very great change had taken place. Her medical attendant was much surprised; he perceived she was dying, and emphatically said, 'It is all over!' Though incapable of expression, a beaming blessed composure pervaded her countenance, and a short time afterwards she resigned her happy spirit, without a struggle or a groan into the hands of her gracious *Redeemer*. . . "

She was thirty-one years old.

Early October 1837

A NEW INVENTION AT DITCHFORD MILL

"TO MILLERS, CORN MERCHANTS, MALTSTERS,
and Others.
SOUTHAM'S PATENT CORN-DRESSING MACHINE is
recommended for effectually drying damp Wheat, Barley,
beans, Oats, and Seeds of every description, in a manner far
superior to the present system of kiln-drying. It is capable of
drying fully two quarters per hour; the fuel required is very
trifling, and it needs but little attention when attached to
other machinery; in a Granary it may be worked by hand.

The space occupied is only 7 feet by 4, including the
brick-work. The Machine, which has been in operation
with good practical effect since the early part of last
October, may be seen in the MILLs of the Patentee,
WILLIAM SOUTHAM, DITCHFORD, near Wellingborough;
or at Messrs BARWELL & Co's Eagle Foundry,
Northampton.

For further particulars, apply, if by letters, postage paid,
and addressed to the Patentee."

(*Northampton Mercury* 20th January 1838, page, 1, col. 4.)

5th October 1837

LINGERING FEUDALISM

The inhabitants of a medieval village virtually belonged to the
lord of the manor. The manorial court over which he or his
steward presided, was a key feature in the organisation of the
community. It regulated the agricultural economy,
appointed village officials, settled disputes, punished wrong-
doers, and, of course, served as a regular reminder of the
authority of the lord. With the changes of the centuries, all
the functions of the court had either been transferred by

statute or custom to other authorities; or had become unnecessary.

A few of the Northamptonshire landowners in 1837 continued to maintain their prestige by the archaic means of convening an annual court. The following notice was issued on behalf of the Duke of Buccleuch, on 5th October (*Northampton Mercury* 7th October 1837, p. 2, col. 4).

"NOTICE IS HEREBY GIVEN,

THAT the General COURTS LEET, COURTS BARON, and CUSTOMARY COURTS of the Most Noble WALTER FRANCIS, DUKE OF BUCCLEUCH and QUEENSBURY, Knight of the Most Noble Order of the Garter, Lord of the Honor of Gloster Fee, The liberty, Hundreds of Huxloe, Polebrook, and Navisford, and the several Manors of Boughton, Weekley, Warkton, Geddington, Newton, Little Oakley, Broughton, Denford, Woodford, Grafton Underwood, Barton Seagrave, Cranford, and Twywell, in the County of Northampton, will be holden at the days, times and places undermentioned.

For the Manor of Weekley,
On Thursday, the 19th day of October instant, at 10 o'clock in the Forenoon, at the Montague Arms, in Weekley.

For the Manor of Warkton
On the same day at 12 o'clock at Noon, at the Duke's Arms in Warkton.

For the Manor of Little Oakley,
On Friday the 20th day of October instant, at 10 o'clock in the Forenoon, at the Manor House in Little Oakley. . . ."
[Similar arrangements for other manors.]

"For the Liberty Hundred of Huxloe,
On Wednesday the 1st day of November next, at 12 o'clock at Noon, at the White Hart Hotel in Kettering, for the several parishes within the said Hundred, namely: Aldwinckle All Saints, Aldwinckle Saint Peter's, Great Addington, Little Addington, Lowick, Woodford, Slipton, Irthlingborough, and Islip. . . ."
[Similar arrangements for the other liberty hundreds.]

"When and where the several and respective constables are required to attend to be sworn, and to bring their fealty and suit rolls; and the several persons summoned on juries; tenants who have come into possession of estates by death or alienation, for which they have not done fealty; and all other persons who owe suit and service are required to attend to pay their respective quit and other rents and reliefs, upon pain and peril of their default herein.

dated this 5th day of October, 1837

THO. MARSHALL, Solicitor, Kettering,

Steward of the said Honor, Liberty, Hundreds, and Manors."

A similar notice was issued at this time, for Lord Montagu of Boughton. It will be observed that the only practical function was the swearing in of the parish constables for the coming year (with a County Police Force still three years away); but this could have been done before any local magistrate. It would be a fair assumption that very few of the vassals bothered to obey the summons.

7th October 1837

KILSBY TUNNEL: ANOTHER FATAL ACCIDENT

". . . an inquest was taken at Kilsby, before G. Abbey, Esq., on the view of the body of John Hart, aged 18 years, who, being employed as banksman at the top of a shaft at Kilsby Tunnel, while in the act of landing a skip of earth, overbalanced himself, and fell to the bottom of the shaft, a depth of 100 feet, when, from the effect of the concussion, his chest was so much affected that he died two hours afterwards. Verdict: Accident."

(*Northampton Mercury* 14th October 1837, p. 3, col. 5.)

17th October 1837

STAGE-COACHES AT THE END OF THEIR TIME

Sam Daniel was one of the drivers of the Northampton coach. In a style of description far from clear, H. O. Nethercote, writing fifty years afterwards, explained what happened when he made a bet with Lieutenant Wellesley of the 12th Lancers, then quartered at Northampton, that, on his "little hack" he could beat the "Telegraph" coach from London.[61] "To ask a horse to go sixty-six miles continuously at the rate of ten miles an hour, seems to approach very nearly the confines of cruelty; but both horse and rider . . . completed the task without suffering any serious fatigue." The coach and the horse both left the Peacock inn at Islington, at a quarter to six on that Tuesday morning, 17th October. Daniel reached Northampton "amid the acclamations of a large concourse of people, one minute and a half earlier than his competitor."

Nethercote tells us that Daniel did not live to experience the reduced circumstances that came to coach drivers soon after the opening of the London and Birmingham Railway. John Harris, another Northampton coachman, was "reduced to driving a one-horse bus about the streets of the town through which for many a year [he] had tooled four well-shaped steeds. Davis, the driver of the "Manchester Telegraph", the fastest coach out of London, "found himself a 'walking postman' on certain remote highways and byways of Northamptonshire. . . . He strove to drown his cares in that usual refuge of the destitute – alcohol".

Arthur Cossons has given us some facts and figures of the mail coaches in 1837.[62] Taking his particulars from Charles Knight's *British Almanac*, 1838, he shows an improvement in the performance of the service, since 1811. Nine mail coaches passed through Northamptonshire from London. The destinations were Holyhead (via Daventry); Liverpool (via Northampton and Welford); Carlisle (via Northampton); Glasgow (via Wansford and Stamford); Leeds (via Kettering); Edinburgh (via Wansford and Stamford); Halifax (via Northampton); Hull (via Peterborough); and Boston (via Peterborough). That was one more route than in 1811. All the mail coaches left London at 8 in the evening. The Northampton arrival time was 2.45 a.m. This was two hours and forty minutes earlier than in 1811. Daventry arrival time was 3.25 a.m.; Kettering, 3.56 a.m.; and Peterborough, 4.24 a.m. The speed was approaching ten miles per hour. The best 1811 speed was 7.43 miles an hour.

Andrew Percival remembered those mail coaches through Peterborough, and wrote about them nearly seventy years later.[31] "For coaches, we were pretty well off. Two mails ran through Peterborough, the Boston Coach, and the Coach to Hull. We used to go shares with the town of Stamford with a London Coach. One of our townsmen ran a coach to Stilton daily, where it joined the coach from Stamford. . . . The Mail Coaches were very comfortable for travelling in fine weather, and an eight or ten hours' journey was very pleasant, provided you did not ride inside. A journey to London or Edinburgh occupied two whole days and nights. The expense of such a mode of travelling was very great, being five or six times as much as the ordinary first class railway fare. Every fifty or sixty miles the coachman would touch his hat and say, 'I leave you here, sir', which meant that you were to give him a fee. The guard would do the same, and when your luggage was put up, the ostler came to you. If you travelled post or in 'a yellow and two' as it was called, you had to pay one shilling and sixpence a mile, beside the toll bars, and threepence a mile for the post boy, as well as something more that he always expected. . . ."

Percival was the son of a Northampton doctor, and took up an apprenticeship in Peterborough in 1833. "When I came . . . and for some years afterwards, the only communication between . . . Northampton and . . . Peterborough was a one-horse carrier's cart, which came twice a week; and I think the large proportion of its business consisted in carrying parcels from the Probate Office at Northampton to the Probate Office at Peterborough. . . . When I wanted to go to Northampton, for many years, I had to get up at six o'clock in the morning, hire a gig to go to Thrapston, where I caught the Cambridge coach, which ran in connection with the coach at Oxford. It cost about four pounds to go home and come back again."

William Hircock, the Kettering farmer, had a little to say

about the coaches of the eighteen-thirties, when he was interviewed by a "representative" of the *Kettering Leader* (10th March 1905). He "used to go by the old stage coach starting from the Royal Hotel at 9 o'clock at night, arriving in London the next morning about 5 o'clock". Hircock had evidently forgotten that the Royal Hotel was still known as the White Hart when he first came to Kettering in 1837. "The coach horses used to be changed at Barton Seagrave and then go on to Higham Ferrers. Mr. Hobson, of Barton Seagrave, used to horse the coach. The horses were generally changed every ten miles or so."

The economy of Towcester was almost entirely dependant on the coaches and other traffic along the Watling Street, the Irish mail route, so the forthcoming opening of the London and Birmingham Railway was a matter of apprehension in that town. We have a graphic impression of Towcester in 1837 from Samuel Cooper Tite, who kept a chemist's shop in that town for many years. In 1889, at the age of 70, he emigrated to Vancouver Island, and on 29th July, he was interviwed for the *Northampton Mercury* (Supplement 3rd August 1889, page 10).

". . . Towcester was a town of inns. Every other house was an inn, and a posting place to boot. . . . Coaches and chaises passed through the town every hour of the day, and almost of the night. Postboys congregated there by the dozens. . . . The large inns had larger stables where horses were kept to work the coaches, and to draw the post chaises. . . .

"A gallant effort was made to compete with the railway. . . . There were heavy gradients between Towcester and Weedon on the high road, but . . . rough stone tramways were laid up the hills on the left side of the road to aid the horses . . . in 1837. . . . About three-hundred men were employed in the work, under the superintendence of the veteran in road-making, George Savage [then living at Stoke Bruerne]. . . . Towcester was then an important posting station, as well as for relays of horses for the coaches. Every third or fourth house was a public house or inn. For instance, there was then the White Horse, the first posting establishment in the town. . . . Almost next to this

... was a posting place called Bell and ——? [which by 1889 had become Richardson's grocery shop]. . . . Next to that, going towards Weedon, was the Dolphin, now the bank. Next was another Dolphin, adjoining the other, and both posting places. Just beyond was the Angel, and a door or two further was the sign of the Tabbard, now altered to Talbot. A little further was the Saracen's Head, a name now supplanted by the Pomfret Arms. Park Lane between the Saracen's Head and the Tabbard was little more than a thoroughfare of public houses. . . . On the opposite side was the Red Lion.

"Foster's Booth was at that time little more than a large booth erected as temporary stabling. The horses there were needed on account of the hills, and there being no inn a wood and canvas booth was thought the cheapest way of providing accommodation for the horses. . . . A hamlet has sprung up and has retained the name."

The anecdotist, Wimersley Bush, had a story of the last days of coaching.[63] It was about the Cosgrove miller, Thomas Dawson, who was persuaded to accompany a friend on a trip to London. They took seats on top of the coach on the Watling Street. Near to London it began to rain. "Dammy" Dawson told his friend that he had no umbrella with him, but he would borrow one in London. "You can't borrow an umbrella in London," said his friend scornfully. "Damn-damn-double damn!" cried the miller. "Why, anyone in Stony Stratford 'd lend me an umbrella" – and back he went to Cosgrove by the next coach. That was the only night he ever spent away from his native village.

---

mid-October 1837

THE CHAPLAIN OF THE NORTHAMPTON WORKHOUSE

The appointment of a chaplain by the Board of Guardians of the Northampton Union was almost certain to engender controversy because an Anglican appointee would not suit the Nonconformists, and *vice versa*. When Broad, a curate at All Saints' was appointed, a handbill was circulated in Northampton which the *Mercury* declared to be offensive (21st October 1837, p. 3, col. 4). Normally the *Northampton Mercury* might be expected to respect the Nonconformist point of view, but the message of the handbill was not simply anti-Anglican: it was anti-chaplain. It said:

"TO THE RATEPAYERS OF NORTHAMPTON
You will soon be called upon by the Collector for A RATE FOR THE RELIEF OF THE POOR. The guardians intend to make this A RATE FOR THE RELIEF OF THE CURATE too.

In page 539 of the second report of the Poor Law Commissioners, they say, 'It is not legal to apply a compulsory rate or tax to any other than the specific purpose for which it is raised.' Tell the Collector, when he calls, that you know of no law that allows of the taking of your money to pay any Clergyman; and that you will not pay until you know that no part of it shall go into the pockets of the Rev. Mr. BROAD.

As the Guardians have undertaken to pay the Reverend Gentleman £50 per Annum (about as much as the maintenance of eight paupers); ought he to be above wearing the Paupers' dress if he is not above taking your money?

Should Mr. B. ever mount the pulpit of All Saints' Church in his Workhouse Dress, how his admirers might exclaim, 'What humility! – surely the days of the Apostles are come again!' "

20th October 1837

THE HISTORIAN OF THE COUNTY ASKING FOR SUPPORT

George Baker had been working for many years on the history of Northamptonshire, relying largely on patronage to finance the project. Without the aid of photocopying, typewriter, word-processor, ball-pens, central repositories of information and fast link-roads, his task must have been overwhelming. When he published part IV in 1836, he addressed his readers, complaining of inadequate financing: "I have lost many subscribers by death and the fluctuations of property since the announcement of my undertaking. Some individuals excuse themselves from subscribing on the plea that they shall not live to see its completion. . . ."

Allowing for purchasers of the latest instalment to read it, and approve of what they read, a meeting was called on Friday 20th October 1837, at the George Hotel in Northampton, with the Marquis of Northampton in the chair.[64] Resolutions of support were passed, and a committee was appointed to carry them out. Among its members were a marquis, two earls, two barons, seven baronets, three members of Parliament, and eight clergymen. Such a high-powered body might have been supposed sufficient to relieve the historian from all anxiety, but not so. Part V appeared four years later, with only eighty-one pages of text, a third of the size of the earlier parts. The work was never completed, and Baker's marvellous collection of material was sold by auction in October 1842.

31st October 1837

PARISH WORKHOUSE TO LET

It has been explained earlier that the Poor Law unions had been given loans from the Exchequer to pay for the building and equipping of the new workhouses, and mention has been made of the Wellingborough Union's sales of property to enable them to pay back the loan (13th March 1837). On 13th September 1837, the Wellingborough Guardians put on sale the redundant workhouse at Bozeat for £81.[65] Now they were about to dispose of the old parish workhouse in Wellingborough itself.

"HOUSE TO LET.
TO BE LET BY AUCTION,
By Mr. CLEAVER,
"At the Town Hall, in Wellingborough . . . on Tuesday, the
31st day of October, 1837, at Eleven o'clock in the fore-
noon.

PART of the FEOFFEE PROPERTY, situate in the Parish of
WELLINGBOROUGH aforesaid, consisting of a MESSUAGE
or TENEMENT, in the centre of the Town, lately and for
many years past used as the Parish Workhouse, consisting
of two rooms on the ground floor, one of which is 24 feet
by 16 feet; three large chambers, two attics, and a good
cellar, together with a large open yard immediately
adjoining, and convenient out-office therein, bounded by a
brick wall dividing the same from the remaining part of the
Feoffee Estate lately occupied therewith.

"The premises adjoin the Town Hall and the High Street,
are well calculated for any business requiring extent of
room, and will be let for the term of one year from the 21st
day of December next, or earlier if desired; and so on from
year to year, until six months notice in writing shall be
given by the landlords or tenant to quit or leave the same at
the end of any year.

"For further particulars, apply to Mr. SANDERSON, the
AUCTIONEER, or to Mr. BURNHAM, Solicitor, all of
Wellingborough."

(*Northampton Mercury* 14th October 1837, p. 1, col. 4.)

The Feoffees were the forerunners of the Town Council,
entitled to charge fees. The Town Hall, mentioned in the
above advertisement, adjoining the old workhouse, still
stands, as a hardware shop.

2nd November 1837

HIGHWAY ROBBERY ON THE KETTERING ROAD

Supplementing the efforts of the county magistrates and the parish constables in dealing with crime, in the days before the Northamptonshire County Police Force, were the associations for the prosecution of felons. Some of these associations still exist, with, seemingly, no other function than the annual dinner. Their very real purpose in 1837 is illustrated by the following advertisement, which appeared in the *Northampton Mercury* of 4th November (p. 3, col. 1):

"BRIXWORTH ASSOCIATION.
TWENTY GUINEAS REWARD.
WHEREAS Mr. BINYON G. DRAGE, Jun. of HOLCOT, in this county, was on Thursday night the 2nd Instant, about eight o'clock, STOPPED and pulled off his horse by three men in dark clothing, about a mile and a quarter from Northampton, on the Kettering Turnpike Road, and ROBBED of a small Pocket Book (with steel spring clasp) containing NINE FIVE POUND NOTES of the Bank of 'Messrs. Percival', Northampton, and several Memorandums. Four Sovereigns, and some Silver, and also a Black Hat with the Name of the Owner printed within side, and Maker's Name, 'H. Thompson, 65 Great Suffolk Street, Southwark.'

Whoever will give such information as shall lead to the conviction of the offenders or either of them, shall receive a Reward of Fifteen Guineas from the said Binyon G. Drage, and a further Reward of Five Guineas from Mr. R. C. Andrew, Solicitor, Brixworth, treasurer of the said Association; and in case either of the offenders shall impeach his accomplices, he shall receive the above Reward, and intercession will be made to obtain him her Majesty's pardon. . . ."

8th November 1837

FARNDON WINDMILL FOR SALE

TO BE SOLD BY PRIVATE CONTRACT.
A POST WINDMILL, with Two pair of Stones; a DRESSING
MACHINE, with Two Cylinders, now standing on EYDON
HILL, to be taken off the ground.
  Apply to Mr. RICHARD HAYNES, FARNDON MILL, near
Eydon. Nov. 8th, 1837."

(*Northampton Mercury* 11th November 1837, p. 1, col. 4.)

11th November 1837

THREE MORE DEATHS ON THE RAILWAY AT
KILSBY

George Abbey, the Coroner, had been to Barby on Thursday
2nd November, to conduct an inquest on view of the body of
twenty-eight-year-old Timothy Butler. He had been oiling an
engine at the Kilsby Tunnel, when he fell backwards on to an
iron bar, injuring his kidneys. Less than two days later he was
dead.[66]
  On 3rd November, the same coroner was at Kilsby, holding
an inquest into the death of Thomas West, aged seventeen.
Some hard clay from a skip fell eighty feet to where he stood
at the bottom of a shaft, and struck him on the head.[66]
  On Saturday 11th November, George Abbey was back in
Kilsby. The deceased this time was Charles Peck, aged thirty.
He also had been at the bottom of a shaft in the tunnel. A
heavy stone from the "heading" had fallen on him and
fractured his skull. This man had died two days later at "the
Infirmary" at Kilsby. The verdict in all these cases was, of
course, Accidental Death.[66] That mention of the infirmary at
Kilsby is a reminder of the great concern felt by the governing

body of the Northampton Infirmary about the number of railway casualties being brought there for treatment (and to die). Evidently the railway company had at last thought it expedient to establish an infirmary nearer to the tunnel workings.

13th November 1837

BULL-RUNNING AT STAMFORD

This was the last year in which the traditional bull-running was successfully carried out. For centuries, on this day of the year, a bull had been turned loose in the streets to chase and be chased by the young men of Stamford. For many years the festival had been controversial: there are disapproving descriptions of it dating from the late eighteenth century. By 1837 it had become political. Tories (flourishing red ribbons) heartily supported the bull-running. Whigs (in blue) were doing their best to oppose it. Richard Newcomb, the proprietor of the *Stamford Mercury* (published in Northamptonshire in the parish of St. Martin's), campaigned against the tradition. As the day approached, the magistrates swore-in a large number of special constables, but they proved themselves unreliable. A Collyweston farmer, Richard Stevens, saved the custom for one more year, by supplying a bull which successfully evaded all barriers to its entry into the town.[67]

14th November 1837

THE STRANGE BEHAVIOUR OF A PROMINENT CITIZEN AT THE NEW WATER MAINS IN NORTHAMPTON

Although the water mains were not yet laid in the town centre, the Northampton Water Company was already advertising its services. Its price list was issued on 10th November.[68] From the 25th of next March, it undertook to supply "any persons with any quantity of water they require, by day and night . . .". The area covered was described as "Northampton and its boundaries". Charges were to be quarterly, and the scale related to the rateable value of the property served. Private houses, inns, beerhouses, bakehouses, stables, slaughterhouses, of a yearly value "of 20 & not exceeding £25" were to be charged five shillings per quarter. Property worth between 80 and a hundred pounds would be charged eleven shillings. The smallest houses were to have the lowest charge of one shilling a quarter.

The talented James Sharp was personally supervising the laying of the water mains in the town centre. On the night of 14th November, a curious disturbance occurred. The outcome was a case heard at Northampton Petty Sessions on Tuesday, 21st November, before the Mayor, and three other magistrates. One of them, D. Hewlett, during the proceedings, found himself involved in the case. Those who gave evidence before this court will tell us now, what they saw on the night of the 14th. Thomas Phipps had been summonsed under the Petty Trespass Act. A complaint had been brought aginst him by the engineer, James Sharp, who went into the witness box first.

Sharp: I hold a contract under the Water Company for laying the mains. On Tuesday last, my men were at work at the bottom of Sheep Street, and on account of the wet weather, it was found impossible to fill the trench before dark. In order to prevent accidents, I ordered lights to be kept burning during the night, at each end of the trench. At one end was placed accordingly the fire-pot which was used for melting lead, and the other end, a lantern with a candle in it. A man was also placed to watch. About half past ten o'clock, I was informed by this man that the candle had twice been knocked out, and the fire upset into the trench. The man said that Mr. Phipps had done it, and that he was gone into the Ram. I told the watchman then on duty, Absalom Payne, what had occurred, and I desired him, if the act was repeated, to take the person into custody. Some time after, while I was standing near the Bear gate, I saw Mr. Phipps come out of the Ram, and deliberately pull down the fire basket. The watchman accordingly took him into custody. I went up to Mr. Phipps and remonstrated with him, telling him at the same time that if he had any pique against the Water Company he was in the wrong, for he was injuring me, not the Company. Mr. Phipps insisted upon being taken to the watch-house, but I replied that I did not wish to give him in charge. I knew him and that was sufficient. My only object was to protect the public against accidents. I should have considered myself deservedly blameable if I had not taken those precautions.

Thomas Phipps: I admit I kicked over the fire-basket. I want to know what connection Mr. Sharp's partner has with the *Chronicle.*

Sharp: I cannot answer that question, for I do not know.

Phipps: The *Chronicle* has attempted to prejudice my case in a most unfair way.

The Mayor: The question is quite irrelevant. The decision of the case is in our hands, and you might assure yourself that we are not prejudiced by anything which may have been published on the subject. The simple question we have to decide is whether you have committed the act with which you are charged, and if so, whether you were justified in doing it.

Phipps to Sharp: Do you have permission from the Commissioners to open the ground? [He was referring to the Northampton Improvement Commissioners, of whom he was a member.]

Sharp: I believe that the Company has the necessary permission.

Clerk of the Peace: I have no doubt they have.

Phipps to Sharp: Do you not consider the light was unsafe and likely to frighten the horses?

Sharp: I do not. While I stood there, I saw three coaches pass, and the horses showed no alarm whatever. I should now like to call James Evans.

James Evans: I am employed by Mr. Sharp. I was sitting, on the night in question, watching the trench to prevent accidents. About a quarter before ten, I went to light the candle in the lantern, which had been put out. I left a boy sitting by the fire-basket. At this moment, several gentlemen came out of the Ram, and told the boy to get up. I could not say who they were. They fixed a string to the fire-basket and pulled it over. I replaced it, and put the fire in again, and in the mean time someone went and put out the lantern.

Phipps: Was it me?

Evans: I could not say.

Phipps: Well, that's no evidence against me.

Evans: I then went towards the lantern, and hearing someone behind me, I looked round and saw Mr. Phipps push down the fire-basket. While I was lighting the fire a second time, Mr. Sharp came up.

Phipps: And I put it out again. That's very fair evidence so far.

Evans: I saw him knock it over a third time. This time I was close to the fire. Mr. Phipps said: "Damn you, old man. You've got your damned old coffee kettle up again." (Laughter.)

Phipps to the Mayor: I beg to caution the witness that he is on his oath.

Evans: I am aware of that.

96

Phipps: It does not look like it.

Evans: Having said those words, he hurled the fire-basket into the trench. I then told the watchman to take him into custody, and while Mr. Payne and Mr. Phipps were together, Mr. Sharp came up and said he should not give him into custody as he knew him, and that was sufficient. Mr. Phipps said if they lit the fire again he would knock it down again. Mr. Phipps stood there some time, and then went with his party towards the lantern, and I saw the light knocked out. I was not nigh enough to see who actually did it.

Absalom Payne: I am a night constable. I was standing near the Ram between eleven and half past, when I saw a party come out of the Ram. I recognised Mr. Phipps among them. I did not know the others. There were five or six. They all went away except Mr. Phipps, who stood a few minutes in front of the Ram by himself. He then went across and kicked the fire-grate into the trench, and I took hold of him. Mr. Sharp came up and said, "I know the gentleman quite well. It's Mr. Phipps: therefore it's all right", or something of that kind. "I shall let him go home, and deal with him another way." Phipps then walked away. I saw the lantern go out, but I did not see who put it out.

James Sharp called no more witnesses, and Phipps next had the opportunity to speak in his own defence.

Phipps: I acknowledge that I kicked over the fire-basket. My motive was that the light was an improper one, and calculated to frighten horses. It was scarcely possible for a horse to pass without being terrified. Another reason was that Mr. Sharp had no business to leave the ground open. Several accidents have happened in consequence of the bad state of the streets. One occurred lately in Bridge-street. The surveyor did not do his duty, so I kicked over the grate. I have a right to do it inasmuch as Mr. Sharp has no business to leave his property exposed. Mr. Hewlett's son was nearly thrown from his horse in consequence of the fire.

D. Hewlett, from the Bench: That is true, but it was in consequence of Mr. Phipps having kicked the fire over and rendering it necessary to re-light it, and thus occasioning a great flame. I passed up the street myself about seven in the evening, and I could not help noticing how clear and beautiful a light the fire produced, without any flame. With respect to Mr. Sharp's right to open the ground, I think the magistrates have a right to consider that the Water Company had obtained regular permission to carry on this work, or their proeedings would have been stopped long since. The question we have to consider is simply this. Did Mr. Sharp take all proper precautions to prevent accidents, and was Mr. Phipps justified in acting as he has done. For my part, I think that if Mr. Sharp *had* done wrong, Mr. Phipps has taken a very wrong method of correcting it. I regret that the case has not been settled before a single magistrate, because Mr. Phipps could then have appealed to the Recorder, and the question would have been set to rest whether any individual has the power to act as Mr. Phipps has acted.

Phipps: I consider, as a commissioner, I have the right to do as I have done, and if I have an opportunity I shall appeal to the Sessions.

The Bench retired to consider. On their return —

The Mayor: We are of the unanimous opinion that Mr. Sharp had used every proper precaution to prevent accidents, and that Mr. Phipps had no right to remove those precautions. Whether the Water Company had or had not obtained the necessary permission to open the streets was a question with which we have nothing to do in this case. We are unanimously of opinion that Mr. Phipps has done wrong, and we therefore fine him sixpence, the amount of damage done, and twelve shillings and sixpence costs.

Phipps: I suppose I shall be allowed time to consider about the payment.

The Mayor: Oh, yes. If you like, we will allow you a fortnight to pay it.

Phipps: I shall lay an information against Mr. Sharp, for lighting a fire in the street.

15th November 1837

TWO DAYS OF ACTION FOR THE BRACKLEY FIRE BRIGADE

In the early hours of Tuesday, 14th November, the Brackley fire engine had been called into Oxfordshire to assist the Bicester firemen at Tusmore House. On Wednesday afternoon, 15th November, the Brackley firemen were out again, at Hinton Field, where fire destroyed the house, barn, stable and several stacks of corn and hay, belonging to Job Lord. The firemen found very little water, and it was so polluted that the pipes of the engine were soon choked. The household furniture was saved; and a hill of beans (literally). One of the destroyed ricks was a gigantic structure composed of a hundred and thirty bags of wheat. The fire was burning from two o'clock until five on Thursday morning.

At first, the fire was supposed to have been caused deliberately, and a man suspected of being the incendiary was arrested on the Thursday and taken before Major Cartwright an Aynho. He was released when it was finally established that Job Lord's young son had accidentally started the fire by discharging a touch-gun (an old-style muzzle-loading gun fired by the application of smouldering material to a touch-hole).

Accounts of both fires were given in the *Northampton Mercury* on 18th November (p. 3, col. 5).

24th November 1837

AN OLD SOLDIER REMEMBERS THE EARL OF CARDIGAN

George Loy Smith was serving in the 11th Dragoons when Cardigan assumed command, in India. In his memoirs,[69] he recalled hearing of the appointment during a spell of treat-

99

ment in a military hospital. The reputation of Lord Brudenell (as he then was) was well known, and it was not good news. Smith described "dreadfully hard" training under the new Colonel, in October. The men were "completely prostrated", which, some would say, was probably good for them.

An incident in November filled Smith with disgust. An old soldier, John Dowling, due for discharge, was found to be drunk on picquet. This offence would have brought a punishment of eight days confinement, under the previous commanding officer, but Cardigan ordered him to be tried by court-martial. The regiment did not know the sentence until all ranks were marched to the riding school, where it was read out to them: corporal punishment. Cardigan apparently had the final decision of whether or not it should be carried out. Asked what he had to say, the old soldier said, "My Lord, I hope you won't flog me. I am an old man just going home. . . ."

"Tie him up," ordered Cardigan, and the farriers began to lay on the lash.

28th November 1837

A FARTHINGSTONE FARMER DISOWNS HIS WIFE

John Herbert inserted the following brief notice in the *Northampton Mercury* of 9th December 1837 (p. 1, col. 3). It was repeated each week until Christmas.

"CAUTION
I, the undersigned JOHN HERBERT, of FARTHINGSTONE, in the County of Northampton, Farmer and Grazier, do hereby warn and caution all persons from selling goods to or otherwise TRUSTING MY WIFE, Ann Herbert; and that after this public notice I will not be answerable for any debt she may contract. Given under my hand, the twenty-eighth day of November, 1837.

JOHN HERBERT."

28th November 1837

ON THE SAME DAY, A NORTHAMPTONSHIRE M.P. EXPOSES A "SCANDAL"

With its huge temporary population of railway labourers, all with homes at some distance, Kilsby was an obvious place to establish a post office. Even before the great national reform of 1840, the Penny Post, there were local penny post schemes. When the approval of the Postmaster was obtained for an office at Kilsby, the Rev. Charles Gillbee, a Conservative, recommended a staunch Conservative named Wood to take charge. He was installed, but his appointment was never approved, and after a time he was replaced by a sixteen-year-old girl, Miss Wall. Her age gave grounds for Conservatives to object, and she was officially replaced – but not by a Conservative.

In the House of Commons on Tuesday 28th November, Sir Charles Knightley (Conservative), of Fawlsey, brought this matter to the notice of one of the Treasury Ministers of the Whig Government.

> Sir Charles Knightley (South Northamptonshire): I can mention an instance of the perversion of Government influence. . . . An application had been made to the Postmaster to establish a penny post-office at [Kilsby]. The Daventry office keeper required information to enable him to appoint a proper person. The clergyman of the place recommended a proper person, but after three months, another person was appointed . . . a young lady only sixteen years of age, and ultimately, the appointment was set aside. The young lady was the daughter of a dissenter. The next person appointed, a lady named Lee, was also a dissenter, and a violent opponent of mine.

> F. Baring: I am afraid I do not perfectly understand the charge of the honourable Member. The points of his statement seem to be that on the recommendation of a clergyman, a penny-post office was established at Kilsby, and that a man named Wood was appointed as keeper of that office, without consultation of the proper authorities. In a few

months, on the recommendation of the Treasury, Wood was removed, and another person appointed in his place; the clergyman of the parish recommended a person who was strongly in favour of the politics of the honourable Member, and the Treasury appointed one who was not quite so strongly inclined to that way of thinking. I can only add that so long as the Treasury has these appointments, the Honourable gentleman is likely very often to have similar grounds of complaint. (Laughter and cheers.)

28th November 1837

ON THE SAME DAY, AN INQUEST AT BRACKLEY WORKHOUSE

The Union Workhouse at Brackley had been open for a year and two months. It had approximately eighty inmates. One of them, Abraham Badby, of the nearby village of Croughton, had been found dead in his bed on Monday morning, the previous day. Except for a new-born baby, no one had died in this workhouse before. There was widespread criticism of the regime in some workhouses, and the Coroner, R. Weston, had been requested to encourage the jury to examine the witnesses closely, for the satisfaction of the public as well as themselves. The *Northampton Mercury*, reporting this inquest, on 2nd December (p. 3, col. 5) did not make clear whether the pressure came from opponents of the new Poor Law, or from the Guardians or the Master, who would be anxious to prove that all was well.

The Master gave evidence first: "I am the Master of the Union Workhouse. The health of the deceased was much as usual at supper on Sunday night. He ate his allowance. That is ten ounces of bread and one ounce of cheese. I never saw him alive after that."

The Coroner requested the supper allowance to be brought

in and shown to the jury. They all said it was sufficient for any man, and more than any of them would have eaten.

Successive witnesses testified that they had never heard Abraham Badby complain; that he was kindly treated at all times. Those who were inmates answered extra questions to say that they were very comfortable and had no cause to complain. The unanimous verdict was "Death by Visitation of God". The Coroner afterwards took the jury to visit the paupers in the house who had not given evidence. The inmates all appeared clean and healthy, and all the jury recognised one old man, Thomas Hicks, well-known in the town. He was asked how he was being cared for. "Why, we have plenty of food, plenty of clothes, and a good bed to sleep on. What can we desire more?"

30th November 1837

HIGHWAY ROBBERS AT OUNDLE

"Mr. Bebee, the Woodford carrier, on his return from Oundle market on Thursday [30th November], when near Barnwell, was stopped by three men, when walking by the side of his cart, near Gypsey-lane, one of whom knocked him down, after which the party robbed him of 23 shillings and his pocket book containing a number of memoranda. A female passenger, who was in the cart, became so alarmed as to be unable to proceed further than Barnwell that night." (*Northampton Mercury* 9th December 1837, p. 4, col. 2.)

The crime took place on the south side of Oundle, probably during late afternoon, bearing in mind the November dusk and the likely time traders were leaving the town after the market. The following incident took place on the same day, at six o'clock, on the north side of the town. If two of the same criminals were involved, it is a fair assumption that they passed unnoticed through Oundle between the two crimes.

"As Robert Everest, son of Mr. Everest of Cotterstock Mills, was returning from Oundle market on Thursday evening, the 30th ultimate, about 6 o'clock, at the bottom of Elbow-lane, not a quarter of a mile from Elmington toll-bar, he was knocked down by two fellows, who instantly fell on him, and took out of one of his pockets, a purse containing eight shillings. Fortunately, they heard the noise of a carriage going along the Peterborough Road, and one said, 'There is a gig coming', on which they immediately left Mr. Everest, who thus saved a watch and some sovereigns. On the same evening an attempt was made by two ruffians to stop Mr. Isaac Cooper, of Polebrook, on his return from market, but his horse shying, he was able to ride off."

(*Northampton Mercury* 16th December 1837, p. 3, col. 5.)

1st December 1837

KETTERING WORKHOUSE CLOTHING

At the meeting of the Board of Guardians of the Kettering Union on Monday the 27th of November 1837, tenders were considered, for the supply of clothing from 1st December to 1st June 1838, for the inmates of the Union Workhouse. The advertisement inviting these tenders, had been issued on 16th November, and published in the *Northampton Mercury* on 18th (p. 2, col. 5). The specifications give us a graphic impression of what Kettering paupers were wearing at the end of 1837:

"MEN'S CLOTHING
Dark brown cloth coats and waistcoats, three sizes,
    at   per suit
Dark brown cloth trowsers [sic.], three sizes,
    at   per pair

Grey worsted stockings, three sizes
    at   per pair
Strong shoes and hightops, from 6 to 10 size,
    each at   per pair
Coarse felt hats, two sizes,
    at   per hat

WOMEN'S CLOTHING

Blue striped cotton for gowns, at   per yard
Flannel, at   per yard
Linsey woolsey, at   per yard
Stays, jean, three sizes, at   per pair
Black worsted stockings, three sizes, at   per pair
Coarse straw bonnets, three sizes, at   per bonnet
Shoes, from three to six sizes, at   per pair
Cotton shawls, two sizes, at   per dozen
Blue spotted handkerchiefs, two sizes, at   per dozen
Strong coarse cloth for aprons, at   per yard
Unbleached cotton, for linings, at   per yard

BOYS' CLOTHING

Fustian jackets and trowsers, three sizes, at   per suit
Grey worsted stockings, at   per pair
Scotch worsted caps, at   per cap
Strong shoes and hightops (different sizes),
    at   per pair

GIRLS' CLOTHING

Coarse straw bonnets, at   per bonnet
Stays, jean, two sizes, at   per pair
Black worsted stockings, three sizes, at   per pair
Shoes (different sizes), at   per pair

CLOTHING MATERIALS

Strong linen sheeting, at   per yard
Strong cotton shirting, at   per yard
Threads, tapes, needles, &c.
Grey and black worsted, at   per lb."

The Scotch caps to be worn by pauper boys were almost certainly the style known as Tam o'shanter, or tammy. The tenders had to be delivered, sealed, at the expense of the tradesman, with the name of a surety for due performance of the contract, together with samples.

5th December 1837

DEBTORS' COURT

Debtors were imprisoned until 1869, although from 1844 those who owed less than twenty pounds could not be put in gaol. If successful arrangements were made to clear a man's debts while he was in prison, then an application would need to be made for his release. The following notice appeared on page one of the *Northampton Mercury* of 2nd December:

> "NOTICE is hereby given, That THOMAS BARTON NOWEN, Esquire, one of her Majesty's Commissioners for the Relief of Insolvent Debtors, will, on the FIFTH day of DECEMBER, 1837, at the hour of Ten in the Forenoon precisely, attend at the COURT HOUSE, at NORTHAMPTON, in the County of Northampton, and hold A COURT for the RELIEF OF INSOLVENT DEBTORS, pursuant to the Statute."

5th December 1837

ON THE SAME DAY, A CHALLENGE TO MORTAL COMBAT

James Wilmot Croxen, of Leicester Street, Northampton, believed himself to have been defamed by John Stanton. He addressed a letter to him, dated "5 Dec. 1837". It said:

"I, James Wilmot Croxen, by the Grace of God, being of sound mind, body and understanding, do this. First, from your having wantonly and wilfully aspersed my character, (not coming under the existing laws of the country) I hereby challenge you to mortal combat. Place — Race-course.

Name time per return, and weapons."

To intensify the blood-chilling horror of the challenge, Croxen added at the foot of the letter, a sketch of a skull and cross-bones.

Stanton, having sought advice, brought Croxen up before Northampton Petty Sessions, at the Town Hall on 12th December. The challenger was bound over to keep the peace towards John Stanton, for three months; himself in the sum of twenty pounds, and with two sureties, each of the same sum.

6th December 1837

A NORTHAMPTON FORTUNE TELLER

The Court that dealt with the would-be duellist, Croxen, also had before it a woman named Walker, described as an "old woman" although her daughter, who was present with her, was only fifteen years old. A complaint had been brought against her by another woman, not named. Let this complainant explain in her own words to the Court:

I went to her house on Wednesday [6th December] and had my fortune told. I went because several of my relatives have been, and I thought it was time the practice should be stopped. I understand it has been carried on for six or seven years. She told a young woman that it would not matter if she got in the family way because the young man would marry her. She told *me* that my husband was gone on a little journey.

D. Hewlett, from the Bench: And was that so?

107

Complainant: No, unless she calls walking up the yard a little journey. (Laughter.) She told me I have a great many enemies, and that my greatest enemies' names begin with N and S. She then took some ordinary playing cards, and told me to wish. She said the wish was a very good wish, and I should have it.

D. Hewlett: And what was your wish?

Complainant: My wish was that her fortune-telling might be done away with.

Mrs. Walker: I'm got to do *something*. Anybody is welcome to use my cards for a few halfpence. Sometimes I get a few halfpence, and sometimes nothing. There are others in the town besides me. I cannot do much washing: I am not strong enough.

D. Hewlett: Your conduct is abominable. You told those young women that they had no chance of being married unless they became prostitutes. I have not for a long time looked upon anybody with more disgust. I am unwilling for the sake of your daughter to send you to prison on this occasion, but the very first time I hear of any young woman visiting your house, I shall send you to the treadmill. . . . We shall dismiss you this time, but your conduct will be narrowly watched, and if I know any person who might employ you as a washer-woman, I shall feel it my duty to inform them what sort of woman they have in the house. I am sure no servant girl could be safe in your company.

(The *Northampton Mercury* investigated the background to this case, and reported on 16th December (p. 3, col. 4) that Mrs. Walker's account of her profits "is very far from accurate. We are assured that her dupes are numerous, and include persons of a far more respectable class than could be supposed in this reading age".

8th December 1837

AN EARTHQUAKE

At fifteen minutes past eleven on the night of Friday 8th December,

> ". . . an earthquake was distinctly felt at Stamford, as well as at several places in the neighbourhood. . . . From Wansford, and other towns within twenty miles, we have received accounts of the alarm occasioned by the visitation: many persons were roused from their sleep."

(*Stamford Mercury*, 16th December 1837).

11th December 1837

EARL SPENCER, SCIENTIFIC FARMER

The third Earl Spencer had already made his national reputation by his statesmanship as a member of the Grey and Melbourne Governments. At that time his main interest seems to have been industrial reform, and a key factory law bears his name: Althorp's Act. Now his chief interest had become farming, and the encouragement of the latest agricultural developments. In November he had taken the chair at the formulation of the Yorkshire Agricultural Society. On 11th December he was at the annual dinner of the Smithfield Club, in London, at the Freemasons' Tavern. As a result of his speech there, the organisation was formed that became the Royal Agricultural Society of England. In this speech, Spencer used a phrase "practice with science", which became the Society's motto. As a prominent Whig, he wisely made the Society non-political by inviting the Tory Duke of Richmond to join him as co-founder.[3]

An anecdote of Spencer at this time is taken from a letter from Alexander Napier, a Norfolk clergyman to his brother, in 1841, writing about Spencer's participation in a battue at Holkham Hall "a few years ago".[70] (A battue is the kind of grouse shooting at which beaters scare the birds into the air to be shot.) Spencer was hidden from view in the cover, and a shot was fired into it. Some of the shot stuck in his thick hair, and some grazed his face. "Out of the cover he comes, scratching his head and with a comical face, walks up to the man that fired the shot with several pellets in his hand, and calling out, 'Allow me, sir, to return your property', hands him the shot. . . ."

12th December 1837

A LOST GRAVESTONE AT RUSHDEN

In 1939, the inscriptions on all the stones then standing in St. Mary's churchyard at Rushden, were anonymously recorded in a notebook later deposited at the Public Library there. The following words were on a stone in the north side:

> "This pail memory of
> departed worth is raised
> over the dust of the
> affectionate Wife of Robert Dickins
> who having lived a life of
> usefulness tranquilly gave
> up the Ghost
> Dec 12, 1837
> Aged 40 years."

12th December 1837

CORBY POACHERS

Although the Earl of Cardigan was serving in India with his regiment, his keepers on the Deene estate were vigilant, and early in the morning of 12th December, they went into action against poachers from Corby. John Milley was involved in this confrontation, as he had been on 10th January. He was gamekeeper on the Earl of Winchilsea's Kirby Hall estate, but the protection of Cardigan's game from poachers must have been regarded as mutually rewarding. On this occasion, some of the poachers were recognised, but one of them was not arrested until five years later. William Williamson stood before the Lent Assizes at Northampton on 1st March 1842, having been indicted in 1838. The charge was "being, in company with three or more persons, in Corby Hill Wood, belonging to the Earl of Cardigan, armed with guns, for the purpose of taking and destroying game". The judge, Lord Abinger, heard James Chambers give his version of the events of December 1837:

"I am gamekeeper to the Earl of Cardigan. In 1837, I lived near a wood called Corby Hill Wood. On the night of 11th December in 1837, Lord Winchilsea's keeper and his assistant, came to me about twelve o'clock, and in consequence of what they told me, I went with them to Corby Hill Wood. I heard some guns fired. There were many pheasants in the wood. I went in the direction of the firing, and when I came round a thicket into an open space, I saw a body of from fifteen to twenty men, armed with guns and bludgeons. With my assistants I separated the men into two parties, and I pursued one party, while my companions went after the other. When I got near the party I was after, John Patrick said, 'Keep back you bugger or I'll blow you down.' The prisoner, Williamson, said a similar exclamation. He was armed with a gun. The men then formed themselves into two lines, four of them pointing their guns at me. When I had been standing there a few minutes, I heard footsteps behind me, and John Milley and another person came up, and said to the men, 'Now, my lads, what are you going to do now?' Others of my party were within call, and I shouted to them, and the poachers made off. On the following day, I obtained warrants against several of them, and Williamson's house was the first we searched. I have not seen him from that day to this."

Asked if he might have difficulty in recognising the poachers in the darkness, the gamekeeper said: "That night was very light."

John Milley gave evidence. He said that he had alerted James Chambers that night because he had heard firing in Corby Hill Wood. He corroborated Chambers' version of what had occurred in the wood. A former parish constable was sworn, next.

Thomas Meadows: I was constable of Corby in 1837 to '38. I had a warrant placed in my hands for Williamson's apprehension, but I could not take him.

The jury found Williamson guilty, and he was sentenced to seven years' transportation.

14th December 1837

A STEAM ENGINE FOR SALE AT WELLINGBOROUGH SILK MILLS

Joyce Palmer has given reasons for the failure of the silk mill at Swanspool in Wellingborough, some time before 1840.[71] The following advertisement from the *Northampton Mercury* of 2nd December 1837 (p. 1, col. 3), suggests that the enterprise was closed down by 1838. When a silk mill was opened in the town later in the century, for a brief period, it used donkey power rather than steam. Mrs. Palmer has drawn attention to an old Mulberry tree in Swanspool Gardens, a few yards from the site of the first silk mill, probably planted as a habitat for silk-worms.

"STEAM ENGINE.
TO BE SOLD BY AUCTION,
By Mr. CLEAVER,
At the White Hart Inn, WELLINGBOROUGH, in the County of Northampton, on Thursday, the 14th December, 1837,

at Five o'clock in the Afternoon. An excellent three-horse high-pressure STEAM ENGINE, with fly wheel and shaft, governors, pullies, &c.; a cylindrical boiler, with tube and fire-box of five-horse power; steam pipes, pump, furnace-work &c.

The above has been at work a few months only, and is now standing at the SILK MILLS, WELLINGBOROUGH. . . ."

20th December 1837

SYRESHAM WINDMILL FOR SALE

"An excellent WINDMILL and FREEHOLD LAND
At SYRESHAM, near Brackley, Northamptonshire.
TO BE SOLD BY AUCTION,
BY J. CLEMENTS,
On Wednesday the 20th December 1837, at the Red Lion Inn, Brackley, at Two o'clock in the afternoon, under such conditions as will then be produced. An excellent POST WINDMILL, containing two pairs of capital Stones; also a four-feet FLOUR MACHINE, with two Cylinders; together with the MILL BANK, containing Seventeen Poles in circumference, round the tail of the said MILL.

May be viewed any day prior to the Sale by applying to Mr. THOMAS ROLLINS, of Syresham; and for further particulars, apply (if by letter, post paid) to Mr. WHITE, Solicitor, or the AUCTIONEER, both of BICESTER, Oxon."

(*Northampton Mercury* 2nd December 1837, p. 2, col. 6.)

21st December 1837

HOW COGENHOE'S CHARITY LAND WAS LOST

Until the enclosure of the open fields, the poor families of Cogenhoe were assisted by the produce of certain strips or lands in them. The Enclosure Award, in 1829, allowed for this by allotting over an acre in one of the enclosed fields called Barley Leys. This plot was known as the "Town Lands". After the 1834 Poor Law Amendment, the parish of Cogenhoe was included in the Hardingstone Union, for the relief of its poor. We have seen on earlier pages relating to Wellingborough, how parish property was being sold to add to the funds administered by the Board of Guardians. Here was a similar situation in Cogenhoe. The Hardingstone Guardians intended to take Cogenhoe's Town Lands and dispose of it.

A meeting of Cogenhoe rate-payers and property owners took place on Thursday, 21st December, in the parish Church, and in a resolution of almost impenetrable verbiage, consented to the Hardingstone Guardians selling the parcel of land "for the permanent advantage of this Parish, as the Poor Law Commissioners for England and Wales shall in that behalf direct."[72]

The poor families of the village were not invited to the meeting. By coincidence, the day of the meeting, 21st December, was St. Thomas's Day, traditionally the day on which bread and flour were doled out to the poor.

21st December 1837

SAINT THOMAS'S DAY IN THE SOKE OF PETERBOROUGH

"Earl Fitzwilliam, with his usual consideration, caused upwards of 500 stones of beef to be distributed among the

114

poor of his neighbourhood in Christmas week; and on Saint Thomas's-day his lordship distributed bread to 1,800 poor persons."

(*Northampton Mercury* 6th January 1838, p. 4, col. 3.)

24th December 1837

DEATH OF A PHILANTHROPIST

The inscription on a tablet in All Saints' Church at West Haddon:

"Sacred
to the memory of
JOHN HEYGATE, ESQUIRE
of West Haddon Lodge, in this parish,
who departed this life
on the 24th day of December, 1837
in the 82nd year of his age.
Endowed by nature and inheritance
with a vigorous and independent mind,
and blessed by providence with worldly fortune,
his life was marked
by various acts of kindness and charity.
He erected a School House
and vested in Trustees
an endowment
for the perpetual and gratuitous instruction
of poor children
of West Haddon and Winwick.
He aided in augmenting the accommodation
for divine worship in this Church
and liberally supported various institutions
in this and the adjacent counties;
especially the Infirmary and Lunatic Asylum
at Northampton.

115

These noble institutions
with the Leicester and Bedford Infirmaries,
two friendly Societies in West Haddon,
the poor of six adjacent villages, and of Wellingborough,
were remembered in his last will;
by which he also bequeathed a benefit
to be annually distributed
amongst the poor of this parish.
These things are not recorded for the purpose
of exalting human and imperfect actions,
nor as a vain eulogium on the dead,
but that the living may imitate this example,
and whilst it is yet in their power
dedicate a liberal portion of their substance
in obedience to the injunctions of HIM who gave it.

POSTSCRIPT TO 1837

We have seen the curtain rise on Victorian Northamptonshire with a survey of 1837 events that is by no means exhaustive. There are, of course, many stories other than those presented in the foregoing pages. Some items were rejected because they do not fulfil the criteria already described. Some are lacking in key elements of explanation or identification, and await further research, or perhaps the accidental disclosure of conclusive information. Others have no precise date and are unable to take a place in the chronological arrangement.

As examples of miscellaneous 1837 topics calling for investigation, consider the following.

When Theophilus Jeyes died in October, he had been Town Clerk of Northampton since the previous century. Why did his posthumous affairs become a case in Chancery? His property, listed in detail, in the *Northampton Mercury* of 31st August 1839, page 3, included two houses in the Drapery, Northampton, perhaps adjacent to the shop of his relative, Philadelphus Jeyes.

Three Shires House stands at the point where Northamptonshire, Bedfordshire and Huntingdonshire meet, on land actually in the parish of Hargrave, Northamptonshire. When the wife of the householder died in 1837, why was he prevented from having her buried in Hargrave churchyard? He had the body interred in the house, and in 1843, when his daughter died, she was laid alongside her mother. They were not buried in consecrated ground until the old man himself died in 1867.[73]

Until 1837, John Harwood Hill was curate at Corby, and at the same time, librarian to the old Earl of Cardigan at Deene. He compiled an extraordinary catalogue of the Deene library in black-letter, illustrated with his own pen-and-ink etchings.[74] The highly-respected, efficient and thorough Joan Wake was the historian of the Brudenell family of Deene, but made no mention of the Rev. John Hill, except in a note, as the father of the Countess of Cardigan's companion, "a Leicestershire clergyman".[75]

The Rev. Hugh Tollemache had been the Rector of Harrington since 1832, and would remain so until his death in 1890. It is well-known in the county that the Tollemache Arms public house in the village was established by him because he objected to the villagers drinking on Sundays. He appointed his coachman as landlord with instructions to remain closed on the Sabbath.

At Lamport Hall, Dodson, the butler to Sir Justinian Isham took on extra responsibilities, adding those of house steward to his own. In recognition of this, his wages rose from £45 per annum to £60.[76] The same source lists the other servants at Lamport Hall: coachman (£52, two suits of livery and two stable jackets, annually); cook-housekeeper (£34); groom (£20); footman (£18); lady's maid (£15); laundry maid (£11); upper housemaid (£10); under-housemaid (£9); dairy maid (£9) and kitchen maid (£8).

Sir Arthur de Capell Brooke, of Great Oakley Hall, founder and President of the Raleigh Club (which later became the Royal Geographical Society), during the year, published a two-volume travel book: *Sketches in Spain and Morocco*.[77]

Sir Henry Dryden inherited the Canons Ashby estate in 1837. He was still in his teens, and a student at Cambridge. He later made a considerable reputation as an archaeologist and historian. In 1875, he delivered a lecture to the Northampton Architectural Society which included a verbal reconstruction of the Hospital of St. John the Baptist in Northampton, as it had been in 1837, apparently using as his main source, the Charity Commissioners' Report of that year. In the twentieth century only one portion of the Hospital survives, as a Roman Catholic church. In 1837, the Master's House still stood, though the Master, Canon Pretyman, had never lived in it. Several of its outbuildings had recently been pulled down. In addition to the non-resident Master, the establishment in 1837 comprised two co-brethren, seven women pensioners, who had lodging, firing, and a daily allowance; and one man, who acted as clerk.

Of the 1,750 miles of highway in Northamptonshire, 313 miles were in the control of turnpike trusts.[78] Thirty-six of these highway authorities controlled roads in the county. The most valuable general account of the turnpikes is the brief description by Arthur Cossons, written in 1950 (*Northamptonshire Past and Present*, vol. I, no. 3). It is surprising that more has not been written about the individual turnpike trusts. Sufficient documentary material survives to enable this to be done. If one is taken as an example – the turnpike road that ran from the east end of Hall Lane in Kettering, to the east end of Abington Street in Northampton – we find that like nearly all the others in 1837, it was losing money. They all had loans which would never be repaid, with interest never paid in full. The statement of accounts for this "Kettering and Northampton Turnpike Trust" for the year "between the first day of January, and the thirty-first day of December, 1837"[79] shows that although £89 3s 5$\frac{1}{2}$d was brought forward from 1836, and an income from tolls of £781 13s 4d was collected during the year; a loss of £34 0s 11$\frac{1}{2}$d was sustained. Expenditure included over £281 on manual labour; and just under £287 on "Team Labour and Carriage of Materials". Materials for "Surface Repairs" accounted for £212, and £13 was the cost of the damage done "in obtaining materials". A salary of £50 was paid to the Surveyor, though no salary was allotted either the Treasurer or the Clerk. The remaining items of expenditure were "Law Charges", "Incidental Payments", and "Lighting the Road" (£3).

One last unanswered question of 1837: who was the "poor old woman" who lived in the village of Wold [Old] and "was particularly fond of tobacco"?[80] "In order to economize her stock and extract all its means of enjoyment, she used first to chew it, then dry and smoke it, and lastly take the ashes for snuff."

Kilsby Tunnel – north entrance

Site of Scarletwell, Northampton

1st January 1838

"OUR FIRE BRIGADE IS ILLEGAL"

When Northampton Town Council met on 1st January, "Fire Engine Establishment" was on the agenda. On the motion that a committee be appointed to superintend the Fire Engine Establishment, Christopher Markham protested against the grant made by the Council for the maintenance of the engines, on the ground that it was illegal and contrary to the provisions of the Municipal Act. The appointment of the committee was, after an argument, negatived.

How could the provision of a fire service possibly be illegal? What was that Municipal law referred to by Christopher Markham? The Municipal Corporations Act, of 1835, had reformed local government in towns with populations over 50,000, laying down what services must be provided. Fire brigades were not included. Corruption and the misuse of ratepayers' money were the main reasons for this legislation, and this Council, the first to be elected under the new regulations, was being careful.

The proceedings of the Council meeting were reported in the *Northampton Mercury* on 6th January (p. 3, col. 5), but the alarming decision on fire engines was under discussion before that. "An inhabitant" wrote to the *Mercury* to protest about it, but his letter missed publication on 6th January. It was printed on 13th January (p. 3, col. 6). It said:

". . . the effect of this vote will be that there will be neither a place to keep the engines in, nor a fireman to work them, and it can require but little foresight to see that, in a very short period, not an engine will be available for extinguishing any fire . . . and this upon the mere quibble that the Municipal Act does not sanction any such expenditure. I cannot imagine a more legitimate object to which the borough fund can be applied, than maintaining the fire engines in a good state of preservation; they are the property of the town (and valuable property too). . . . The Council are selected for the regulation and good government of the town, and as much required to protect this property as any other for which they are the trustees for the time being. . . ."

This disturbing problem was not solved until 6th August, when the Council voted to pay the Mayor a salary (which *was* legal). It was agreed that the Mayor would donate his salary to the upkeep of the fire engines.

2nd January 1838

A BOZEAT MAN "COLTED" AT ROADE

George Hooton, of Bozeat, went to work on the London and Birmingham Railway at Roade on New Year's Day. On 2nd January he had his watch taken from him. James Hafford, a fellow railway labourer, who had taken the watch quite openly, was arrested and taken before the Northamptonshire County Sessions on Friday 5th January. Earl Spencer was in the Chair, and he was about to learn something of the customs of the railway navvies. The descriptive comments come from the *Northampton Mercury* of 13th January (p. 4, col. 1).

George Hooton: I live at Bozeat. I am a labouring man. I was working at the railroad, at Roade, on Tuesday night last when the prisoner, Hafford, came up to me and asked me what time it was. I took the watch out to tell him, and he snatched it from me.

The Roade Parish Constable gave evidence of the arrest. When apprehended, Hafford told him that he had left the watch as a pledge for three shillings' worth of beer. They went to a beer-house, and there the watch was produced.

The accused man now had the opportunity to give his defence.

James Hafford: It is the custom for new-comers to stand three shillings for beer. Hooton had no money, and gave us the watch voluntarily. I have witnesses.

The first defence witness was a labourer named Perkins. He began:

"I am a navigator . . .",

and then he was stopped by Spencer, because he was too drunk to be intelligible. Next appeared another railwayman named Bates, "of no ordinary dimensions". When he was directed to kiss the Book, he looked at it with a "ludicrous expression of disbelief", and repeated the words: "Kiss the Book." With some difficulty he was made to understand that he really was required to give the volume a real kiss.

Earl Spencer: Do you understand the nature of an oath?

Bates: No. I'm sure I do-an't.

Spencer: Do you realise that you are supposed to tell the truth while giving your evidence?

Bates: Yes, I know that . . . I am a navigator. I was there when Hooton gave up his watch. It is the custom to "colt" a fresh man.

Spencer: Did you drink some beer after the watch had been taken away?

Bates: I did, but I did not know it was from the watch. . . . They told me I would be "colted" on Saturday night.

This was enough to convince the jury that Hafford was not guilty.

3rd January 1838

BLISWORTH: DEATH ON THE RAILS

A short distance down the line, on the day after George Hooton had given up his watch, blood was shed on the rails – twice.

"On Wednesday last a labourer on the Rail-road at Blisworth, was accidentally thrown from a train across the rails, and the whole of the waggons passed over him. The poor fellow was killed on the spot." This brief report was carried in the *Northampton Mercury* of 6th January (p. 3, col. 5). The inquest was held on Friday, 5th January, before George Abbey, at Blisworth. The deceased, twenty-two years old, was Richard Jaynes, who, "as the trams were passing along the railway at the usual pace, most imprudently endeavoured to run under the chain connecting the waggons with the steam-engine". He fell, and sixteen waggons passed over his breast. The jury, in returning a verdict of accidental death, said that no blame could possibly attach to any one but the unfortunate man himself. This, and the following report, were in the *Mercury* of 13th January (p. 3, col. 5).

On the same day, a boy named George Clark, employed on the railway at Mill Orchard, near Blisworth, "was unhooking a gang-waggon, when he fell, and his leg and thigh were so severely lacerated that it was found necessary to bring him to the Infirmary. There are hopes of his recovery."

January 1838

SOME MIGHT HOPE THE FOX WAS EVEN FASTER

"The Gentleman in Black" had a comment on the style of the Pytchley Hunt at this time, in *Bailey's* Magazine, June 1862.[81]

"The Pytchley . . . have always had a reputation for immense speed. Under Mr. George Payne in 1838, when Jack Stevens hunted them, they 'could almost fly when scent served them, and their fox was a straight goer'."

January 1838

THE SAD END OF A PASTORATE

James Robertson had been the Pastor of the Cheese Lane Chapel in Wellingborough since 1826. Suddenly, in January 1838, he was afflicted with a mental illness not easy to diagnose from contemporary descriptions.

He had been an accomplished classical scholar, and a respected theologian. He was a regular contributor to the *Eclectic Review*. Thomas Coleman, in describing his character and ability, makes use of phrases that invite admiration *and* revulsion.[82] "His intellectual power was considerable . . . his skill in criticism was great; while he was a man of inflexible integrity, pre-eminently without guile − a sincere and steadfast friend, with much kindness of heart. His stern and unbending regard to principle sometimes occasioned a roughness of exterior, and occasionally appeared to assume an austere and unkind aspect. . . ."

The church books say: "In the month of January, 1838, it pleased God to visit with a painful mental affliction the Rev. James Robertson . . . so as to disqualify him totally from conducting the services of the sanctuary, or holding any intercourse with the people of his charge." For several months, neighbouring ministers stood in for him. "The friends, however, at length . . . perceiving the congregation on the decline, were led anxiously to deliberate on the course which . . . the welfare of Zion required them to take; at the same time keeping in view their obligations to their honoured and afflicted pastor. After frequent consultations among themselves and various ministers . . . and much prayer, it was suggested, that as no symptoms of returning health appeared, the connexion ought to be dissolved. . . . The friends perceived that such a proposal must come from them, rather than from their pastor himself; but the state of his mind being such as to unfit him for the transaction of business, it became, on their part, a matter of necessity and painful duty. Accordingly, in the month of September, 1838, a letter to this effect . . . was addressed to Mrs.

Robertson, after which other correspondence took place, which it is unnecessary to detail, and the relation terminated."

The unfortunate pastor died, at Wellingborough, on 23rd June, 1842, and was buried in the Cheese Lane burial ground. Along with all those at rest there, he was disinterred in 1901, and laid in the London Road cemetery in an area marked by a large granite cube. The tablet placed by his widow at the right side of the pulpit at the Cheese Lane Chapel (the site of which is lost beneath the large shopping mall) referred to his illness. "For upwards of four years before his death he was the subject of intense mental and physical suffering, which much beclouded his fine intellect; and the deep waters of tribulation went over his soul. . . ."

15th January 1838

WELLINGBOROUGH FROZEN

"The thermometer at Wellingborough, on Monday morning last, at half-past eight, in an elevated and north-east aspect, was down to 1, being 31 degrees [fahrenheit] below the freezing point. Such extreme cold has not occurred for many years."

(*Northampton Mercury* 20th January 1833, p. 3, col. 5.)

The reading at Wootton on the same day, was 23 degrees below freezing.

21st January 1838

AN INTRUDER IN THE KITCHEN AT
GUILSBOROUGH HOUSE

In the Annual Report of the Northamptonshire Archives Committee for the year ended 31st March 1968, P. I. King, the County Archivist gives an enticing description of a recent acquisition (p. 11).

> "Amongst a miscellaneous group acquired ... is an amusing letter written to Thomas Bateman, a London barrister, by his mother at Guilsborough in 1838. Apart from saying she has sent his skates up by the Rocket, she gives a long account of how she dealt with her servants who were guilty of hiding her cook's lover in the scullery."

The letter is indeed entertaining,[83] but a rigmarole. It was written on 24th January by Mrs. Mary Bateman, the wife of a clergyman who had a living in Leicestershire, though their home was Guilsborough House. "My dear Tom" was Thomas Bateman, of the Middle Temple, London, and he paid for the receipt of the letter the next day, 25th January. His "skaits" had been sent the previous Saturday "by the Rocket", a road service, not a joking reference to the London and Birmingham Railway.

> "When I wrote to you last I think I told you that we heard of a man coming every Sunday – he made his appearance again. I having given her notice on monday the 15th – last sunday the 21st the cold made me stay from Ch: I did not think he wd come after she had notice to leave – but soon after all had gone to Ch. Dan barked just so that I felt . . . some one had just come in. I ran up to the garret stair window – saw her talking to a man who walked up with her to the kitchen, went in and shut the door – I went down into the kitchen, look'd at him for a moment and asked if he wanted Mr. Bateman – he said no he did not want Mr. Bateman he came to speak to the Cook – I ask'd him what his name was – she call'd out, he is my Brother – at the same instant he spoke and said his name was Tailby. –

she said you mean Tyrrel – I look'd surprized, and said how very strange that this man does not know his own name, and asked her if she cd declare he was her Brother – she wd not speak . . . and I then asked her if he was the same man that was with her last sunday – she said yes – then I said I do not believe you are her Brother and the sooner you leave this house the better – I discharge you from ever coming on this errand again – I expect you will go this instant out of the House – and tell your real name he said he did not care for this ground or for me either and he did not choose to tell his name. The Cook scream'd very loud that she wd go with him – I said sh shd. not but he said she should come out and speak to him upon wch she ran out at the Scullery door – and he went out at the other – I sent Lyne out after some time to tell her to come in and him to give his name and leave the premises – he sd he should go soon – but wd not tell his name – I kept the doors fastened till he was gone – but like a fool that I was I did not prevent Lyne from letting her in – when she came in she said she wd go in the morn'g – I told her she must not go till Mr. Bateman came home (he was at Kibworth) – and I sh'd think you will blame me for not preventing her coming back into the House – she said she wd leave that night when the altercation first began – but I think she seems to be too cunning to have gone till she was sent, on acct. of forfeiting her months wages – I never went into the kitchen on monday, but order'd Mary and Ann to get the dinner – saying I did not choose to speak to her – Papa came in from Kibworth late – and after dinner we told him – when he sent for Lyne and made him tell how often the man had been here – and that he had had all his meals for fourteen sundays – he then sent for Mary and Ann – and with a good deal of trouble made them say the same – and ask'd whether they did not confess themselves guilty of a Breach of trust in seeing that man regularly fed – and letting him hide himself, wch they were obliged to say he did, by going into the Back Kitchen every sunday when the master came in at the other door – Mary very reluctantly said she did so know or something like it . . . he gave the two maids a very good Lecture – and then sent a [message?] by Lyne to the

Cook to desire she wd be quite off before 12 the next day —
and she might apply to the Magistrates for her wages next
saturday when he would pay her what they order'd. But
the next morning he was ill with a cold . . . so I persuaded
him to let me pay her up to the day she went — she said she
had agreed for a month's wages or warning. I said here is
the money up to this time in my hand, and if you choose to
take it you will sign the receipt wch I laid before her — she
then signed it and I pd her in the presence of three
witnesses. I then told her that Mr. Bateman would consider
of what steps would be taken in consequence of her hiding
the man in the house various times, giving him food,
refusing as she did to the last to tell his name — and for
slipping back the lock of the scullery door — wch she did on
sunday after I had locked it and brought away the key . . . I
staid in the kitchen after the man first went and kept the
doors fastened and while looking about I found she had the
roast Beef keeping warm for him in the hot closet. I made
her bring it out and told her I saw plainly it was keeping for
the man's dinner — after dinner came in she went out and
staid as usual till time for Prayers . . . I wd not let them call
her in that night, wch I find they used to do for prayers —
but went into the kitchen after they came into the parlour
to see that the doors were fast. . . . I sent for Robin to put on
padlocks — to show her that in future it shd. be made safe.
now is there any thing we can do to the woman we think of
finding out the man's name — who I believe is Cooper a
mason of Long Buckby — and sending him a written
discharge — just to let him know that we know him — it is
strange the servant all persist in saying they never once
heard his name. I said so to Mrs. Booth and it struck her that
he is a married man. . . . I shd like to have a Line from you on
saturday to tell me what I ought to have done in this case . . .
and whether we shd have given ourselves much trouble by
with-holding her wages . . . will you send me down a copy
of what we should say — (the only object is because they
were so obstinate about the name), we wish to let them
know he is discover'd — and if he shd prove to be a married
man Papa says he will send a person over to Lamport to tell
her friends of it . . . will my having paid her off prevent our

punishing her in any way if Papa wishes it — he wd not have
given her the wages . . . tell Aunt I fear the Beef is less tender
than I expected . . . give my kind love to aunt and Jos
"and believe me yr loving mother *M B*"

24th January 1838

MORE RAILWAY MISHAPS

"On Wednesday morning last [24th January] between 11
and 12 o'clock, as the engine employed on the railroad
between Roade and Ashton, was passing the latter place, a
large flake of fire issued from the chimney, and fell upon
the thatch of a barn in the occupation of Mr. Weston, baker.
The roof was immediately in a blaze, and in less than ten
minutes it had fallen in upon a horse which was in the
barn. . . . Every effort to save the poor animal was fruitless
and it suffered a horrible death. The wind was blowing
freshly . . . and the fire extended to the adjoining stables, a
hovel and a piggery, all of which were completely
destroyed. Three fat pigs and nineteen sheep were saved
with great difficulty. The premises were the property of the
Duke of Grafton and were insured."

(*Northampton Mercury* 27th January 1838, p. 3, col. 6.)

"On Thursday last [25th January] . . . Gawthorn, employed
upon the rail-road, fell, while unlocking a gang waggon,
and his leg was so dreadfully fractured that on being
brought to the Infirmary in [Northampton], it was found
necessary to resort to amputation as the only chance of
saving his life."

25th January 1838

ROTHWELL ("ROWELL") STARTING A FIRE-FIGHTING BUSINESS

There is, of course, irony in the caption above. The parishioners of Rothwell did not decide to put their fire engines out to hire; but possibly prompted by Northampton's decision not to fund its own engines, they voted to make a charge to any community which called on Rowellian assistance at a fire. A meeting of "Rowell" parishioners at the New Inn, on the 25th of January, under the chairmanship of John Tordoff, was reported in the *Northampton Mercury* of 3rd February (p. 2, col. 5). It was resolved that the fire engines would not in future be sent to any of the neighbouring villages except under three new regulations. On consenting to pay one sovereign per year towards the repairs of the engines, "they shall have the use of them whenever they may be required, with a DIRECTOR for each, and a sufficient number of hands to work the same". Parishes that did not subscribe would be denied the use of the fire engines "without a Guarantee of £5 2s. 6d. from some responsible person of the place where they may be required, previous to their removal from Rowell. The third requirement was that a waggon or waggons must be sent to carry the engines there and back "carefully".

"The keys of the Engines will be found at Mr. Lawrence Turner's, from whom all further information may be obtained. . . ."

mid-February 1838

BREACH OF PROMISE AT THE ANGEL IN PETERBOROUGH

An action for Breach of Promise, Watkin v. Daniels came before the Court of Common Pleas, London sittings at Nisi

Prius; before Mr. Justice Coltman and a common jury. Counsel for the plaintiff was Mr. Serjeant Talfourd. Let his words explain what this case was about.

"The plaintiff in this case is Miss Jane Watkin, a young woman who has resided at Peterborough in the county of Northampton, the greater part of her life; and the defendant, Mr. William Daniel, who is sixty years of age, is the widower of the proprietor of the Angel, one of the principal inns and posting houses of the town. The plaintiff, whose age is between 29 and 30, is one of a family of six children . . . and their father resides chiefly at Bourne . . . where he carries on business as a journeyman saddler; but the daughters live with their mother at Peterborough. Some of them there engaged in the business of milliners and dressmakers. . . . In the year 1831, the plaintiff was engaged by the defendant to live at his hotel in the capacity of housekeeper. She filled that situation for several years, living as one of the family. In the course of that time, after about a year, the defendant made repeated professions of attachment to her. Subsequently she was brought to bed of a child by him, and at his house, which, however, she left about a fortnight afterwards, as soon as she had sufficiently recovered, and returned to her father's home. That was in the year 1833, and the defendant was then in town − in London. Upon his return, he behaved with great affection towards the plaintiff, and upon one occasion, said to her, 'Don't cry, my girl. Wait till you have your strength again, and then I'll take you to church and make you my wife.' That kindness of behaviour continued for a length of time. At various intervals, he renewed his promise of marriage, and on the 24th of October, 1835, he obtained a licence. He went to the plaintiff and appointed the following day for the ceremony to take place. But on the next day, instead of appearing, he sent a message, excusing himself on the ground of illness. The same state of things continued until the spring of 1836, when the defendant, on one occasion, went to the plaintiff's house and charged her with some improper connection with his son, telling her still that he would marry her if she could clear herself. One of her sisters wrote immediately to her father at Bourne . . . and he came to Peterborough. Shortly, however, the defendant acquainted the plaintiff and her relatives that he was perfectly satisfied that his son, who had given him the original information, acknowledged that it was untrue. All the family had persuaded him to say it in order to set his father against the plaintiff and prevent the marriage. His visits were continued, and in August 1836, shortly before the marriage of the defendant's daughter, he declared that, as she came out at one door of the church, he would take the plaintiff in at the other. In 1837, the defendant expressed a desire that she should go to London, and he said that if she would go to town, he would come to her and marry her in a month. She did go to London in April 1837, and since the month of May in that year, has resided in Panton Street, Hanover Square, with two of her sisters, one of whom was engaged as a dressmaker in a house of business. This, with the small assistance afforded by her father, supported the three of them. The defendant kept up an affectionate correspondence with her, but his letters grew colder and less frequent, and the plaintiff, having lost all hope, resorted to this present mode of obtaining compensation for the injury which she has sustained from the non-fulfilment of the defendant's promise."

The licence of 1835 was put in as evidence and read. It was made out for William Daniels to marry Jane Watkin, dated October 7, 1835. Letters were also produced:

"April 13, 1837.

"My dear Girl,

"In your last letter you branded me with being cold, but you know better. I hope you and the baby are well. The dinner of the coachmasters is not yet fixed, and till then I cannot come to town. . . . God bless you, yours, &c.,

Bill Daniels."

"May . . .

"My dear Girl,

"Though absent neither you nor my girl are forgotten. Since you left we have been very busy respecting the posting. . . . Yours and no other. God bless you, Bill Daniels."

"July . . .

"My dear Jane,

"In your last letter I could not comprehend entirely what you meant, I still entertain the respect which I always had for you. . . . Enclosed is a Gift to my little girl. Love to all, Yours truly,

Bill Daniels."

"October 2. 1837

[In reply to the plaintiff's attorney's formal application for the fulfilment of his promise, threatening this action in the case of his refusal.]

"Sir, I have received your letter. The conduct of Miss Jane Watkin has been such as to induce me to desert her for ever. The child I will maintain. She may send it by any of my coaches, and I will send it to the union, where it will be properly taken care of. Yours respectfully, W. Daniels."

Mr. Serjeant Wilde (for the defence) to the jury: Upon the record there must, beyond all doubt, be a verdict for the plaintiff, and only the question therefore of the amount of damages remains. Upon that point, I believe that you will agree with me, when you have heard the evidence that it will be my duty to submit to you, that there is the least possible claim for any damages at all. You will be satisfied that there is good reason for fearing that the plaintiff had formed a criminal connection with the defendant's son, even before the birth of the child. The bare suspicion of such a connection is more than sufficient to deter a man from marrying. . . .

———Chambers: I am a farmer. I live at Peterborough. I am a sporting friend of Benjamin Daniels, the son of the defendant. I have frequently seen Benjamin taking great liberties with the plaintiff. On one occasion, at the latter end of 1832, wanting to speak to the defendant, and not finding him at the bar, I went to number ten, which was Miss Watkin's bedroom; and upon opening the door and

134

entering the room, I discovered her and Benjamin Daniels together on the bed in a very indecent position. He said something, but I did not remain long enough to hear it. Benjamin was very frequently in that room. Whenever I could not find him in the bar, I went there to seek him. The door was not bolted at all on the occasion I have mentioned. It was broad daylight, and the blinds, if there were any, were up. The next day I mentioned it to my brother, but I have never spoken of it again until about three weeks since, when, upon my brother's inquiring, I told him again.

William Daniels' daughter and her husband, named Donkin, both gave evidence for the defence. They both described scenes of indecent familiarity between Jane Watkin and Daniels' son Benjamin. Donkin said that he told the defendant of them several times when he heard talk of a licence. His wife said that she had talked to Jane about her conduct, and that Jane had admitted that brother Benjamin was paying his addresses to her, and had promised to marry her. "She was fretting, and when I asked her the cause, she replied that my brother had deceived her. That was before the birth of the child."

Mr Serjeant Talfourd urged on the jury to utter incredibility of the story told by the defence witnesses.

"The defence would have been a good legal case against the action, but it has been brought forward merely in mitigation of damages. The plaintiff should have been given notice of this attempt to blast her character and prospects, so that she might have prepared to meet it. Mr. Chambers has brought in facts which he never mentioned except to his brother, until very recently. Therefore, if his evidence is true, those facts could have had had no influence on the conduct of the defendant. The other witnesses are almost like defendants in the action. . . . The story which they told today was the same story which Mr. Daniels himself, in the spring of 1836, after hearing it from Mr. Donkin and from his own son, had investigated and declared to be unfounded. Nay, further – had shown that he believed it to be unfounded, by renewing his former visits and attentions to the plaintiff. It is abundantly clear that the defendant's son and family have got up this story with a view to preventing a marriage to which they felt strong, and perhaps not unnatural objections. . . . The defence which has been set up – merely to save the defendant's pocket – is disgraceful. For that paltry consideration he comes here to heap upon his own son's head the most inconceivable infamy of being thus connected with a woman to whom he knew his father was paying his addresses, and with whom he would soon have been united in marriage. . . . No amount of damages, however great, could at all repair the cruel and grievous injuries which the defendant has inflicted upon my client. . . ."

The judge directed the jury to find for the plaintiff and assess damages. The verdict was indeed for the plaintiff, with damages of £400.

13th February 1838

"PICKWICK" ON DAVENTRY RESERVOIR

Six weeks of unremitting frost had encouraged widespread skating. Samuel Cox the younger went to the north end of Daventry Reservoir and made a delightful sketch of the crowds on the ice. With the spire of Daventry church in the distance, the entire surface appears to be holding up a large proportion of the male population of the town, gliding, swaying or just standing, most of them clad in their high hats and frock coats. Tradesmen's lean-to stalls and fires are to be seen. In the very centre of the foreground is a portly figure in white knee-breeches, who could be Samuel Pickwick. The activity portrayed is so closely reminiscent of the famous illustrations to the Dickens book by Hablot K. Browne *(Phiz)*, that one might be caused to wonder which came first. In fact the Pickwickian episode on the ice pre-dates the Daventry sketch by a year. The picture was advertised in the *Northampton Mercury* of 3rd March 1838 (p. 3, col. 3):

"Festivities on the Ice and Banks of the New Reservoir near Daventry, Tuesday February 13, lithographed by HULMANDELL from a drawing by S. Cox Junior of Sheaf Street, Daventry."

Samuel Cox and Samuel Cox Junior are described in directories as "Artists". The picture reappeared as a postcard, in Daventry, in the early twentieth century.

The *Northampton Herald* of 17th February 1838 (p. 3, col. 2) reported "a noble sheet of ice" on Tuesday, 13th February, covering more than a hundred acres. A whole sheep was roasted on the ice, carved and distributed. On the evening of this "beautifully fine day", there was a fireworks display. Two days later, "the gentlemen of Daventry Cricket Club played a game on the ice . . . numerously attended . . . and well played."

18th February 1838

ESCAPE FROM WELLINGBOROUGH LOCK-UP

". . . Charles Middleton, who had been apprehended by Packe, one of the Northampton Police, on Saturday, on a charge of Assault, broke from the Hole at Wellingborough, on Sunday last and has not since been heard of. He made a desperate attempt to escape from Peake's custody on his apprehension. He lodged at a house in Chapel Place in [Northampton] and asked permission to go upstairs to put on his coat and hat. Packe, suspecting that he meant to make off, if possible, followed him closely, and saw him jump out of the window into a field leading to the Race Course. Packe immediately followed, and succeeded in overtaking him. At Wellingborough he effected his escape by breaking a hole through the wall."

(*Northampton Mercury* 24th February 1838, p. 3, col. 8).

24th February 1838

OUTWORKERS ONLY

Mechanisation of the boot and shoe industry was two decades away. The shoe factories of 1838 were warehouses from which the raw materials were distributed to out-workers who made up the shoes in their own homes or in workshops adjacent to them. With the factory system spreading in other industries, some shoe manufacturers must have considered the advantages and disadvantages. They would have concluded that costs could be kept at a minimum with the shoe-stitchers continuing to work at home.

The following advertisement appeared in the *Northampton Mercury* of 24th February 1838 (p. 3, col. 3):

"T. WALESBY.
(FROM THE LATE W. PARKER'S)
WHOLESALE BOOT & SHOE-MANUFACTURER,
WOOD STREET, NORTHAMPTON
T.W. having understood that a report is in circulation, that he wishes to engage work-people on the "Factory System", takes this opportunity of distinctly stating that such report is wholly unfounded, and that he is decidedly opposed to that system."

27th February 1838

A DISPUTE ABOUT A BURIAL VAULT AT CHIPPING WARDEN

At the time of the Assizes, one of the courts dealt with civil disputes. This was the Nisi Prius Court. At the Northampton Lent Assizes, Sir Joseph Littledale heard the strange case of Hitchcock v. Walford on Tuesday, 27th February 1838. The unidentified barrister for the plaintiff explained:

"This is an action of trespass. The plaintiff is a gentleman living at Chipping Warden, and the defendant is the Rector of that parish. . . . The father of the plaintiff, Mr. W. Hitchcock, of Chipping Warden Grange, died in the year 1812, and a large monument was erected to his memory in the church-yard of Chipping Warden, by his executors. In 1813, a sister of the plaintiff, Elizabeth, died, and was buried in the same vault; and in 1814 another sister, Mary, was also buried there. In 1822, George, the son of the plaintiff's father, and half-brother to the plaintiff, died, and on that occasion, the widow of Mr. Hitchcock, who had, in the interim, married a gentleman named Bawcutt, applied to the executors under her first husband's will, for an enlargement of the vault, in order that room might be made for the reception of her son. The vault was accordingly enlarged about five feet on the west, and the new portion was arched over and covered with two stone slabs. The coffins of the two sisters, Elizabeth and Mary, were then removed into the new part of the vault, and in 1833 Mrs. Bawcutt was laid by the side of her first husband, Mr. W. Hitchcock. No objection was made to the original erection of the monument by the then incumbent, Mr. Hubbard, nor to the enlargement of the vault, by his successor, Dr. Lamb. In 1833, when Mrs. Bawcutt was buried, the defendant was the Rector. More recently, the aisle of the parish church being in a state of dilapidation, the churchwardens entered into an agreement with the Rector for its repair, which the latter undertook for the sum of two pounds. In making those repairs, it was found that the south transept also required some fresh paving, and the defendant directed his labourers to take up the two flat stones which covered the new part of the vault of the Hitchcock family, and appropriated them to the purpose, observing that they had long been a nuisance. The plaintiff, however, remonstrated, but without effect, and he then applied to the Bishop, who expressed his disapproval of the course which Mr. Walford had pursued, but stated that he had no power to interfere. Mr. Hitchcock again addressed the defendant by letter, which was returned unopened, and he then sought redress by the present action."

The barrister for the defence, also unidentified, stated the Rector's case:

". . . No right to erect the original monument has been shown. Supposing that right to have existed, it did not include the power of extending the vault, as had been done in 1822. The stones are mere slabs, without inscriptions, and being annexed to the parson's freehold, were his property. Even if that were not the case, the property is not the plaintiff's, but is the surviving executors' under his father's will, who had paid for them."

Barrister for the plaintiff:

". . . The right of both making and extending the vault was fairly to be presumed. Not one of the three rectors has ever offered the slightest objection to either. . . . There is an express exception to the ordinary rule as to materials attached to a freehold, in the case of a church-yard, where the freehold is a trust, and at all events, whatever power might lie in the parson to prevent a removal of the stones while they are attached to his freehold, or to remove them himself; the severance being made, he ceases to have any claim to their disposition; and he has certainly no right to appropriate the material to his own use. The executors only acted during the minority of the plaintiff, who was residuary legatee, and the individual whose fund was diminished proportionally by the expense of the stones."

This second contribution from the plaintiff's side needs translating. It means that the plaintiff really did own the stones. The executors did not own them, because they acted for him only while he was under-age. As the main inheritor of his father's property, he really is the one who should complain when the stones were removed.

The decision of Judge Littledale also needs translating. He said:

"The property of the tomb must be considered as in the plaintiff still, as upon the pleadings. Many important points have been raised. I will nonsuit the plaintiff, reserving him leave to move in the alternative to enter a verdict or for a new trial."

This means that he declared the plaintiff to be the owner of the tomb, but his complaint could not be taken any further. He was, however, giving him the option of a new trial if he wanted it.

Sure enough, on 24th November 1838, at the Court of Common Pleas in Westminster, in this matter of Hitchcock v. Walford, Serjeant Goulbourn applied to have the case entered in the list of new trials. He founded his application on an affidavit sworn by the plaintiff, Hitchcock, to the effect that the defendant, the Rector, had recently declared that as soon as he could obtain the judgment of the Court in this dispute, he would bury the first pauper who died in his parish in the vault in question.

No record has come to light of a clear satisfactory outcome of this case.

6th March 1838

MURDER AT EASTON-ON-THE-HILL

Elizabeth Longfoot was murdered between three and four o'clock on the morning of Tuesday, 6th March. She was an eccentric woman, described as "old", but still in her forties.

Henry Goddard, the Bow Street Runner, was called into Northamptonshire for the second time, to work on the case. His first investigation in the county had been in July 1837. In 1842 he was to become the first Chief Constable of Northamptonshire. His memoirs[84] are not very helpful to a modern student, because, writing many years later, his memory was at fault, and he made mistakes. The body of Elizabeth was not found floating "on the surface" of a well. She was found lying behind her kitchen door.

Much of the evidence is confused and confusing, because of the attempts to induce the accused men to testify against one another, and the consequent accusations and counter accusations. In fact the prosecution case was bungled, as will be seen.

The events of the morning of the crime will be reserved until the account of the trial, in which Easton-on-the-Hill villagers gave their eye-witness testimony. A report in *The Times* says that magistrates questioned over a dozen suspects and released them all except three brothers named Archer, who were released on the following day when Andrew Porter, a baker, was arrested. One of the Archer brothers, John, was eventually charged.

Goddard says that he was the only officer in town when the messenger arrived at the Bow Street office to request assistance. He travelled by the night mail and arrived at Stamford early the next morning. He met William Read, the senior police officer of the Borough of Stamford, and together they went to Easton to see the scene of the crime. They measured footprints, but Goddard says that the size of them caused them to suspect a large-footed "lay-about" named Stancer, whereas, Read said that the foot-prints led them to John Archer. Goddard goes on to say that Stancer's sister reported him missing since the murder. He and Read trailed the fugitive from Easton to Bourne, Gosperton, Deeping, Peterborough, Spalding, and finally Uppingham, where he was arrested, with money in his possession.

On being lodged in Oundle bridewell, and charged with being accessory to murder, Stancer admitted that he was present when the murder had been done, but that the murderers were Jack Archer and Richard Woodward.

Goddard and Read set off on the trail of Archer and Woodward, through Weedon, Crick, Colly Weston, Barnack, Market Deeping, Duddington, and finally back to Easton-on-the-Hill, where they were found and arrested. The two prisoners were placed in different lock-ups, Stamford and Oakham, "so that there should be no communication". Woodward asked Goddard who had given the evidence against him, and was told that it was Stancer. He admitted that he had been concerned in robbing the woman's house, but not in murdering her. He said that he was a bricklayer by trade, and wanted money to "take him to America". His only part in the murder, he said was to force the back door open with a mortar chisel.

Before the magistrates, Stancer was admitted as an

approver (one who gives King's evidence), and the other two were committed for trial at the next Northampton Assizes.

The *Lincoln Gazette* of 5th May 1838 carried the following report:

"John Stansor [sic], a labourer, who absconded from the village [of Easton-on-the-Hill] on the morning of the murder of Elizabeth Longfoot . . . has been taken into custody. He was discovered concealed at Willow Hall near Peterborough, and has made a voluntary confession implicating himself and . . . John Archer and Richard Woodward, both of Easton, in the robbery and murder. . . . He stated that the two men and himself having framed the design to rob her, they also determined on murdering her to prevent the possibility of her appearing against them in a court of justice. The hour of four o'clock on the morning of the 6th March having been fixed upon, they went to the house, and were proceeding to remove some boards when she was alarmed by the noise, and she suddenly opened the door of the house and ran into the street crying 'Murder, thieves'. She returned however, almost immediately, to the house, and just as she was going to the window of the wash-house, Archer rushed from a dark nook close by and knocked the old woman down. He pressed his knuckles against her throat, and after a short struggle, she was dead. Woodward then took a 'plough-line' from his pocket and having fastened it round the neck of the deceased, they hauled the body into the house, and shut and locked the door. They then secured the money, silver spoons and other things, left the house by the back way, and divided the plunder at a pond in an adjoining field. Woodward admitted that the statement made by Stansor, which was repeated in his presence, was correct, and seemed to think that he had some right to expect mercy, as his was not the hand that accomplished the murder. Archer strongly denied his guilt. After the magistrates had heard all the evidence the three prisoners were committed to take their trial for murder at the Assizes."

At the Summer Assizes at Northampton on 17th July, there

was a surprise. Woodward, Archer and Stansor were brought up, but instead of pleas being heard, an affidavit was read. "Mr. Farrant, a surgeon," and William Read, the Stamford constable, had been on their way to the Assizes in a gig, when the horse fell. Read had broken his arm and was "otherwise so severely injured to render his attendance impossible." The prisoners were remanded till the next Assizes. Whether the affidavit was at fault, or, more likely, the *Northampton Mercury* reporter, the information was incorrect. "Farrant" was not a surgeon: he was Farrer, the Magistrates' Clerk who was to testify that he had taken down Stansor's deposition. He and Read were, of course, vital prosecution witnesses. The surgeon was almost certainly the one who signed the affidavit to certify their incapacity.

The case did not come up at the next Assizes, perhaps because the two injured witnesses had not recovered. The postponement was for eight months, the case eventually coming before Lord Denman at Northamptonshire Lent Assizes on 4th March 1839. The case took all day, and according to Goddard was still being heard at eight o'clock in the evening. Richard Woodward and John Archer only were on trial, although John Stansor was produced to give evidence for the prosecution, during the course of which he said that he had been charged with the murder.

> The first witness was H. Broughton: "I live at Easton . . . and I knew Mrs. Longfoot. She lived near me and was about 40 or 50 years old. . . . She was a person of eccentric habits, and for the last few months appeared to be deranged. She had an orchard and used to sell the fruit. The boys used to annoy her. . . ." (Broughton kept a boarding school for young gentlemen, and he was referring to his pupils.) "I have heard her raving and abusing in the street. I heard her being murdered on Tuesday morning, March 6th. I live about 80 or 90 yards from the spot. I heard her cry out, about a quarter to four that morning. She was raving in the street in her habitual way, and I did not think anything of it."

> John Hudson: I live at Easton. . . . I heard her cry "murder"

three times on the morning of March 6th. . . . My daughter was in the room with me, and went to the window.

Lawrence Thompson: I live opposite the house of the deceased. . . . On the morning of the murder, a little before four o'clock, I heard a woman cry out "Murder!" three times. I got up and dressed myself in about four minutes, not putting on my stockings. I went to the window and opened it. I heard a noise like vomiting. My brother went with me to Mrs. Longfoot's gate, which we found locked. . . . There is a yard between the gate and the door, in which there is a well. There was a hay stack. . . . I heard a key turned in the door. I remained about three minutes, and then went to the window shutters of the bottom room, in the street. I saw a light within the house, and went across the road to a high piece of ground whence we could see a light in the upper room. . . . I left my brother watching, whilst I went to feed my horses.

Richard Thompson confirmed his brother's evidence, and added: "I waited at the door about five minutes, and then went to Mrs. Eaton's wash-house, where I saw the washerwoman. I went to bed and got up about a quarter to seven o'clock, when people were running to Mrs. Longfoot's. I went, and saw her lying dead on her back just within the door. About the entrance to the door, near the deceased's feet, there were marks of blood and the print of a man's knee."

Sarah Claypole: I live at Easton, and knew the deceased. I was going to work at Mr. Broughton's in the morning of the murder, about half past six o'clock. I saw her pattens and a shoe in the yard, just within the gate. I mentioned this at Mr. Broughton's, and Anne Wild and James Newman went back with me. Anne Wild said, "Poor creature, here she lies!" I saw marks outside the door, on the slab, as if she had been drawn through the dirt into the house.

Pattens were wooden shoe soles raised on slats, used to slip on when walking through mud as found in unpaved streets.

145

From Sarah Claypole's evidence, Anne Wild was the one who found the body. This is her testimony:

"I am a widow . . . I went back with Sarah Claypole to Mrs. Lightfoot's, and found Newman listening at the door. I picked up the shoe and pattens, and seeing the key inside the door, I put my hand on the latch, and the door opened. I saw the body with feet towards the door, and the face towards the window. . . . The bonnet and cap were pushed quite back. I moved the head, and blood trickled from the left side of the face. There were marks of blood outside, and the print of the knee of corded breeches. . . . The place was in great disorder, and a bunch of keys was hanging in a drawer. The beds did not appear to have been slept in. . . . There was a half-burnt candle in a candle-stick on the stairs. Next day I observed black places on the neck, as if made by pressure of knuckles."

By "next day", Anne Wild meant at the inquest. She had not quite finished at the trial: she was re-called after a recess to answer a question about the scene of the murder.

"An hour or two after I had been at the deceased woman's, I saw the door of the back kitchen open."

The Easton-on-the-Hill constable, Thomas Allen, gave an account of his visit to the scene of the crime. Then he was cross-examined by Mr. Miller who was representing the prisoner Woodward. He agreed that he had not known the whereabouts of Stansor until Woodward had told him that he might be found at Bourne. He said that a warrant was out against Stansor – for poaching.

The next witness was Mark Wilson Jackson, a Stamford surgeon:

"I saw the body lying on a table in the room next the kitchen. The side and head were bloody. Next day, before the Coroner, I examined the body. I found a wound, half an inch long and a quarter inch thick, on the left side of the head. It was in incised wound, as if from the sharp end of a mason's hammer or a mortar chisel. This wound might have knocked her down, but could not have killed her. On the right side of the neck and lower jaw, there were the marks of a man's fist, such as, by long pressure, would cause suffocation. I opened the body, and found the lungs distended, and full of black blood, which would result from strangulation. . . ."

William Read, "Chief Constable" of Stamford was called. He was at the house at eight o'clock, and examined the knee mark in the blood.

"The woodwork of the kitchen window seemed to have been taken out by a chisel. I examined Whitehead's premises, which are much lower down than those of the deceased. There is a wall between the haystack and the yard, and these premises. Near the haystack, I saw footmarks of one man, as if he had come over the wall. I measured the footmarks and examined the shoes of the prisoners. Archer's feet correspond in size, but there were marks of nails, but no nails in his shoes. I got the shoes from his house, and his mother said they were his Sunday shoes. In consequence of having intercepted a letter, I took the prisoner into custody on Wednesday, April 4th, at Willow Hall in the county of Cambridge."

Mr. Miller, for the defence: How long after the murder was it that you compared Archer's shoes with the marks?

Read: I compared them on the day after the murder.

Miller: What did you say to Stansor about his being admitted to Queen's evidence?

Read: I never said anything to him.

Many expected Stansor's evidence to be decisive. He was the next to give evidence.

John Stansor: I am brought out of gaol to give evidence against the prisoners. I have been charged with the murder myself. I have known the prisoners ever since they were lads. About a fortnight before the murder, I saw them at the opening of the Fox and Hounds, one Friday night. Woodward said, 'Stansor, I want you to go along with Archer and me, to do old Tetty.' I said, 'No, I won't have

147

nothing to do with it. It's a comical job. . . .' Archer came up
. . . and after a good deal of persuasion I agreed to go [They
drank together, and then Stansor drank with others.] We
went up the street and the clocks were striking three.
Woodward pulled a chisel from his pocket, and said that
would do to open the boxes. . . . We took the casement out
with it, and Mrs. Longfoot came to the window and
[shouted]. . . . She then came out into the yard, and swore
and blustered about, whilst we hid behind the haystack.
Samuel Mitchell passed, and asked what was the matter.
She told him to go on; it was nothing to do with him. We
parted that morning, and on the Wednesday following,
Woodward [renewed the proposition]. . . . About nine
o'clock on the night of the murder, I saw Woodward and
Archer. Archer refused to go and drink in the public house,
telling Woodward that he would come when it was time to
go, and say 'Robin Hood, come out'. I went to my sister's
and lay down. It was three o'clock when Woodward came
and rolled a stone against the door. Two sisters of mine, and
a brother, were upstairs. He opened the gate, and propped
it open with a stone, and told me to stay and watch. Archer
put his head through the window, but he could not get in.
Woodward did. He got in, and went to the door, and
called, 'Tetty'. She came downstairs and went into the
street, shouting and swearing. I stood against the haystack.
The others were by the well. She could not see us. She
locked the door and took the key with her. . . . When she
came against the window, Archer knocked her down with
his left hand, and Woodward struck her with the chisel.
Archer fell on her and throttled her. He was kneeling on
her, and she was gurgling in the throat as if she was sick.
Woodward put a cord round her neck, and took the key
out of her pocket, and unlocked the door. Archer pulled
her into the house with the cord. I was going away [but] . . .
Archer cursed me for my cowardice. . . . I went in, and as
soon as the door was locked, we heard persons come. . . . I
followed the others upstairs with a candle. It was burning
on the table when we got in. Woodward drew the curtains
in the upper room. He took the keys out of Mrs. Lightfoot's
pocket, and opened the drawer. There were sovereigns in

it. Archer put these in his right hand pocket. We found money and bills in other drawers, which Woodward and Archer pocketed. Woodward saw two persons crossing the road. . . . He took the cord off her neck, and as we went out, Archer pointed to the body and said, 'There the old bitch lies.' Woodward said, 'If it weren't so late, we would throw her into the well, and then it would be thought she killed herself.' We all three went into a close called the Brook, and divided the money. I got three sovereigns and five shillings. On the same morning, I went to Bourne and stayed three days. Woodward came to me on the Saturday, and threatened to murder me if I got found out by changing the sovereigns. He told me to go in search of a job, and to keep out of the way because Archer was already taken up. I quitted Bourne and wandered about a hundred miles, going by the name of Thomas Islip. I was taken at Peterborough on suspicion of this murder. . . . On the following Tuesday, I confessed.

Thomas Masters: I know the prisoners, and Stansor. I was at the opening of the Fox and Hounds. I saw them there. . . .

Samuel Mitchell: After the opening of the Fox and Hounds, I went home about half past three in the morning. I saw Mrs. Longfoot near her house, storming in the street. . . . I found a stick on the morning of the murder, near the spot . . . [a stick produced].

Thomas Messam: I live at Tolthorpe . . . I saw Stansor and Woodward together at Bourne.

Henry Goddard: I am a Bow Street officer, and I was sent for in consequence of this murder. I saw Woodward on 12th April in Stamford gaol. He said, 'If you can promise a free pardon, I'll tell you about the murder at Easton. I said that was out of my power. . . . He then made a disclosure to me, and afterwards . . . before the magistrates.

At this point, Goddard was stopped from saying anything further about Woodward's statement. The reason would have been that the most acceptable evidence was the statement itself. Goddard left the witness box and his place was taken by the Clerk to the Stamford magistrates.

149

Nathaniel Farrant: I am Clerk to the magistrates . . . at Stamford. The examination of Woodward took place on 12th April. No promise or inducement was held out.

The statement (referred to as "The Examination") was handed to Farrant and he read it. It referred to Woodward's visit to Stansor at Bourne, but described it as a "meeting". It alleged that Stansor told him how he had murdered Mrs. Longfoot alone and kept all the money himself. It said that the incident Woodward had asked Stansor not to mention was the attempted robbery, earlier, in which he, Stansor and Archer had been involved.

Henry Goddard, re-called: This was subsequent to the examination of Stansor. . . . On April 14th, I saw Woodward again, in custody, and he told me that . . . he and Archer went with a ladder to Mrs. Longfoot's house. They raised it in the street, but failed to get in through a window. They agreed that they would have to murder her to rob her. . . . Woodward confessed to participating in the murder, and said that Stansor's statement was true. . . .

Richard Whitehead: I am a farmer at Easton. Some days before the murder, I missed a ladder from my stack-yard. I saw it about a week later in Mr. Phillips' yard.

William Brown: I was in Northampton gaol on 6th April, for cutting down some poles. Archer and Woodward were brought into the yard I was in. Archer spoke of the murder. When Mrs. Longfoot came in he stood behind the gate, he aimed a blow at her, but missed. Woodward struck her, and then again with the chisel. Woodward put a cord round her neck and dragged her indoors. Her shoe and patten came off. . . . Woodward took what he could find upstairs. Stansor remained in the yard. He had five sovereigns and five shillings. They left in different directions. . . . These particulars were related to me at different times in the prison-yard. I saw Woodward in July, in the "Glory Hole". I was there for stealing Mr. Morton's ducks. He showed me a letter, and he told me, as a secret, that he had a double-barrelled gun hidden under a stack. Woodward was in Number eleven, and I was in Number ten. We used to talk to each other between the iron rails. Woodward said he had some money in a hole in Mr. Rayson's grounds, and some sovereigns in the ceiling of his brother's house.

Mr. Miller, for the defence, cross-examining: Have you heard of a reward of a hundred pounds for the conviction of the prisoners?

Brown: I have.

Miller: My Lord, I should like to have Allen, the constable of Easton-on-the-Hill re-called.

The parish constable took position in the witness box.

Miller: Did you search Woodward's house at Easton?

Thomas Allen: I did.

Miller: Did you search the roof?

Allen: I searched the roof, but found no money.

Miller addressed the jury. His "eloquent, fervid and effective" speech endured for four hours. One of the important points he raised was whether it was possible for prisoners in Northampton gaol to communicate with each other in the manner described by William Brown. Lord Denman, the judge, evidently took this point, and although it was late in the day, he sent for the Governor of the gaol before commencing his summing up. Mr. Grant, the Governor of the prison was present in Court when Denman finished.

Grant: It is impossible that the prisoners in their cells could converse in whispers. They would need to speak as loud as I am now giving evidence, and there is an officer continually on duty, so they must surely be heard, and would be liable to punishment in close confinement.

Henry Goddard, in his memoirs, says that the jury had a "long retirement" but they were in consultation for a short time. They found both prisoners not guilty.

Goddard says that the verdict caused "surprise and astonishment" to the Judge and "everyone in court". He also tells us that later inquiries proved that prisoners in

Northampton gaol were fully able to communicate with one another in the manner described by Brown. The modern reader may well decide however, that the prosecution was using Stansor to "frame" Woodward and Archer. That is certainly what the defence counsel, Miller, wanted the jury to believe.

Patrick Pringle, the editor of Henry Goddard's memoirs,[84] quotes the *Annual Register* description of the reaction to the verdict in Easton-on-the-Hill. The inhabitants were called to assemble by "the call of a drum", and attacked Archer's house. His furniture was smashed and scattered in fragments in the streets. Woodward's property was subjected to similar treatment. The uproar did not abate until after midnight, but the villagers were unable to find either Archer or Woodward.

7th March 1838

NORTHAMPTON AND THE RAILWAY: THE TOWN WAKES UP

A common fallacy obstinately repeated by historians of the railway, accuses Northampton and its municipal representatives of refusing to have the London and Birmingham Railway through the town. The notion was first contradicted by Joan Wake in 1935 (*Northampton Vindicated; or Why the Main Line Missed the Town*); and again in 1959, by Victor Hatley.[85] The Act for building a railway from London to Birmingham received the Royal Assent in May 1833. It included the proposed route. Northampton was not on it.

Early in March 1838, it dawned on many prominent Northamptonians that they should be taking steps to establish some kind of link between the town and the track. Over a hundred names were appended to a petition on 6th March. Whigs and Tories signed, so there was nothing political in this.

To the Worshipful
GEO. PEACH, ESQ.
MAYOR OF THE BOROUGH OF NORTHAMPTON.

WE, the undersigned, request you will, at your earliest convenience, call a Meeting of the Inhabitants of this Town, to take into consideration the Propriety of applying to the London and Birmingham Railroad Company, for a Station at the nearest and most convenient Situation for the Town and Neighbourhood of Northampton, and to take such further steps to accomplish that object as the Meeting shall think proper to adopt."

This came into the hands of the Mayor on the following day, and arrangements were made to have it printed by Ratnett, as a poster, together with the names of all the petitioners, and the Mayor's footnote:

"In compliance with the foregoing Requisition, I appoint a PUBLIC MEETING of the Inhabitants of Northampton, to be held in the GUILDHALL, on THURSDAY next, the 8th Instant, at Eleven o'Clock in the Forenoon. —— Dated this 7th day of March, 1838.

GEO. PEACH, Mayor."[86]

This was the beginning of the campaign which was to have two objectives: the establishment of a suitable station on the main line at Blisworth; and the construction of a branch line into the town.

12th March 1838

THE REVIVAL OF THE BARONY OF VAUX OF HARROWDEN

Henry Knollys, sixth Baron Vaux of Harrowden died in 1662 without issue, and his title fell into abeyance.[87] Harrowden passed "by marriage to the Fitzwilliams of Wentworth

153

Wodehouse (not . . . Milton . . .)".[88] Early in 1838, George Charles Mostyn, of Kiddington in Oxfordshire, was one of three men seeking to have the title revived in their favour. The other two were Robert, Earl of Pembroke, and Edward Bourchier Hartopp.[89] A committee of the House of Lords was appointed to investigate the claims. Mostyn and Hartopp both traced their descent to daughters of the third Baron Vaux; but Mostyn's ancestor was the older daughter. The Lord's committee found that the title had been created by writ in the early Tudor period. It was recommended that the abeyance be ended by writ, and so, with the Queen's approval George Mostyn was summoned to Parliament as Baron Vaux of Harrowden. He never owned Harrowden Hall: it was bought back by his grandson in 1895. That was Hubert Mostyn, who succeeded to the title on George's death in 1883.

15th March 1838

THE STANWICK ENCLOSURE AWARD

The Stanwick Enclosure Act had received the Royal assent on 27th June 1834. Its purpose was to authorise the process of enclosing the old open fields of the village. This task was to be carried out by three Commissioners, none of whom was to have any interest in Stanwick lands, with the assistance of two similarly independent surveyors. Nearly four years later, their work was complete, and the Award was published on 15th March. It is preserved in Raunds Parish Council Office, exquisitely presented, bound in leather, a pleasure to handle.

It begins with the oaths of the three Commissioners, John West, Henry Dixon and Charles Paul Berkeley, all from parishes remote from Stanwick. The surveyors, John Allen and Walter Ray, follow with their own oaths. The public roads are next described. One of the duties of the Commissioners was to alter the routes of roads and paths to conform to the rearrangement of the fields.

"One public carriage Road and Highway of the width of thirty three feet leading from and out of the village of Stanwick near the homestead of George Gascoyen the elder, Esquire, in a southward and south westward direction along the present track to its junction with the public road in the parish of Chelveston.

"One other public carriage Road and Highway of the width of thirty three feet leading . . . near the Church Yard in a north eastward direction through and over Dry Close Corner Piece to the present Road and thence along the remaining part of the road into the parish of Raunds.

"One other public carriage Road and Highway of the width of thirty three feet leading from Raunds public Road in the parish of Raunds near the north west corner of Stanwick Pastures in a southward direction along the present track by the west side of Stanwick to its entrance into the parish of Chelveston.

"One other public carriage Road and Highway of the width of thirty three feet leading from and out of the village of Stanwick near the Manor Farm Homestead belonging to William Drayson Esquire, in an eastward direction along the present track to a certain point opposite the north east corner of a certain old Inclosure belonging to the Devisees in trust of the late Isaac Robinson deceased, and thence in a southward direction to its junction with the Back Lane Road and thence in an eastward direction along its present track to its junction with the Raunds and Chelveston Road near the west end of the Lane leading to Stanwick Pastures.

"One other public carriage Road and Highway of the width of thirty three feet leading from and out of the Stanwick and Chelveston Road opposite the Manor Farm Homestead in a southward direction along the present track into Yew Bridge Lane. . . ."

There follow descriptions of two other roads adapted to fit the new field boundaries: Back Lane Road and Cotton Lane Road. "No. VIII" is an example of a newly created road:

"And one other public carriage Road and Highway of the width . . . leading from and out of the village of Stanwick at the west end thereof in a westward direction through and over a garden and the scite [sic] of certain sheds and out-buildings belonging to a cottage in the occupation of William Martin and thence into through and over part of an old Inclosure called Nether Close and Spinney adjoining belonging to the Reverend John William Coventry Campion and through and over the same into over and along other part of the said Inclosure called Nether Close into Carter's Leys and from thence near the present track to its junction with the Cotton Lane Road."

As in other parts of the county, the word "Cotton" is an archaic plural of "cottage".

There was no change to any turnpike road.

Private roads affected were named as "Long Tip Private Road", "Cock Close Private Road", "Stanwick Mill Private Road", and "Brook Furlong Private Road". Four footpaths were named.

The duties of the Commissioners included the re-cutting of any water-courses, so as to keep them to the borders of the newly enclosed land. Those named were "Watery Lane public Watercourse", "Moors Slade public Drain and Water-course", "The Upper Meadow Brook and public Water-course", and "The Upper Meadow public Drain".

The allotment of land to the Stanwick inhabitants, and those needing to be recompensed for loss of former rights, come next. Finally, inside the rear binding is the enclosure map, in delicate water colour, and quite delightful.

24th March 1838

A SKELETON AT WALTON

Walton is now part of Peterborough's urban sprawl. In 1838 it was a separate village to the north-east of the city. On Saturday, 24th March, a labourer on Canwell's farm was digging a drain. Very close to the surface of the ground, he uncovered a human skeleton, lying in a "huddled" posture. Its skull was in very good condition, and the teeth perfect. Just above the head was what was considered to be a Roman spear-head, and next to that, an earthen vessel made of materials "not indigenous to the area". Some boys crowded round to see the disinterment, and for their "amusement" the earthenware object was smashed. This discovery was reported in the *Northampton Mercury* on 7th April 1838 (p. 4, col. 5).

26th March 1838

HONEST JACK VISITING THE WORKHOUSE BEFORE BREAKFAST

John C. Gotch, of Kettering, rose early on Monday morning, 26th March, and went to inspect the new workhouse, nearing completion. It was one of G.G. Scott's design, with a central octagonal block. It still stands, as St. Mary's Hospital, but the centre has been modified. That evening, John Gotch did not attend and chair the Kettering Vestry meeting as he usually did, even though Poor Law matters were discussed. Instead, he wrote a letter to himself, setting down his reservations about the functions of the workhouse. The letter, signed "Honest Jack" is in the Gotch collection at Kettering Public Library, and was reproduced as Appendix III in *Kettering Vestry Minutes AD 1797-1853* (edited by S. A. Peyton: Northamptonshire Record Society Volume VI, 1933).

"I have no doubt whatever that when you saw . . . all the conveniences with which it is provided that you pronounced them all to be very good. for here are not only large and small sleeping rooms but water closets, and every other convenience that seems necessary for to live and sleep in . . . a *Chappel* i think they call it, for to promote their *spiritual* as well as their temporal welfare . . . if families according to their moral character are to be placed in these different apartments, it would very much increase their comfort, & spread happiness through the whole house. but upon enquiry i found that these were . . . for the seperating of single familyes into 4 parts and thus cruelly tearing asunder man and wife, parents and children, thus breaking those bonds that nought but death should break . . . can a Dissenter get much benefit thereby, while he has set before him doctrines that he cannot believe and while he reflects on his condition and that his family so near him and yet be denyed the priviledge of seeing them. You must surely think that anything but religion will fill his mind and instead of loving, will he not hate those who under the pretence of freindship have placed him in this prison, not for crime but because he was poor. . . .

So consientous were you with others a little time ago that your conscience would not allow you to support the Church, but now you can cram the poor with this unwholesome food, as though they had no mind nor understanding. Can these things be long endured. No, a stronger arm than yours will here Sir be lifted up for the needy and render useless all these tyranical schemes.

"Adieu for the present. when i have an opportunity i shall resume the subject.

"Yours affect^ly Honest Jack"

On 16th August 1838, the old workhouse in Hog Leys (west side of modern Silver Street) was sold, together with its garden, the lock-up house, and twenty-five cottages and a mill-house, all parish property. The details were advertised in the *Northampton Mercury* of 4th August 1838 (p. 3, col. 2).

30th March 1838

RICK BURNING AT LONG BUCKBY

"HARLESTONE ASSOCIATION.
SEVENTY-FIVE POUNDS REWARD
WHEREAS some Person or Persons, about nine o'clock on the night of Friday the 30th day of March last, maliciously SET FIRE to a CLOVER RICK, standing in the Rickyard of Mr. THOMAS MARRIOTT, of Long Buckby; whoever will give such information as may lead to the apprehension and conviction of the Offender or Offenders, shall receive a REWARD of £75; £25 to be paid by the undersigned Somersby Edwards, and the remaining £50 by the said Thomas Marriott.

And if any one will impeach his accomplice or accomplices, so that he or they may be apprehended and convicted, he shall be entitled to the same Reward, and application shall be made to procure her Majesty's pardon.

SOMERSBY EDWARDS
Treasurer and Solicitor to the said Association
Long Buckby, 6th April, 1838."

This advertisement was printed in the *Northampton Mercury* of 14th April 1838 (p. 1, col. 1).

1st April 1838

SMOKED BACON AT KILSBY

Earl Spencer was in the chair at the Northamptonshire Easter Sessions on Thursday, 5th April.

Henry Fletcher, James Ball, Joseph Webb and Thomas Oxlam, labourers on the railroad, were indicted for stealing 25 pounds of bacon, the property of Joseph Faulkner, of Kilsby.

Joseph Faulkner: I keep a public house at Kilsby. On Sunday last, the prisoners and two other men came to my house about two o'clock, and had some beer. About four o'clock, I went into the room where they were sitting, and I saw that Ball was not there. While I was in the room, a great piece of bacon came tumbling down the chimney, into Fletcher's lap. In a minute or two, another piece came down, and fell into Oslam's lap; and shortly after, the prisoner Ball came tumbling down the chimney with some more bacon. I accused him of stealing my bacon, but he said the other prisoners had wagered with him that he could not get up the chimney. They refused to give up the bacon, and my wife went for the police. Meantime the prisoners forced their way from the house, taking the bacon with them.

John Dew: I am a police officer at Kilsby. I met the prisoners about three hundred yards from Faulkner's house. There were two other men with them. Oxlam said: "Here comes one of them bloody police. We shall be all taken." He had a piece of bacon partly concealed under his jacket. A few minutes later, when I had been given information of the robbery, I went after the prisoners, and took them into custody. The other two absconded.

Charles Churchill: I am a police officer at Kilsby. . . . I observed Fletcher say to Ball: "You did not tell them we had the bacon, did you?" And Ball replied that he did not.

All guilty. Six months' imprisonment, with hard labour, in the house of correction.

2nd April 1838

A WARNING TO VAGRANTS FROM THE CONSTABLE OF BYFIELD

"To VAGRANTS & GYPSIES
NOTICE is hereby given, That all PERSONS found

BEGGING or ENCAMPING with tents, carts, or horses, or making fires, contrary to law, in the public ways of the several parishes of Aston-le-Walls (with the hamlet of Appletree), Upper and Lower Boddington, Byfield, Edgcott, Eydon, and Woodford, with the hamlets of Farndon and Hinton, will be PROSECUTED as the law directs.

WM. ROCHFORT, constable.

Byfield, April 2d, 1838."

(*Northampton Mercury* 7th April 1838, p. 1, col. 2.)

7th April 1838

RUSHDEN IN 1838

There is some obscurity about the sale of the Rushden Hall estate. In 1985, the respected historian of Rushden, David Hall, quoted Northamptonshire Record Office documents to show that the estate had been sold by Thomas Williams to John Barrington Browne in 1836, though the transaction was not completed until September 1838.[90] It is true that the Hall was offered for sale by auction on 20th May 1836, but in 1838 at least three contemporary sources give the occupant as John Fletcher, and on 7th April it was offered for sale by private contract.

The contents of the Hall were auctioned on 15th and 16th March 1838 "under an assignment for the benefit of creditors", on the premises. The advertisement of this sale, in the *Northampton Mercury* of 10th March, names John Fletcher Esq. as the owner. Among the items offered in that auction, and worthy of comment, were a "Grand Six octave Pianoforte", two bidets, an invalid's chair, "37 vols of racing calendars from 1784", a shower bath, a sandwich service, two meat safes, two salting leads, "a useful milch cow" and a four-wheeled pony chaise.

The advertisement for the sale of the Hall itself was printed in the *Northampton Mercury* of 7th April (p. 2, col. 4) and 14th April (p. 1, col. 4).

"To CAPITALISTS
RUSHDEN, Northamptonshire
TO BE SOLD BY PRIVATE CONTRACT,

A most desirable ESTATE, at RUSHDEN . . ., comprising that fine old Gothic Mansion, "RUSHDEN HALL", with the Gardens and Appurtenances, and SEVERAL CLOSES of excellent Pasture and Arable Land adjoining, containing together 157 Acres or thereabouts, more or less, with the FARM HOUSE and Buildings, the SWAN PUBLIC HOUSE, and several other HOUSES and COTTAGES, the greater part Freehold, but the Copyhold part thereof being Fine certain is equal in value to Freehold. Also an ALLOTMENT of LAND, containing about 58 Acres, adjoining the Road from Rushden to Newton Bromswold.

"The Mansion House Estate may be purchased either with or without the residue of the Property; and two-thirds of the Purchase Money may remain secured on the Estate for a term of five years at $3\frac{1}{2}$ per cent.

"Rushden is in a good sporting part of the country, in the midst of three Packs of Fox Hounds, the Pytchley, Oakley, and Earl Fitzwilliam's, and in the neighbourhood of four Market Towns. . . .

"The Parochial Rates are moderate:

Immediate Possession may be had of the Mansion House, together with the Pastures Closes, which have been lately occupied therewith. . . ."

John Cole described the Hall in 1838.[91]

". . . The Hall is at present occupied by John Fletcher, Esq., and is situated nearly in the centre of Rushden . . . surrounded by plantations, gardens and orchards by which it is completely screened from the village. . . . A full sounding bell, hung at the top of the house, having the rope guarded by a casing of wood down to the ground floor, has been a fixture in the mansion from time immemorial. This bell yet continues to be rung by the family at certain times during the day, and may be heard throughout the extent of the village."

On the east side of the Hall, Cole described a plantation of "spiry fir" beyond which could be seen the spire of the parish church. "The west entrance into the park is flanked by a row of aged trees on each side, principally Wych elms, sixty three in number, which form a noble avenue; at the extremity of which, the tall church spire affords a fine relief. . . " Cole was somewhat disorientated: he was describing the east avenue. He wrote several paragraphs on the trees around the estate. One special tree was "a fine Walnut tree, for which the late Thomas Fletcher Esq., was once offered the sum of one hundred guineas, for the purpose of its manufacture into gun stocks".

Written before photography, and before the industrial transformation, John Cole's description of the village is valuable. "The church-yard of Rushden commands a pleasing view down a luxuriant valley, beyond which, rising hills stretch far away in retiring beauty; and being well-wooded afford a fine prospect. . . ." The village extended for a mile, "the houses being irregularly placed in all directions, some with their gables to the street; others retreating, and are here and there intersected by orchards, and interspersed with straggling shrubs; and rural lanes strike off the principal street to an interesting vale, along which a clear stream winds its variously meandering course, having rustic bridges thrown over it; and being occasionally belted by plantations, with cottages on its winding margin, orchards near the stream, a planted nook of forest trees, outbuildings . . ., and a farm-house, while the tall spire of the church occasionally graces the scene, from a green, lawn-like opening; at another bend of the rippling brook, the water impetuously murmers as it forms a . . . cascade, diverging into two streams, and near it the road curves off to the ascending hill, forming the elevated green mount in front of the . . . church".

Cole confessed that in wintry weather the lanes became wet and dirty.

During these early days of April, the Seed-Time bell was rung. Cole explained that "to call up the sower to his task, at the early hour of four o'clock . . . one of the bells of the church is sounded in an awakening manner".

7th April 1838

PATTENS

Some of the women of Rushden, without doubt, wore pattens when the road was muddy. Many a pair stood waiting on the door step, to be slipped on to their owner's feet when she had an errand along the unpaved street. Elizabeth Longfoot wore pattens on the March night at Easton-on-the-Hill when her murderers struck. There were churches that forbade the wearers of pattens to enter.

The *Northampton Mercury* of 7th April 1838 carried the following advertisement (p. 3, col. 4):

"To Boot and Shoe Manufacturers, &c, &c.
B. LEE & SON
BOOT AND SHOE-TREE, FRENCH CLOG,
AND PATTEN MAKERS
BRADSHAW STREET, NORTHAMPTON
BEG most respectfully to inform the Trade and the Public in general, that they intend to carry on the above business in its various branches, and hope by strict attention and punctuality, to meet with that patronage and support which it will be their anxious study to merit."

7th April 1838

JOHN HERBERT PRETENDING TO BE DRUNK, AT ABINGTON

The list of those committed to gaol during the week ending 14th April 1838 includes the name John Herbert, locked up for robbery. The *Northampton Mercury* of 14th April described what had happened (p. 3, col. 5).

The victim was Thomas Luck, who was returning home to Moulton, on Saturday night, 7th April, carrying a bundle containing nine pounds of mutton, a sheep's head, two pounds of sugar, two ounces of tea, two ounces of tobacco, two ounces of coffee, and a handkerchief. At Abington – the north side of the parish, on the Kettering road – he was overtaken by Herbert, pretending to be very drunk. Seeing some straw on the road, Luck advised Herbert to lie down and sleep it off. He placed his bundle down and began to move some of the straw to the side of the road where Herbert would not be "run over". Suddenly, Herbert snatched up the bundle and ran off with it.

Spencer, the constable, was given sufficient information to enable him to apprehend the villain during the course of the following week.

18th April 1838

A SHOEMAKER'S WIFE ON A DUNG-HILL

One of the cases before Sir John Bernard Bosanquet in the Civil Court at the Northampton Summer Assizes on Thursday 19th July was Webberley and Wife v Elliott the elder, an action for assault on the plaintiff's wife. Webberley was a shoemaker at Welton; and the defendant, Richard Elliott was his landlord.

On the morning of 10th April, Mrs. Webberley had been out near her dwelling, when she found a basket. Two little girls were nearby, and Mrs. Webberley told them that if anyone enquired about the basket, they were to direct the owner to her. In the meantime she would take it in for safe-keeping.

The basket, containing a bottle and one or two other items, was the property of a surveyor named Crow, who had been at work near the place. He was putting up at the public house kept by the defendant's son, John Elliott. Mrs. Elliott, his mother, who sometimes assisted there, hearing of the finding of the basket, insinuated that Mrs. Webberley had intended to steal it. Not surprisingly, Mrs. Webberley soon heard what had been said, and went to the public house to demand an explanation. The old lady's husband arrived at the scene while hot words were being exchanged, and committed the assault on Mrs. Webberley, forcing her out into the yard, and thrusting her upon the dung-hill.

The verdict went to the plaintiff, and Richard Elliott was ordered to pay forty shillings damages, and forty shillings costs.

11th April 1838

MORE ACCIDENTS ON THE RAILWAY

George Abbey, the Coroner, conducted yet another inquest on the body of a railway labourer, on Wednesday 11th April, at Flore (spelt "Floore" in the *Northampton Mercury* account (14th April, p. 3, col. 6). The deceased, Nightingale, had been excavating hard clay at Nether Heyford, when the heap he had got out fell in on him. He died of his injuries, on the way to the Infirmary. The verdict was "accidental Death".

On the next day, Henry John, a Welshman, was riding on a loaded train at Ashton, when one of his fellow workmen accidentally knocked him off the truck. He fell on the rails, and the following trucks ran over his right foot. His leg was amputated at Northampton Infirmary.

12th April 1838

"I THINK YOU ARE GOING TO BE DROWNED"

The Rev. John Wing was the Rector of Thornhaugh. His second daughter, Ellen, was about to be married to the only son of Steed Girdlestone, of Stibbington House. On Thursday morning, 12th April, at ten, young Girdlestone called to take his fiancee and her mother for a sail on the Nene. As the ladies left the house, the Rector, with mock seriousness – or perhaps, genuine concern – said: "I think you are going to be drowned."

An hour later, the sailing boat, carrying Girdlestone, Ellen, her mother, and a boy named Britton, taken aboard to "assist in managing the sail", was 150 yards below the staunch at Wansford. Suddenly a gust of wind threw the boat on her side, and the whole party was precipitated into deep water.

A Wansford surgeon, Mr. Clapham, who happened to be passing on the Peterborough road, saw the mishap. Other persons arrived, with grappling irons. Girdlestone and Britton were able to get to the shore, but the two women were not recovered for nearly an hour. The bodies were carried the mile to the Thornhaugh Rectory in post-chaises, where pathetic but futile efforts were "long persevered in for their restoration".[92]

14th April 1838

ANGRY WORDS ABOUT THE RAILWAY

The first two pages of the *Northampton Mercury* of 14th April carried a comprehensive account of a meeting of county businessmen at Towcester, the purpose of which was to formulate an approach to the London and Birmingham Railway, making a case for a first-class station at Blisworth. Editorial comment on page 3 turned its attention to the previous Saturday's *Northampton Herald*, which had, itself, in a long leading article, insisted on the importance of first-class stations at Blisworth and Wolverton.

Victor Hatley has referred to this issue of the *Herald*, saying that it "hinted" that the Company was punishing the town of Northampton for opposing the line from the outset, by declining to provide an adequate station at Blisworth.[85] He refers to the paper's nickname, *The Lying Herald*, and observes fairly that it was engaged in a "spiteful anti-London and Birmingham campaign". The Editor of the *Mercury*, de Wilde, accused his rival of assailing the directors of the railway "for not having thought fit to advertise in [its] columns . . ., and for having received repeated importunities for advertisements with . . . a scornful silence".

The actual words used in the *Herald* in regard to the supposed attitude of the Company, were:

> "An opinion is very prevalent in this town and neighbourhood, that Northampton is now being punished by the Directors for its former opposition to them in Parliament."

It may well have been true that such an opinion was prevalent; but a Company policy of "punishment" was deserving of de Wilde's derision. It would have meant "that the Directors feel it to be in their interest to have a station at Blisworth, but that they choose to run counter to that interest for the sake of punishing a few members of the Old Corporation". De Wilde went on to say that "the only town and neighbourhood in which it ever prevailed was that of his own imagination [the un-named managing editor of the *Herald*] – with him it originated. . . . To suppose that the Directors are influenced by any other consideration than the general interest of the shareholders is an absurdity".

In regard to the Company's decision to advertise in the *Mercury* but not in the *Herald*, de Wilde provided statistics to show that the *Mercury* always carried more advertising than its rival; and "by referring to the last Parliamentary return, it will also be found that while, during the five months ending with November last, the circulation of the *Herald* was 26,000, or 1,300 weekly; that of the *Mercury* was 38,000, or 1,900 weekly . . .".

The Managing Director of the London and Birmingham Railway was Captain Moorsom, of whose supposed radicalism the *Herald* heartily disapproved. "It is curious," wrote de Wilde, "to see with what a keen nose he pursues an advertisement, and how he condescends to canvass, again and again, 'a red hot Radical' as he politely styles Captain Moorsom. . . ."

15th April 1838

"ABSCONDED FROM THE KETTERING WORKHOUSE"

With a wide range of denominations worshipping in the town, no one at the workhouse in Kettering would have thought it unusual for a male inmate to leave the premises to attend one of the churches on a Sunday. Joe Rowlatt was visually handicapped, and unlikely to stray. By the following Thursday, the Master would have been fairly certain that he was not going to return. A reward was offered for his apprehension, and a notice issued by the Guardians. It was printed in the *Northampton Mercury* on 21st April (p. 3, col. 3). Why should it matter that a pauper moved on? He was still wearing the Union suit.

"KETTERING UNION

ABSCONDED from the Kettering Workhouse, with the Union clothing, on Sunday last, under pretence of attending public worship, JOSEPH ROWLATT, of the parish of Kettering.

The said Joseph Rowlatt is nearly blind, about 55 years old, walks erect, with long stick – height, 5ft. 8in., dark complexion, grey hair, and rather stout made. He had on, when he left, the workhouse dress, consisting of a dark brown cloth coat, waistcoat, and trowsers, nearly new.

Whoever will apprehend and bring the said Joseph Rowlatt to the Union Workhouse, at Kettering, shall receive a Reward of ONE SOVEREIGN, on application to Mr. CURTIS, the master.

By order of the Board,

W. J. F. MARSHALL, Clerk.

Kettering, 19th April, 1838."

17th April 1838

COUGH MIXTURE FROM THE RECTOR
OF KETTERING

William Hircock was born at Laxton in 1810. Nearly a
century later he gave a series of interviews in which he
recalled his impressions of Kettering when he first moved
there to work at the Rectory.[93] That was in 1838 when Dr.
Henry Corrie became Rector (inducted 17th April). Corrie
had been curate there until 1837, moving to Blatherwycke as
Rector, where Hircock worked in the Rectory garden. By
popular demand, the doctor moved back to Kettering as
Rector when the previous incumbent died.

"When I came to Kettering," said 94-year-old Hircock, "my
first job was to lay out the garden at [the] Rectory. The path
then ran round the kitchen garden, so I made the present road
to the front, branching off to the rear." Corrie combined "the
curing of souls with the curing of bodies. Every morning the
old kitchen at the Rectory was full of patients, who came, at
times from a distance, suffering from all the ills that flesh is
heir to. Here a tooth would be extracted; there a bottle of
cough medicine given, and so on, until with grateful thanks
the patients had vanished, to leave the reverend gentleman to
peruse his London paper, which was about the only one that
came into the town. In those days, newspapers cost eight-
pence." The Rector allowed literate inhabitants to pass his
papers among themselves.

"The churchyard was then an open space, and there, the
children of the town used to congregate amongst the
tombstones. . . . A number of old trees then fringed the
churchyard, and these were an eyesore to the incumbent,
who desired that the old decayed trees should be cut down,
and new ones planted in their place." Hircock felled the old
trees, "and planted new saplings, which are now [1905] the
tall stately trees forming the border to the churchyard. . . . In
front of the church was an old farmyard, belonging to Mr.
Roberts, which he kindly gave to the Ecclesiastical authorities
to make the present main entrance. . . ."

This last reminiscence, of 1905, is a contradiction of his

1904 recollection that the old farmyard, which stood between the west front of the Church and the George Hotel, was given to the Church by the Duke of Buccleuch.

"What was Kettering like when you came here?"

"It was a dirty village with a population of four thousand some hundreds. . . . There were hardly any pavements – poor pebbly things. Filth ran down the streets, not in drains, but on the surface. . . . The trade of the town at that time was the silk and plush weaving and woolcombing. One factory I remember in School Lane. Another one was in Uppingham (now Rockingham) Road. . . . There was only one banker and one shoe manufacturer – the Gotch's were bankers and shoe factors. This house [Hircock's own dwelling since his marriage to Dr. Corrie's housekeeper] was the last in Montagu Street except the Swan public house, and mud houses on what was called "the waste". Nearly all the houses were thatched. Tradesmen's windows had very small panes . . . Rose's used to brew in an open yard. Bakehouse Hill was occupied by a faggot stack, a little bakehouse and a pump. Kettering was a wonderful place for water, and springs could be seen everywhere before they got cut off. Some of them ran along the street. There was one across Montagu Street (Swan Street as it was then) and one at the bottom of Gas Street, called Goose Pasture then. . . . The weighing machine stood at the top of Gold Street. Waggons used to go out, of a morning, to fetch coal from Market Harborough, and that was the place where all the stuff was weighed. . . . I remember the lock-up well – the old roundhouse at the top of Workhouse Lane. The Puzzle was a wagon hovel. . . .

"On a bright moonlight night the peaceful inhabitants . . . would be aroused from their slumbers to hear the watchman . . . 'Twelve o'clock – all is right. Lie still,' or 'All's right. Moon shines bright'. . . .

"Kettering did not boast a corn exchange. The merchants – true there were only a few – did their buying and selling under the portico of the 'White Hart' [later 'Royal', much later 'Perequito']. . . .

"I can remember Kettering when Mr. Reresby's butcher's shop was the boundary on one side of the town, the old mill on the Rockingham Road (which is now pulled down and the Rockingham Road schools built on the site) was the other. . . ."

17th April 1838

MURDER AT BRAUNSTON

On Tuesday night last, a dreadful murder was committed on the body of a respectable female, who kept a small grocer's shop, at Braunston. The murder was discovered early on Wednesday morning, by a woman who went to the shop for some rain water, and who discovered the unfortunate female with her head nearly severed from her body and her limbs greatly mutilated, and affording evidence of a severe struggle having taken place between her and her murderer. Suspicion at first attached to a man who lives at Staverton, and travels about the country with sweetmeats, but after a long and minute investigation he was completely acquitted on Thursday night. Yesterday another person was taken up on suspicion, and the inquest was again adjourned. The murdered woman was possessed of some property, and lived in her own house. A box which contained a considerable sum of money, was found with the key fixed in the lock. It is supposed that the murderer had in vain attempted to open it, and had been compelled to leave the object for which the horrid deed had been committed. . . ."

(*Northampton Mercury*, p. 3, col. 5.)

The Inquest on the body of Ann Chown, single woman, about 46 years of age, of The Green, Braunston, conducted by George Abbey, Coroner, was resumed on Saturday, 21st April 1838.

Elizabeth Bennett: I live within a few yards. About eight o'clock on Wednesday morning, the 18th of April, I went for some soft water which she was in the habit of selling.

172

The front door was not locked. When I opened it, I saw her lying dead on the floor. The floor was covered with blood.

James Stubbs, surgeon: I examined the body. I found a wound in the forehead over the left eye, two inches in length, extending into the brain. Taking away part of the skull, I found that a piece of bone from the orbit of the left eye had been driven into the brain. There were also two flesh wounds near to this, each of them an inch and a half in length; a wound on the left cheek an inch and a half in length, with a fracture of the upper part of the cheek bone; three wounds on the left jaw, one on the upper lip an inch long; two teeth knocked out; a wound on the left arm an inch and a half in length and an inch wide. The immediate cause of death was, of course, the severe injury inflicted on the brain. It appeared to have been occasioned by a blunt but heavy instrument; and a sharp instrument seemed also to have been used. A bill-hook or a coal-peck might have inflicted both descriptions of wounds. At least eight or ten blows must have been struck. There was blood on the floor, on the wall, on the clock-case, and on the mantel-piece, but no impression on fingers.

——— Simons: I am constable at Braunston. I examined the house. There are two rooms on the upper floor: one which the deceased used as a bed-room; and one in which she kept her trunks and various goods. In this latter room, which has a window in it, looking towards the street, I found a chest of drawers containing five drawers. Four of them were open, and one was closed but not locked. The open drawers had linen in them, which had been turned over. In the lock of one of the trunks in the room, there was a key with a bunch of other keys attached to it. The key in the lock was not the right one. It was removed with difficulty. The proper key was one of the others in the bunch, and when I opened the trunk, I found in it a red pocket-book containing twenty-two pounds and ten shillings in gold; a purse containing nine sovereigns; a bag, and some rags containing gold amounting to seventy-three pounds and eleven shillings altogether. In another trunk in the same room was a tea caddy, which contained twenty-two pounds, five shillings and sixpence in silver, and a savings bank book. The key of this trunk was found in the cupboard below the stairs. There is no reason to suppose that anything had been taken away. In the bed-room which faces the back, the bed had the impression of one person having lain upon it, but it had not been slept in. A gingerbread-baker named Feavers was understood to have kept company with the deceased. I found him at his own residence at Staverton. I later found out that he was at Daventry from nine in the morning of Tuesday, the day the murder was committed, till four the next morning, at the house of Elizabeth Baker, who keeps a grocer's shop there. A porter, William Green, in the employ of Messrs. Pickford, is a distant relative of the deceased, and he was also examined, but nothing was found to justify detaining him.

Joseph Hemmings: I am a boatman. I heard the deceased in conversation with a man, at five minutes past eight on the evening of the murder, as I was passing by the house. I paid no attention to what was said. The voices were not very loud.

Mary Foster: I saw a light from the window of the upper room facing the street, between half past eight and nine. The curtains were drawn quite close. I thought it strange because I have never seen them drawn since her mother died about two years ago. I have seen a light in that room only once before.

William Boyce, labourer: I live in the yard into which Mrs. Chown's back door opens. There is a gate which is a common entrance for all. I locked it at precisely eight o'clock.

Verdict: Wilful Murder by Person or Persons Unknown.

Editor George de Wilde, of the *Northampton Mercury* made some deductive remarks on this case, on 28th April (p. 3, col. 4):

"It seems pretty clear that the murder was committed between five past and half past eight. Green was proved to be at the wharf from seven until a few minutes before eight;

and at the Ship public-house from five or ten past eight until eight-thirty. His movements have been traced till eleven o'clock, when the light was seen in the upper room. At this very time the murderer was in all probability ransacking the drawers. It is not unlikely that he was disturbed by the noise of Boyes locking the gate at that time. the key left in the lock was ample proof of a hasty retreat. The deceased was uncommunicative, and none of her neighbours or relatives knew that she kept money or property in the house. She always represented herself as being very poor, and used frequently to borrow a shilling or sixpence for a day or two from neighbours. The house was her own. It was said that she paid the purchase price of seventy pounds entirely in silver, supposedly using up all her savings. She had told one of her neighbours that on the previous Sunday night, someone tried the latch of her door. A short time previously, she had visited a solicitor at Daventry to make her will, but on learning the fee, went away saying that she could not afford it. She died intestate, and the whole of her property falls to her niece. A reward of £100 of 'government' money is offered."

23rd April 1838

ASHTON: ANOTHER ACCIDENT ON THE RAILWAY

"On Monday [23rd April] . . . John Yarrell, Joseph Anton, and Matthew Faulkner, labourers on the London and Birmingham Railway, at Ashton, were riding on a train waggon loaded with stones and dirt, which they were going to empty, and whilst going at the rate of about eight or ten miles an hour, one of the wheels broke, and the waggons immediately upset, almost burying the unfortunate men. They were extricated as soon as possible, and taken to the Infirmary. Yarrel was found to have sustained an extensive fracture of the left hip, with great bodily injury; Anton a very severe compound fracture of the arm in two places; and Faulkner a compound fracture of the left leg. Yarrel, who was a fine young man of 18, after suffering the most excruciating pain, was seized with mortification, and died early on Thursday morning. Anton and Faulkner are at present doing well. An inquest was held on the body of Yarrel on Thursday last [26th April] before G[eorge] Abbey . . . when a verdict of accidental death was returned."

(*Northampton Mercury* 28th April 1838, p. 3, col. 5.)

There are similarities between the *Mercury* account and the description of an accident at Ashton in Osborne's *London and Birmingham Railway Guide* [pp. 147-150]. Margery Fisher, of Ashton, referred to this in 1953, describing Osborne as "pompous but racy".[94] The trucks were carrying stones from Blisworth quarry to the bridge being built over the Hartwell Road. After the derailment, the men were dug out from the pile of clay and stone. The man with a fractured arm (Anton, if this is the same accident) walked six miles across the fields to his home. Sympathetic housewives climbed the bank "each evincing a great desire to touch with their fingers the mangled limb" of the youth with the leg injury (Faulkner?), who was "grey-faced and weeping" as the "rough-looking foreman, smoking his pipe" offered hesitant words of comfort.

24th April 1838

DUMB CAKE

On St. Mark's Eve, unmarried girls in Northamptonshire held parties, limited to three in number, to make "dumb cake". Strict silence was the rule, and all domestic animals were put out of doors, so that they did not disturb the proceedings. As the clock struck midnight, each girl broke off a portion of cake and ate it. Then, walking backwards, each went to her bed, still maintaining silence. The spell could be broken by a single word. All those who were destined to be married women would see, it was believed, a vision of their future husbands. If such an image was not seen, then a post-retirement noise in the house — knocking or rustling — was accepted as a favourable sign. It would not have been possible to blame banished pets. Girls fated to remain single would dream of funereal matters: shrouds, newly-dug graves and similar.[95]

2nd May 1838

THE DUTIES OF THE CHAPLAIN AT WELLINGBOROUGH UNION WORKHOUSE

". . . THE Guardians of the above Union having determined upon ELECTING A CHAPLAIN to the Union Workhouse, at Salary of Fifty Pounds per Annum, hereby give Notice that they will receive Applications from Clergymen of the Established Church, for such Chaplaincy, at their Meeting, to be held at the TOWN HALL, WELLINGBOROUGH, on WEDNESDAY the 25th of APRIL instant; and that such Applications will be considered at the said Meeting, and the Appointment of the Chaplain made on Wednesday the 2nd of May next. The Duties required will be one full service every Sunday (Morning and Evening alternately), and to visit the Inmates of the House frequently every week.

Clergymen willing to undertake the above Office are requested to forward Applications to the Clerk of the Union by Tuesday Evening the 24th Instant.

By Order of the Board,
HENRY M. HODSON, Clerk.
Wellingborough, 12th April, 1838.

(*Northampton Mercury* 14th April 1838, p. 2, col. 4.)

Thomas Sanderson, M.A., Headmaster of Wellingborough Grammar School, was appointed on Wednesday, 2nd of May.

May 1838

A WALK ALONG THE NENE VALLEY

John Cole walked through the meadows from Welling-borough to Higham Ferrers, one day in May 1838.[96] Before describing the route, he listed its "characteristics" – elevated terraces at the side of brooks, "foot-bridges, three-barred styles, rude planks; a winding river and horse-drawn barges; sheep tracks; Roman foundations; ancient mills and bridges, spired churches; willow plantations; . . . the nodding panicles of grass, concealing the winding track. . . .

"The first distinguished object on the route from Wellingborough, is the mill, well-known as Kilburn's. . . . We then enter a red-land lane, which during the refulgent weather of May, glitters like gold, and where hawkweed and dandelion . . . adorn it, and the convolvulus spreads a flowery carpet . . . over the dry path, while the upper portion of the hedge-row is enriched with the simple hare-bell. . . . On mounting the hill of the mill-lane, in a field to the right, a clump of five sister elms beautify the scene. . . .

"Diverging into the meadows, we approach a Roman emcampment. This fortification was an oblong . . . containing in the area, about eighteen acres. . . .

"Mr. Goosey's house is about mid-way between Welling-borough and Ditchford. . . . Near Chester House, the dwarf elder . . . flourishes; and here the finest series of the holly, glossy-leaved and shining in the sun, ornaments that portion of the avenue near the house. . . .

"An elevated path at the side of a little rivulet, conducts to . . . a water-mill called Ditchford-Bridge. . . .

Near the willow-spinney on the Nen between Ditchford and Higham [are] . . . elegantly-formed insects . . . in great numbers among the rushes. . . .

"Between Ditchford and Higham staunch is a spring of water of a peculiar tincture, called Whey-well; so named . . . from being the colour of whey. This locality is a celebrated place of rendezvous for starlings. . . .

"Due front, the handsome spire of Higham rises to view, and on our left the curious tower of Irthlingborough. . . .

"Making our arrival at the Higham Wharf, and ascending the hill, over a gate to the right, looking downward, is a charming view. . . The various ranges of trees . . . down toward the meadow-land, assume peculiar angular combinations of rich effect. . . ."

5th May 1838

A NORTHAMPTON INSCRIPTION LOST AND REDISCOVERED

An erstwhile visitor to Northampton wrote over the pen-name VIATOR, to the *Northampton Mercury* on 24th March 1838 (p. 3, col. 6) about an architectural feature no longer to be seen.

". . . In passing through Northampton in former years, I was struck with the appearance of a house situated at the western corner of St. Giles's Square, having the following inscription on the parapet, in large stone letters, similar to those which are to be seen at Castle Ashby, taken from Lucretius, the Latin poet: 'ERIPATUR PERSONA, MANET RES.' The substance of the passage . . . is as follows: that we should seek to learn a man's character in the time of danger and adversity, as at that time the real feelings are called forth; the mask is torn off, the reality remains. Both that inscription and the house itself . . . have undergone the transforming hand of time, and are no more. What event the inscription was meant to commemorate . . . I have no means of knowing. . . . One would almost imagine from its position, that it was in memory of some calamitous event. . . ."

From its position in the town, it would be safe to say that the house was likely one of those rebuilt after the great fire of

179

1675. That would explain the words. On 5th May, the *Mercury* printed another letter from VIATOR:

". . . I have since learnt . . . that the same inscription still exists in a different form, on a small square tablet of stone, inserted in the wall of the same house, on the western front, as follows: 'B.B. 1705. ERIPATUR PERSONA, MANET RES.'. . ."

7th May 1838

RESISTING ARREST AT WELLINGBOROUGH

Chief Justice the Right Honourable Sir Nicholas Conyngham Tindal presided over the Crown Court at Northampton Summer Assizes on 17th July 1838. One of the cases he heard concerned an adventure at Wellingborough. Charles Allen stood indicted for assaulting and maliciously cutting and maiming John Kingston; and for resisting apprehension for a felony. He was defended by the same active Mr. Miller who had defended the men accused of the murder of Elizabeth Longfoot.

John Dorset Old: I am Master of the Union Workhouse at Hardingstone. In April 1837, I was a constable in Wellingborough. At that time, I had the prisoner Allen in custody. A charge was made against him by Mr. Jones, draper, of Wellingborough, of stealing some prints from his shop. On this charge he was taken before Mr. Hill, remanded, and locked up in the cage. He was locked up about ten in the morning, and between twelve and one, he made his escape. I saw no more of him till this day.

John Kingston: I am a butcher, and a constable, in Wellingborough. On 7th of May last, I went to the prisoner's father's house in Wellingborough, with Luke Knight, another constable. I stayed below, while Knight went upstairs and brought the prisoner down. Knight told him he was apprehended on a charge of felony. The prisoner said nothing, but he went into the pantry to put his shoes on. He was using a knife to do this. When he came out, he stood at the door, with a knife in each hand. Knight took out the hand-cuffs, but the prisoner said he refused to be taken without a warrant. Upon this, Knight went away, leaving the prisoner and me together. When Knight was gone, he said he would make his escape, and rushed upon me with the knives. There was a scuffle, and my hand was cut. The prisoner then escaped up the stairs. I remained below. Meantime, Knight came back, and we then saw the prisoner standing at the top of the stairs with three open razors and a knife in his hands. He threatened to murder whoever attempted to take him. I armed myself with a chair and went upstairs. The prisoner then assailed me with a clothes pole. With Knight, I succeeded in over-mastering him, and he then threw himself on the bed and cut his throat with a razor.

Miller: Did you tell the prisoner that you came to apprehend him for breaking prison?

Kingston: No, sir.

Miller: Did Knight?

Kingston: No, sir.

Miller: Here is the record of your examination before the magistrate [Paper was produced and placed in his hands]. It states that you and Knight told the prisoner you came to apprehend him for breaking out of prison, where he had been confined on a charge of felony.

Kingston: That is true, sir.

Miller: Did you have a warrant with you?

Kingston: No, sir.

Miller: Did Knight have a warrant?

Kingston: I do not know that, sir.

Luke Knight: I am a constable at Wellingborough . . . I found the prisoner concealed behind the bedstead, and I told him

181

I was come to apprehend him for breaking out of prison, and likewise for being remanded on a charge of felony [sic.]. I had no warrant, and the prisoner refused to be taken without one. I then went away to ask Mr. Jones whether he had a warrant, but he had not, and I returned to the house. I found Kingston with his hand bleeding, and the prisoner was at the top of the stairs, with knives and razors in his hands. When Kingston went upstairs, he stood at the top with a pole, and there was a razor at the end of it.

Andrew Fernie: I am a surgeon, in Oxford Street, at Wellingborough . . . I dressed Kingston's wound. It was a slight cut, apparently done with a knife.

E. Jones: I am a draper, at Wellingborough . . . [gave evidence about the loss of several pieces of cotton print, and the apprehension and remanding of the prisoner Allen on the charge of stealing them].

Miller (addressing the jury for the defence): The prisoner must be acquitted. . . . The constable not having had any warrant, and the attempt to apprehend him being unlawful. It does not appear that the prisoner has broken prison – which being in itself a felony, would have justified his apprehension without a warrant. It was merely stated that he escaped – which would have been a misdemeanor only, and for which he could not be apprehended without a warrant. There is no evidence that the slight wound inflicted upon the constable was not merely an accident.

The Chief Justice: . . . There are two points for your consideration. First, whether he is guilty of a felony. Secondly, whether, supposing him not to be guilty of a felony, he is guilty of an assault. The question of whether he was justified in resisting the apprehension without a warrant, depends upon the question whether he had broken out of prison.

Verdict: Not guilty of the felony, but guilty of assault upon Kingston, the constable, which the jury considered to be brutal and violent.

Sentence: Three months' hard labour.

Charles Allen was again put to the bar, charged with stealing twelve yards of cotton print, and property of E. Jones, draper, of Wellingborough. No evidence was offered. Acquitted.

10th May 1838

THE LUNATIC ASYLUM APPROACHES COMPLETION (ST. ANDREW'S)

"NORTHAMPTON.
GENERAL LUNATIC ASYLUM.
A MEDICAL SUPERINTENDENT and a MATRON to the above Institution are wanted. Parties desirous of the Appointment are requested, on or before the tenth of May next to send their Applications, together with Testimonials to Mr. HARDAY, the Secretary, who will be ready to give any information as to terms, &c. which may be required.
Candidates for these Situations must have been previously connected with some similar establishment; and with the view of uniting the two offices, a married Gentleman could be preferred.
By order of the Committee
SPENCER, Chairman.
April 7, 1838."

(*Northampton Mercury* 14th April 1838, p. 3, col. 1.)

11th May 1838

A DREADFUL COACH ACCIDENT

"A dreadful coach accident occurred yesterday at Weedon. The Greyhound coach to Birmingham had pulled up at the

Bull Inn, to change horses, when the coachman incautiously parted with the reins before the horse-keeper took charge of the horses. The animals immediately started off, turning the corner into the inn yard, through which they galloped, and made off towards Stowe. There seems no reason to believe that no serious mischief would have ensued if the passengers had kept their seats. Unhappily, a gentleman threw himself off when the coach was near the bridge at Stowe, and pitching on his head, was killed on the spot. Several other passengers were injured more or less, but none seriously. The [deceased] is supposed from the papers found upon him to be an American merchant. The horses proceeded to Foster's Booth where they drew up without further mischief."

(*Northampton Mercury* 12th May 1838, p. 3, col. 5.)

Stowe, in this account, is Stowehill. The bridge where the fatality occurred was the one on the main road over the Grand Union Canal.

11th May 1838

CLARENCE MEN WANTED

"HALLAM & EDENS
CAN now give PERMANENT EMPLOY to sober, settled, smart BOOT and CLARENCE MEN. No others need apply.
Northampton, May 11, 1838."

(*Northampton Mercury* 12th May 1838, p. 3, col. 1.)

Hallam and Edens had premises in St. Mary's Street, in Northampton. We shall hear more of the Clarence style boot later in the year.

12th May 1838

A DESCRIPTION OF THE PUBLIC BATHS AT NORTHAMPTON

"NORTHAMPTON PUBLIC BATHS,
ALBION PLACE, WATERLOO.

THE Directors of the above establishment most respectfully acknowledge the liberal patronage with which the Baths were honoured during the short portion of last Season they were open to the public, and which has stimulated them to increase the accommodations to those Ladies and Gentlemen who may wish to enjoy the luxury or convenience of warm or other Baths. The right wing of the Building is appropriated to Ladies, and the left wing to Gentlemen.

The Directors have the pleasure of announcing that the whole of the interior arrangements are now complete, including a Plunging Bath exclusively devoted to the use of Ladies. In addition to which a commodious

TEPID SWIMMING BATH

has been fitted up, 44 feet long by 22 feet wide, with dressing rooms attached; and that they have made an arrangement with the New Water Company to supply the same with a continued running stream of water; they therefore anticipate a still more extended patronage, and which they hope permanently to secure.

Cards of Terms may be had at the Office of Mr. FREEMAN, Market Square, and the Premises.

May 1838."

(*Northampton Mercury* 12th May 1838, p. 3, col. 2.)

In April, Becket House had been offered for sale after the death of its owner, James Chamberlain. This was a large house at the corner of Waterloo Terrace and the New Walk (facing what is now Becket's Park). One of the advantages, along with "beautiful views of the river" and "pleasure garden well stocked with choice fruit and other trees" was convenient proximity to the new Baths in Albion Place.[97]

However, despite this early interest shown in the Baths by influential residents of the town, the establishment did not do well, and in March 1842 the premises were offered for sale.

17th May 1838

MANY LEAKS ABOUT THE TOWN

On Thursday 17th May, the shareholders of the Northampton Water Works Company met at the Guildhall for the purpose of receiving the report of the Directors. This was an adjourned meeting. The general supply of water had originally been intended to start on 25th March; but it was mid-May before the works were finished and brought into operation. There was a steam engine of eight horse-power, supplied by the Butterfly Iron Company. The shareholders were told that it was "of very superior workmanship". The report congratulated the Company on "the ample supply of pure spring water . . . amounting already to at least 100,000 gallons per day, without in the least diminishing the supply to the public pumps, which have been kept up in the same manner as heretofore".

A shareholder named Brown wished to know the cause of the many leaks about town. "Are the pipes defective?" The admirable engineer Sharp explained:

> "The main cause is that the fire plugs in first use are not as yet swelled sufficiently in the sockets to make them water-tight. There is no defect in the pipes. We have not found a single bad joint all over the town."[98]

23rd May 1838

A RAILWAY ACCIDENT AT WHILTON WHARF

"On Wednesday last, William Fieldhouse, aged 15, working on the railway at Whilton Wharf, while engaged in unhooking the waggon from the engine, slipped, and his left leg falling on the rails, it was passed over by the whole train consisting of ten loaded waggons. His leg was so dreadfully crushed that the foot merely hung on by the tendons. On his arrival at the infirmary, he was in so exhausted a state as to be unable to bear amputation which was, in consequence, postponed until the following morning. . . ."

(*Northampton Mercury* 26th May 1838, p. 3, col. 5.)

Exactly a week earlier, on 16th May, just over the border at Denbigh Hall in Buckinghamshire, Thomas Cooling, a railway worker, fractured his leg and was "brought to our infirmary".

29th May 1838

OAK APPLE DAY

The Northampton tradition of crowning the statue of Charles II, on the portico of All Saints' Church, with a garland on 29th May, is well-known. Other Northamptonshire villages had festive activities on that date. Here, John Cole, in characteristic purple prose, describes what was happening in Rushden on 29th May 1838:[99]

"The 29th of May is a day of much rejoicing here. The display of oak boughs is general. The battlements of the church and the houses are enlivened with these verdant honours waving in the ambient air. Those youngsters who do not display a small slip of oak about them are pinched by others, until they 'charm the ear with melodious numbers'; and at length produce by a shew from the fruitful woods; in addition to which, one is chaired on a hurdle wattled around with the oak, which some of the company carry with wandering steps about the village."

4th June 1838

"UNFORTUNATES" ON THE STREETS

"A meeting was held at our town hall, on Monday [4th June 1838] to take into consideration the best means of restoring to virtue and comfort such of the numerous unfortunate girls haunting our streets, as may be anxious to abandon their present mode of life. Several respectable and benevolent gentlemen were present, but the meeting was adjourned to Monday next, to enable a greater number to attend. It is contemplated to establish a Penitentiary, and we are informed that several philanthropic individuals are favourably disposed towards the object."

(*Northampton Mercury* 9th June 1838, p. 3, col. 4.)

11th June 1838

THE HIGHAM FERRERS ENCLOSURE ACT

One day in 1838, John Cole walked across the river valley from Higham Ferrers to Irthlingborough.[100]

" . . . On returning through Higham, I was much struck with the appearance of all the cows of the parish, about 100, which were feasting on the Common, where they are from 4 o'clock in the morning until 6 in the evening, and being there at that time – I witnessed the pleasing scene of their retirement for the evening: up the whole length of the town, preceded by a boy blowing a horn, in order that those who had cows might be on the look out."

Cole was observing a ritual whose days were numbered. On 11th June, "An ACT for Inclosing Lands in the Parish of Higham Ferrers in the County of Northampton" received the Royal assent. Dozens of enclosure acts for parishes in Northamptonshire had been passed already, but this one was rather special. Why? See the second of the introductory clauses:

"WHEREAS there are within the Parish of Higham Ferrers . . . divers open fields and commonable and waste lands and grounds:

"And whereas the Queen's Most Excellent Majesty, in right of her Duchy of Lancaster, is Lady of the Manor of Higham Ferrers within the said Parish of Higham Ferrers, and as such is entitled to the soil of the waste lands within the said manor; and her said Majesty in the same right is also entitled to divers land and grounds within the said parish:

"And whereas the Right Honourable Charles William, Earl Fitzwilliam, is lessee for a term of years of the said Manor of Higham Ferrers, and also of the said lands and grounds within the Parish of Higham Ferrers aforesaid, belonging to the Queen's Majesty as aforesaid:

"And whereas the Mayor and Corporation of the Borough or Town of Higham Ferrers aforesaid are or claim to be Lords of a Manor within the limits of the said borough or town, called the Borough or Town of Higham Ferrers, and also are or claim to be entitled to the soil of the waste lands within the said manor. . . .

"And whereas the estates of the several proprietors in the said open fields and commonable and waste lands and grounds lie intermixed and dispersed in small parcels, and in their present state are incapable of any considerable improvement, and the owners and persons interested therein are desirous that the same may be divided and inclosed and specific shares thereof set out and allotted to them respectively, in lieu of and in proportion to their several and respective estates, rights and interests therein; but as such division and inclosure cannot be effected without the authority of Parliament:

"May it therefore please your MAJESTY,
That it may be enacted, and BE IT ENACTED by the Queen's Most Excellent MAJESTY. . . ."

Victoria then, had a personal interest in this enclosure act. The penultimate clause above explains exactly why all these enclosures had been, and were being, carried out. The traditional lay-out of the land prevented improvements from being brought in. The text of the Act continues, appointing a trustworthy man, lacking personal interest in the outcome, to take charge of the operation:

"That Edward Gibbons, of Castor, Gentleman . . . is hereby appointed the sole Commissioner for dividing, allotting and inclosing, the said open fields . . . and for carrying this Act into execution, subject to the rules, orders and regulations in this Act contained. . . ."

Eighty-four paragraphs on forty-eight pages set out those "rules, orders and regulations". The Commissioner must make a declaration on oath. The Surveyor, Richard Hayward, of Thorpe Malsor, must also make a declaration. They must appoint a clerk, hold meetings, ascertain boundaries, settle disputes, award costs, extinguish rights of common ("by notice for that purpose under his hand, to be fixed on one of the outer doors of the Parish Church . . . on some Sunday before Divine Service"); shorten boundary fences, set out drains, alter water courses, stop up, divert or widen roads; set out a ten-acre area "as a place of exercise and recreation for the inhabitants . . ."; set out gravel pits for materials for the roads, order the fencing of enclosed land, borrow money, keep cattle off the new roads; and so transform the landscape and the way of life of many of the townsfolk of Higham Ferrers.

A curious clause of the Act is number 69:

"And be it further enacted, That the said Earl Fitzwilliam, as such Impropriator as aforesaid, shall immediately after the making of the allotment aforesaid, be for ever exonerated and exempted from providing and keeping a bull and a boar for the use of the inhabitants of Higham Ferrers aforesaid."

In the *History and Antiquities of Higham Ferrers* . . . (1838), John Cole describes another Higham Ferrers custom that would soon come to an end. Even as the Queen was affixing the Royal Seal to the Act, this tradition would have been in the planning stage.

"In hay-time a holiday takes place at higham respecting the King's-close. The several tradesmen who enjoy allotments, assemble in the meadow, when the planning of the respective portions is made, and their several lots assigned, each being marked by a willow-bough. A dinner is also provided and the accounts audited. Each person's payment for irrigating the land, &c. amounts annually to about four shillings. . . . Three-pence from each is required for the surveying, and sixpence from each member who does not attend."

The work of the Commissioner and Surveyor of the Enclosure was completed, and the Enclosure Award issued, on 27th December 1839.

18th June 1838

A BUSY SHEPHERD

On Monday the 18th inst., Amos Hollis, shepherd to Mr. Henry Coles, [of] Aldwinckle Green . . ., after going his regular round of attending the whole of his master's flock, sheared the extraordinary number of one hundred and ten sheep, the whole of which were done in a most creditable manner, and afterwards, the same day, performed the whole of his regular shepherding."

(*Northampton Mercury* 30th June 1838, p. 3, col. 6.)

20th June 1838

BREAKING OUT OF THE OLD GAOL
AT PETERBOROUGH

Andrew Percival, writing in the early twentieth century[31] recalled a curious escape from the Minster Gaol at Peterborough in 1838.

> ". . . A person walking through the Minster-Yard saw a head pop up out of the pavement. A body followed, walked off, and was never heard of again. The man had simply undermined the foundations of his cell with a knife or bone and disappeared."

The abbots of Peterborough Monastery had judicial rights over their extensive lands, and kept a prison. After the Reformation, the Bishop of Peterborough continued to maintain a prison, just inside the gate of the Cathedral precincts, until Queen Elizabeth I agreed to its jurisdiction being transferred to Lord Burghley. His descendant, the Marquess of Exeter, still maintained it in 1838.

The *Northampton Herald* of 23rd June 1838 (p. 3, col. 3) described the escape in more detail. Two brothers had been committed to the old gaol for pig stealing.

> "The cell in which they were confined adjoined the Minster-yard, and they had contrived to undermine the wall, and obtain a free passage by boring."

The attempt was made at two o'clock on the Wednesday morning of 20th June.

> "All was seemingly quiet, and the elder of the brothers safely emerged into the yard. Just as he had obtained his freedom from the terminus of the undermined passage (which they had most admirably concealed with a flagstone) a policeman passed him, to whom he cooly wished a 'good night', and passed on unobstructed. Not so fortunate, however, was the fate of the other, for no sooner had he raised his head above ground, than the same 'guardian of the night' perceived that all was not right – gave an alarm – and on the awakened gaoler going to his cell, he found him safe in bed, but alone. Means have been

taken to secure the remaining offender more effectually, but of his brother and partner in guilt, no trace has been found."

20th June 1838

THE DEATH OF ANOTHER RAILWAYMAN

On the day before the completion of the Kilsby tunnel, a railway worker named Embray became the last accident victim before the trains started to run through the county. His death was not noticed by the *Northampton Mercury*, but the *Herald* explained how he came to be killed.

> "He was turning the rails on for the engine and gang wagons to proceed on the line, when unluckily he did not get out of the way with sufficient expertness, and the engine and ten loaded wagons passed over him, nearly severing his legs from his body, and otherwise injuring him."

From this account we might understand that he was careless in operating the points. He was taken to Northampton, but died before reaching the Infirmary. The inquest verdict was "Accidental Death". The accident occurred north of Weedon, near Brockhall.

21st June 1838

THE LAST BRICK IN THE KILSBY TUNNEL

The first brick had been laid on 7th October 1835. At one o'clock on Thursday afternoon, 21st June 1838, all the bricks were in place except one. In the measurement of the time, the completed tunnel was one mile and six-hundred and sixty-six yards long. The horseshoe-shaped profile had a span of twenty-six feet.[101] 1,250 men and 200 horses had been working on the project, and it had cost £300,000 – treble the original estimate. The enormous problems caused by the quicksand account for the additional expenditure. It had not been located in the original survey.

Now a large crowd of spectators waited at the south entrance to see the last brick inserted. A brass band marched into the tunnel through the stone portal, followed by Charles Lean, the superintending engineer. Hundreds of people closed in behind, carrying lanterns, candles and flambeaux, to light the interior.

The *Northampton Mercury* published a description of the ceremony on 23rd June (p. 3, col. 5), only to correct it with a revised version on 30th June (p. 2, cols. 4-5).

The band was playing "See the Conquering Hero Comes" as the procession reached the largest of the two big ventilating shafts. A platform stood a few yards beyond, and Lean ascended. The spectators had already given "three times three cheers" for the tunnel, before entering it. Now they gave the same for Charles Lean, and as Robert Stephenson climbed up to the platform, followed by other engineers, they cheered him too. "After a few minutes' preparation, the last brick was inserted, cemented with a silver trowel, a present to Mr. Lean from the workmen. This having been proclaimed to the surrounding multitude, wine was presented to those on the platform, and the last bottle dashed against the crown of the arch. The national anthem then struck up, the vaulted roof of the tunnel giving it additional effect. The party then proceeded, the band playing before them. . . ." Under another ventilation shaft, the engineers stepped into a skip and were taken up, as "a salute of guns was fired".

The spectators marched through the entire length of the tunnel to the northern entrance. There a large amount of soil still to be removed blocked their exit. "They could only be restored to the light of the day by climbing up ladders. . . ."

The *Mercury's* revised version describes "a splendid dinner" at 5 p.m., under a large marquee, with "Mr. Forster presiding". This was probably Frank Forster, who had formerly been the engineer in charge of the section of track construction between Blisworth and Kilsby. Lean was on his right and Robert Stephenson on his left. Next to Lean was Robert's father, the great George Stephenson. While they consumed "every delicacy of the season", the band played "several airs". When the cloth had been removed, "the Queen was toasted. Then *God Save the Queen* was sung by three gentlemen invited for their musical ability. Then a toast to the Army and Navy, followed by the glee *Ye Gentlemen of England.*

While supervising the work of the tunnel, Robert Stephenson took a house in Kilsby which is still standing. In 1925, A. E. Treen wrote about it.[102]

"It is a pretty, stone-built villa surrounded by a flower garden with a vine tree entwined over the front entrance. In the garden is an excellent model of the entrance of Kilsby tunnel, above which, suspended on the garden wall, is an ancient sun-dial. . . ."

Treen was "courteously received" by the occupant, Molly Pittom, at Cedar Lodge, and she showed him "relics of Stephenson". The reclusive Miss Pittom lived until 1979, leaving £108,715 to the National Trust. Cedar Lodge was sold by auction.[103] The contents of the house were sold for £28,000, perhaps including priceless Stephensoniana. Whatever 1838 mementoes there were, they meant little to Molly: she wore old rags, and cycled to Rugby every day to borrow a newspaper, keeping her bicycle in the bath.

23rd June 1838

A "SCOUNDREL" DEFENDS HIMSELF AGAINST A "CUTTLE FISH"

The ceaseless war of words between the two rival newspapers of Northampton's Market Square brought forth accusations and counter accusations, accompanied by insults, nearly every week. The origin was political: the Tory *Herald* had been founded to counter the influence of the Whig-sympathising *Mercury*; but a variety of contentious topics kept the war going. In June 1838 there was an accusation that the *Mercury* was disohonestly stimulating its circulation figures. Newspapers had carried a stamp tax since earlier times of public unrest when a government had considered it unwise to allow the poorer classes easy access to the printed word. Northampton papers in 1838 carried, in the top right hand corner of the front page, a small pink stamp to certify payment of the tax.

On Saturday 23rd June, the *Mercury* came out with fierce editorial words directed at its rival (p. 3, col. 3).

"Naturalists inform us that the cuttle fish, when pursued by an enemy, possesses the singular faculty of discharging a black liquid, and shrouding itself from observation amidst the discoloured water. The cuttle fish is but a type of our Tory contemporary. Whenever he is hard pressed by unanswerable argument, or an incontrovertible fact, he immediately calls his assailant scoundrel, fool, and liar, and endeavours to effect a retreat under the cover of his own dirt.

"We have no wish to intercept the retreat of our opponent. We are as anxious as he can be, though from very different motives, to terminate the controversy, utterly distasteful to the public, and into which nothing but his own malice and folly has forced us. We are quite content to leave it to others to decide whether the preposterous accusation which he thought proper deliberately and repeatedly to bring against the conductors of this journal, of having committed to the flames some thousands of imprinted papers for the fraudulent purpose of increasing our apparent circulation in the official returns of stamps, has been supported by one tittle of evidence. . . .

"One word at parting to the Editor of the *Herald*. . . . We beg to tell Mr. Litchfield that expressions such as he has ventured to apply to us, shall be used by no men, be he who may, with impunity. We tell that reverend journalist who, not finding occupation enough in superintending his two benefices, devotes a large portion of every week to the task of editing a libellous newspaper, that in designating the proprietor of this journal as a 'scoundrel', a 'knave', a 'disgrace to the Bench of magistrates', a person 'guilty of gross dishonesty, aggravated by foul lying', he has uttered language as false as it is scurrilous. . . ."

23rd June 1838

MAINS WATER NOT FOR DRINKING AT THE INFIRMARY

At the weekly meeting of the Infirmary management committee at Northampton on Saturday, 23rd June, the new mains water in the town came under discussion. It was decided to ask the Water Company to lay a pipe from their main "which passes along the northern boundary of this property", into the garden. A maximum of twenty two shillings was to be spent on this, with a further annual expense of one pound. The purpose of this supply was simply for watering the garden. Water for drinking and cooking was to come as before from the Infirmary well.[104] Exactly six years later, this decision to reject mains water for human consumption at the Infirmary was repeated, and the sinking of another well was authorised.

24th June 1838

THE FIRST PASSENGER TRAINS THROUGH NORTHAMPTONSHIRE

Passenger services on the London and Birmingham Railway commenced running from Euston to North Buckinghamshire in the spring of 1838. The terminus was a former inn, Denbigh Hall. From there, Birmingham passengers were carried in horse-drawn vehicles through the county of Northamptonshire to Rugby, where they were able to board another train. The official opening of the complete line did not take place until September, but with the completion of the Kilsby tunnel, the Company evidently regarded the track to be finished. Unostentatiously, in a very brief advertisement tucked away on the fourth column of the second page of the *Northampton Mercury* of 23rd June, the first trains from London through to Birmingham were announced:

"LONDON AND BIRMINGHAM RAILWAY
—— The Public are informed that on Sunday the 24th Instant, and on every succeeding Sunday until further notice, the TRAIN which now leaves London at 9½ A.M. for Denbigh Hall, WILL RUN TO BIRMINGHAM, and that an ADDITIONAL TRAIN will leave Birmingham at 10 A.M. for London, stopping at all the stations.
    By order,

R. C. REED	Secretaries to
C. R. MOORSOM	the Board.

London, June 18, 1838"

From Monday to Saturday, of course, the work-force was fully employed clearing, levelling and fitting at the track-side – but the track itself was complete.

28th June 1838

CORONATION FESTIVITIES

During the week before the Coronation, blackened boards were put up in the centre of Northampton. The largest was the size of a "cottage-gable", and the smaller ones were of "coach-wheel" size. The effect was "sombre and melancholy", but on the great day they were back-grounds of the illuminations. "Brilliant devices in gas and lamps abounded in all the principal streets. . . ." The balustrade in the portico of All Saints' Church was hung with sheet iron, mounted with lamps forming the motto "Church and Queen". A variegated crown was suspended over the statue of Charles II, and on either side were placed a coronet and mitre. "Many flags and banners were displayed from public and private edifices; home exteriors had oak-boughs, evergreens, flowers." Mr Greville, the chemist, had a star at his shop with a centre in changing colours, and there was "a particularly fine Star and Garter on the north front of Waterloo House". The bells commenced ringing at half-past four in the morning, and throughout the day occasional peals were heard. The shops remained closed; crowds came out into the fine weather; and there was music. The latter was provided by the Northamptonshire Militia band, Wombwell's Menagerie musicians, and itinerant performers. Some said that there was no good music. The Mayor and Corporation, and Liberal politicians dined at the George Hotel. It was regretted that the opposing parties felt unable to celebrate together: the Tories dined at the Angel. No tables were "spread in public" for the "lower classes", but £700 was distributed to the supporters of the two political parties. Fifteen hundred children of the Anglican Sunday schools assembled in the Barrack yard and were provided with plumcake and tea. The dissenting Sunday schoolchildren formed in the Market Square and proceeded to Hagger's Brewery where they were likewise fed.[105]

Earl Fitzwilliam, in a House of Lords speech, described the Coronation as "a useless pageant, suitable only for barbarous ages", but he contributed £20 to Peterborough's "Fun and

Frolic" committee. The Bishop of Peterborough gave £15 towards the £200 collected. In Wellingborough, the public procession was praised because "no banners appeared carrying party slogans. The workhouse inmates there were served with plum-pudding and roast beef, and "a moderate portion of ale".[106]

At Kettering, there was a procession of the Trades, with banners and insignia, and at 3.30 p.m. public tea-drinking on the Market-Hill, free for all females and for boys under eight.[105] Years later, a Wellingborough doctor told how his father, Charles Wright, at the Kettering celebration, distributed snuff to the old people from a warming pan.[107]

Earl Spencer gave the best oak tree to be found on his estates for a Coronation pole at Long Buckby. It was 78 feet high and surmounted by a crown. Bells began at 4 a.m. and the pole was then raised. At Syresham, a fiddler played for dancing from 6 to 9 p.m. At Higham Ferrers, tickets were given out to any one, for meat, bread and beer, so over 700 people had a special dinner in their own homes. There were donkey races, foot races, climbing poles, and jumping in sacks. At 10 p.m. a ball was given by the gentlemen for the ladies of the town, at the Town Hall which was "elegantly decorated". The ladies were given tea there, and the male adults were given tickets for more beer.[108]

At Gayton, "persons employed on the railway" were included in the festivities. At Braunston, an "early rustic ball" was opened by R. H. Lamb "leading down the Hon. Mrs. Adams in good style". Then followed "the big and little, light and heavy, young and old, all running, walking, bustling, jumping, dancing, each telling with their feet their several capacities for such fantastic trips". At Weedon Bec, there were "races for hats run by boys, climbing up a soaped pole for a leg of mutton [which] was won by a little chimney sweeper from Northampton". A statistician recorded the celebrations at Brackley: "1,067 persons consumed 760 lbs. of meat, 926 pints of ale, 1,022 lbs. of flour, 254 lbs. of plums, served at the Market House."[110]

The day at Irthlingborough "was ushered in by a merry peal and the discharge of a powerful detonating ball. A blue flag waved from the top of the steeple" [The tiny point on the tower, then and now, is hardly a steeple]. "Victoria" was the inscription on the flag, which was joined by a white one ("God Save the Queen"), and a pink one ("Religion and Loyalty"). At ten o'clock, a royal salute was fired "by the detonation of seven balls in honour of her Majesty's departure from the Palace. . . . At four o'clock, the Rector addressed the assembled multitudes around the Cross, and read them the account of the coronation of King Solomon, and requested the National Anthem might be sung. This was done in excellent style, and the earth rang with the acclamation of loyalty". Cake was then served. It had taken the whole morning just to prepare the tables and seats. As elsewhere, the men were given ale to drink, and the women and children, tea.[109]

On the following day, at Cold Ashby, "the broken meat that remained was made into soup for the poor".[110]

There were three days of celebration at Geddington. On the second day, Friday, 29th June, a barrel of ale was consumed at the Eleanor Cross. "Then various sports – wheel-barrow running, jumping in sacks, boys dipping for oranges." On the Saturday evening, there were "gingling matches, women running for gown pieces and money".[111]

Mary Ann Smart, of Ringstead, was asked to recall the Rushden Coronation events, in 1911, at the age of 93. She said: "We had legs of mutton and pieces of beef, and cherries for dessert, in the Rectory orchard in a big barn."[112] That was the *old* Rectory, and in 1911, the barn was long gone, replaced by Frederick Knight's shoe factory. Mary Smart, a native of Rushden, was newly married at the time of the Coronation of Queen Victoria.

The most miserable person on Coronation day was at Croughton. "David French was drunk and disorderly on the Queen's Coronation Day and was accordingly placed in the Stocks. . . ."[113]

30th June 1838

AT THE COUNTY GAOL

It is possible to abstract from the published Accounts of the County of Northampton for the year ending 30th June 1838 those items relating to the prison. The prisoners consumed soup to the value of £271. 5 shillings and elevenpence halfpenny. Their bread cost £607 14 shillings. Spent on clothing, bedding and furniture was £119. and threepence. The Governor's salary was £255; that of the Chaplain, £210. The turnkeys and the baker earned only £182 for all of them. The surgeon's contract cost £50, and the Matron's pay was a mere £35. The cost of conveyance of convicts to the hulks (for transportation to Australia) cost £179. 17 shillings. Altogether, the expenses of the Gaol amounted to £2,832. 2 shillings and twopence-halfpenny. (The cost of maintaining all the County's bridges was only £319.) There was a small amount of income. The Treasurer of the Borough of Northampton paid £257 for the Borough prisoners to be held (there being no Borough gaol yet). Work done by prisoners earned just under £7. The paymasters of regiments at the Barracks (38th and 88th) paid £40 to be able to confine soldiers under sentence at the Gaol. Other soldiers held there, deserters and others passing through, earned for the County just over £21 from the Army.

Dr. Bisset Hawkins, Inspector of Prisons for the Southern and Western District, in his Third Report (1838), page 77, says that the diet in Northampton Gaol was 24 ounces of bread daily, two pints of soup and two pints of gruel. The addition of gruel had been made "in consequence of six cases of decided scurvy having appeared in the gaol in 1837". The surgeon had found "a considerable number of other prisoners were getting weak and losing flesh and were likely to have become ascorbutic . . .". Dr. Hawkins observed that nearly all the male cells held three beds and were "inconveniently small" for that number. He likewise complained that they were not well lighted, "except when the sun was on them". They were too dark for the inmates to work properly, nor read. There was no heat in any of the cells. "Solitary confinement is quite impracticable in this prison as a general system, on account of the unfitness of the cells to contain a prisoner night and day constantly."

It is interesting to note from the County's Accounts, mentioned above, that £88. 16 shillings and ninepence had been spent on coals, and £26. 6s. on gas lighting during the year. Evidently neither of these expenses was for the well-being of the prisoners, held in the 76 cells. Approximately fifty a year were being sentenced to solitary confinement.

There were problems at one of the smaller lock-ups of the county, the House of Correction at Oundle. The County had spent £39. 5 shillings and sixpence halfpenny on this establishment, including the Keeper's salary of £12, and £2. 10 shillings for "the carpenter and the draper".

On 2nd July, five magistrates at Oundle Petty Sessions compiled a petition to Quarter Sessions, listing their complaints about the House of Correction. Evidently they were not satisfied with the reception of their complaints: five months later, they published the text of their petition in the *Northampton Mercury* of 15th December 1838.

"To the Magistrates of the County of Northampton, assembled in Quarter Sessions. The Remonstrance of the undersigned Justices of the Peace, acting for the Division of Oundle . . . touching the state and condition of the House of Correction at Oundle. Sheweth,

"That the House . . . is a small building, two storeys in height, with two small yards before it, fenced with walls on three sides, and in front with pallisades; beyond the yards is a court, into which the Keeper's house opens; and on the east side of this is a garden appertaining to the prison, and through which is the path leading to it.

"That the prison contains two lower and two upper rooms, one of the lower rooms is used for a sitting room, the rest of them for bedrooms, containing in the whole, three beds.

"That the smallness of the place prevents the introduction of any means [of] hard labour, and thus the law for certain offences cannot be carried into full effect.

"That the Magistrates have nevertheless deemed it

expedient to commit to it no less than 64 prisoners (of whom 51 were males and 13 females) in the course of the twelve months ending January 1837, and that the Magistrates both of the Oundle Bench and of the Bench at St. Martin's Stamford Baron, use it on occasions of a minor description, their distance from the county gaol being, in the former case, thirty miles; and in the latter, thirty six.

"That Dr. Bisset Hawkins, Inspector of Prisons, has recently visited the House of Correction and has pronounced it to the Keeper to be in a very unfit state.

"That we . . . consider it to be a point of great importance to the ends of justice . . . that there should be a House of Correction at Oundle. . . . For this purpose we hope we may be permitted to suggest that, in addition to the present accommodation, a sitting room and two bedrooms be erected for female delinquents, or for the better classification of prisoners. And also a mill for hard labour" [signed by five named justices].

4th July 1838

A NEW STAGECOACH

Eleven weeks before weekday trains would traverse the county, it was possible for London passengers to travel every day from Denbigh Hall just over the border, and Birmingham passengers from Rugby. This was already affecting the coach operators, and they were adjusting by running frequent services to the rail terminals, and planning new east-west services. This caused keen competition between coach firms.

On Wednesday 4th July at 2 p.m., a new coach named Victoria, left the Angel Hotel in Northampton for (King's) Lynn. It was "performed" by Thomas Shaw, every day except Sunday, and travelled by way of Wellingborough, Thrapston, Oundle, Peterborough, Thorney and Wisbech. It returned from Lynn at six in the morning.[114]

Throughout July and August, an argument was carried on, in the form of rival advertisements, between Shaw, of the Angel, and William Elworthy, operating coaches from the Ram Inn, Northampton, about misrepresentation, personal insults and threats. Shaw had begun a service to both of the rail terminals.

The supposed superior safety of coaches over that of the railway, had been used to keep the more nervous passengers on the London coaches, which, of course, were still running. A series of coach accidents, however, dealt a further blow to this traffic. There had been the spectacular accident of 11th May. Increased coach traffic related to the Coronation brought two more accidents. The Holyhead mail left Birmingham without lights in the confusion of the festivities of 28th June. In the darkness early the next morning, on the Watling Street north of Towcester at Dirt Hill House, it collided head-on with two northbound coaches, one in the act of overtaking the other on a hill. Horses were killed and passengers injured.[115] The *Lincoln Gazette* of 7th July 1838 reported the following mishap.

"The coach that connects Denbigh Hall with Stamford was upset on Monday night [2nd July] on its return. The downward railway trains are bringing such multitudes from the Coronation, and to proceed to the waters [spa visitors], that the coaches are in extraordinary use, and the driver of this was unable to get a drag. He was particularly careful, but descending the hill halfway between Kettering and Stamford, the accident occurred. Several Lincoln passengers were in the coach, and Mrs. Franklyn's wrist is broken, but no other serious injury was experienced by any one except the driver, he being much hurt."

The drag that the driver was unable to procure, had no connection with the soothing qualities of tobacco; it was an iron shoe to attach to the wheel to prevent the coach gathering too much speed on a hill.

5th July 1838

RAILWAY CRIME

The most interesting of many cases heard at the Quarter Sessions at Northampton on Thursday 5th July was a railway case. Thomas Sutton was indicted for stealing a quantity of cast iron, the property of the London and Birmingham Railway Company, at Weedon Beck [sic.]

Police constable ————: The prisoner is a coal hawker. I saw him loading his cart with iron, at twelve o'clock at night, close to the railway. There was about seven hundred-weight. The prisoner said he had bought it of two men who would be coming back again directly. I concealed myself behind a hedge, and the prisoner jumped into the cart and was about to make off. I made my appearance again, and took him into custody.

Edward Lea, engineer: I have seen the iron. It is the property of the Company. It consists of what we call "chairs" for the rails.

Earl Spencer was the Chairman of the Sessions. He asked the accused, Thomas Sutton, if he had anything to say in his defence.

Sutton: I bought the iron from two men. The bargain was made at a public house at Harlestone, over eggs and bacon, and ale. I have a witness who will prove this.

—————— Freeman: I am a hawker of pickled salmon. I was at the —————— public house. Some gentlemen were regaling themselves with ale and eggs and bacon. Mr. Sutton was one of those gentlemen.

Earl Spencer: Do you know what they were saying?

Freeman: No, sir. I do not know what they were saying.

The verdict was "guilty".

Spencer: Is there anything previous?

Clerk: The prisoner has been previously convicted of felony.

The sentence was Seven Years' Transportation.

5th July 1838

A WINDMILL FOR SALE AT BRIXWORTH

"TO BREWERS, BAKERS, MILLERS, AND OTHERS.
BRIXWORTH, NORTHAMPTONSHIRE
TO BE LET BY PRIVATE CONTRACT.
A Very commodious MESSUAGE or Tenement, with BAKEHOUSE, Brewhouse, Corn & Flour Chambers, good Cellars, Stable, Yard, and convenient Out-offices, situate at BRIXWORTH . . . now in the tenure of Mr. James Perkins.

"Also a POST WINDMILL, in good repair, situate not far from the village of BRIXWORTH, and adjoining the road leading from thence to Scaldwell, with the small Close of Grass Land in which the Mill stands.

"The house consists of a parlour, kitchen and cellar, and four bed-rooms. The premises are very complete, in a good state of repair, and well supplied with water, and are conveniently situated for trade. There is a well-established connexion in the business of a Brewer, Baker, and Miller, and a very good opportunity is now offered to persons desirous of engaging in the business. . . ."

This advertisement was issued from the Kettering office of Lamb and Nettleship, solicitors, on 5th July 1838, and appeared in the *Northampton Mercury* on 7th July (p. 2, col. 4). The windmill changed hands, but was again advertised for sale in 1841.

5th July 1838

"NORTHAMPTON BRANCH RAILWAY"

This was the heading over a handbill issued on 5th July, in Northampton. Those who issued it did not identify themselves, so its presumable purpose was preliminary information. Perhaps those concerned were already well-known. The first positive move to bring the railway into Northampton centre came from the London and Birmingham Railway itself, late in 1842. It was planning the Blisworth-Peterborough line by then, and it needed the support of those with influence in Northampton.

"THE object of this Branch" said the leaflet, "is to connect the Town of Northampton and its neighbourhood, and the range of country to the north and east of it, with the London and Birmingham Railway; and it is proposed that it shall commence at some convenient and eligible spot in the Town of Northampton, and join the London and Birmingham Railway near the point where it crosses the Grand Junction Canal, at Blisworth.

"The advantages of the Branch to the trade and property of Northampton and the neighbourhood, are rendered sufficiently obvious, when it is considered that it will be the means of concentrating the trade and traffic of the county, and keeping up and probably increasing its present market; on the other hand, should there be no direct communication with the London and Birmingham Railway, the trade and traffic will be greatly dispersed, and passengers, instead of collecting in one spot, will find their way to the neighbouring stations of Wolverton, Road, Blisworth, or Weedon.

"It appears that this Branch must be an object of great importance and profit to the London and Birmingham Railway Company, for a great number of passengers, who, in going to Birmingham would otherwise join at the Weedon Station, and in going to London at the Wolverton Station, will, when the branch is completed, meet at Northampton. It will also be a great advantage to them, in respect of the saving both of the power employed and the time occupied in stoppages, to be able to concentrate their traffic in as few places as possible; and on the opening of their whole line, some difficulty will be experienced in regulating the stoppages of their different trains, so as to clear the rails of one class of carriages before the arrival of another, an object which will be greatly assisted by turning the traffic of the Northampton range of country immediately off the main line, and collecting it together in one place. The London and Birmingham Company, besides these conveniences, will derive a much greater profit than will be required to pay a good rate of interest for the outlay expended in completing this branch; and although they would not be willing, from the press of business already in their hands, to undertake the formation of it themselves, there can be no doubt of their readiness to offer a handsome precentage to any company which would complete it in a satisfactory manner, and at a moderate cost. It is well known that they have already agreed to take the Branch to Aylesbury at 5 per cent on the outlay, and when it is considered that Aylesbury does not contain one-third of the number of inhabitants which Northampton contains . . . it may be fairly supposed that they will be willing to enter into a satisfactory arrangement for taking this Branch. Should this object be effected, the . . . Company, instead of making a Station at Blisworth . . .would have a *Station at the Town of Northampton*, and run a certain number of carriages into the Town . . . which will allow of their other trains running without stoppage from Weedon to Wolverton.

"A Company for the accomplishment of the above object is now in the course of formation – Preparatory levels have been taken in several different directions, from which it has been ascertained that a very favorable and inexpensive line may be obtained. It will now be necessary that a more complete survey should be taken, in order to place the Company in a position to treat with the Directors of the London and Birmingham Company, and it is hoped that the exertion of the Directors to effect so desirable an object for the general benefit of the Town, will be cordially supported by their fellow Townsmen, with as little delay as possible, as a Fund to be raised by a deposit of One Pound per Share, on a certain number of Shares, is absolutely necessary to enable the Directors to defray the preliminary expenses."

7th July 1838

HORROR IN A NORTHAMPTON BAKER'S YARD

On Monday 9th July 1838, an inquest was held in the Guildhall, Northampton, before George Abbey, Coroner, on view of the body of Charles Clarke, a six-year-old boy who had drunk concentrated sulphuric acid from a ginger-beer bottle on the previous Saturday. The story is told here by witnesses, in the words they used at the inquest.

John Barker: I am a butcher. I live in Wood Street. The deceased was the son of a friend of mine, Mr. Charles Clarke, a baker, living in Wellington Street. The boy was about six years of age. On Saturday last, a little after two o'clock, I was in Mr. Clarke's yard, hanging up a hide, assisted by Mr. Clarke, and we both, afterwards went into the house for the purpose of taking a glass of porter. While there, I heard something fall. I thought it was in the bakehouse, near at hand, and I immediately saw the boy, running, crying, from the bakehouse towards the street. I ran after him, and I saw something coming out of his mouth. I caught him behind the ear and turned him round. The child was then very sick, and he pointed to the bakehouse door and moaned really bad. Something seemed to be burning the front of his dress. He looked up at me and put his tongue out. It was as white as paper. I said, "For God's sake, what has the child been drinking?" Mr. Clarke's servant then took him from me, and I ran for Mr. Percival, the surgeon, who came right away. Several children were playing in the bakehouse with the boy, while I was in the

210

yard. The eldest was about seven years old. The father and mother both have excellent characters. I went to the bakehouse afterwards and saw Mr. Clarke pick up a bottle and hurl it at the dung-hill. As he did so, part of the contents burned his trousers.

Sarah Clifton (much affected): I am servant to Mr. Clarke. I had just finished cleaning the parlour on Saturday afternoon, when I heard the boy crying, and I said, "Somebody is beating Charles," but I heard a second scream, and I went out, and saw him running out of the bakehouse. I called the master, who immediately came, and Mr. Barker. I saw something running out of the boy's mouth. His mouth was burnt. His pinafore and other parts of his dress were burnt. Mr. Barker went for Mr. Percival. I was in the bakehouse when the master took the bottle off the board. He put it against the pigsty. I broke the bottle. The master, in his fright, forgot to do so, and he said I had done right. His coat and trousers were burnt. He is very fond of his children. The bottle contained oil of vitriol, and it was brought by Edward Ashby, the brewer, on Tuesday, for cleaning the copper, and after he had cleaned it, he put it on top of the copper. I took the bottle from the brewhouse to the bakehouse, to do the cleaning with it, but I changed my mind, and I said to the brewer, "Edward, you may take it back with you." But if he heard me, he forgot to do so. I learnt from the eldest of the children, who was playing with Charles, that he took up the bottle, and said to his playfellows, "I will have some pop. Will you have some?" And he drank some. The child must have got on the board for it, because I put it on as far as I could reach.

Edward Ashby: I am a brewer. I live in Wellington Street. I was at Mr. Clarke's house on Tuesday, and I was not there again from that time up to the time this happened. I brewed for Mr. Clarke on the Monday, and I turned and cleaned the copper on Tuesday, and I used oil of vitriol for that. When I had done with it, I put it on the copper. When I looked for it, it wasn't there, and I suspected it had been moved by the servant maid. I went to her, and told her not to be foolish, for it was vitriol, and very dangerous. She laughed, and said it was all right. She would not give it me back again, and I did not know where it was.

Coroner: Did the servant tell you to take it away?

Ashby: I never heard her tell me at any time to take it away.

Coroner: What sort of bottle was the vitriol in?

Ashby: It was a stone, flat bottle. It would hold about half a pint. There was about three parts of the vitriol left. The bottle was corked, but not labelled. I use it mixed with about three parts water, but the bottle contained pure oil of vitriol. I have never used it for that purpose before. It was given to me by a dyer, and he warned me about how dangerous it was.

Coroner: There is a discrepancy in the evidence of the servant and the last witness. I should like Sarah Clifton to be re-called to clear this up.

Clifton: I told Mr. Ashby to take the vitriol away with him.

Ashby: I never heard anything of the kind.

William Percival: I am a surgeon. I live in Abington Street. About two o'clock on Saturday afternoon, I was called to attend the deceased. I found him with swelled lips; mouth and throat a great deal burnt, and vomiting. I asked what was the matter, and was told that he had swallowed oil of vitriol. From appearances, I thought there could be no doubt of it. It seemed pretty clear that the child had actually swallowed some. I gave him some medicine to counteract the effect of the poison, and I saw the child again about five o'clock, when I found him in the same state, not at all better. He was perfectly sensible, but speechless. I directed them to go on as before. Being obliged to go out, my son called about nine, and found the child in the same condition. He died about a quarter past twelve, ten hours after the accident. I have no doubt that death was occasioned by taking mineral poison, and oil of vitriol is a very strong one. A very small quantity would occasion death, possibly half a teaspoon, in a case like the present one.

George Abbey, Coroner, to the jury: There can be no doubt whatever, that death was caused by the child incautiously taking poison. But at the same time, there has been a great neglect in allowing vitriol to remain on the bakehouse board so many days. Had the neglect been very gross, it would have been your duty to find a verdict of manslaughter, but as it is, you would not be justified in arriving at that conclusion. You do have it in your power to state whether blame attaches to any person.

Verdict: Death in consequence of having incautiously taken oil of vitriol.

Coroner: I hope the young woman will be more cautious in future.

9th July 1838

MORE VITRIOL AT LONG BUCKBY

Too soon to be prompted by the reports of the distressing accident of 7th July, came a sequel. On the day of the inquest – perhaps even while the inquest was in progress,

"a gentleman at Long Buckby, in a fit of despondency, purchased of a druggist in the town three ounces of oil of vitriol, all of which he attempted to swallow, but was only able to take about half an ounce. As soon as the act was committed, he repented, and ran to a druggist, who took him to the surgery of Mr. Dix, in the most excruciating torments, and where he vomited great quantities of blood. Mr. Dix and his assistant, by the most unremitting attention, and the greatest perseverance, literally drenched him for several hours with the proper antidote, viz. the carbonate of magnesia, mixed with milk. He is now, after the acutest sufferings ever witnessed, recovered, and truly grateful for the means that were used for his preservation."

(*Northampton Mercury* 28th July 1838, p. 3, col. 5.)

11th July 1838

WORKHOUSE EDUCATION

The Guardians of the Wellingborough Union assembled for their meeting on Wednesday 11th July with the intention of appointing a schoolmistress to live in the workhouse, at a salary of £12 per annum.

"The Person appointed will be required to instruct the children in Sewing, Knitting, Reading, Writing, and common Arithmetic . . ."

stated the advertisement in the *Northampton Mercury* of 30th June 1838 (p. 2, col. 6).

"Candidates for the situation must send their Testimonials as to Character and Ability, and stating their Age, to the Clerk of the Union. . . ."

13th July 1838

ANOTHER UNEXPECTED DEATH IN NORTHAMPTON

Hidden without a heading in the third column of the third page of the *Northampton Herald* of 14th July 1838, was this brief report.

"A coroner's inquest was yesterday afternoon held in this town, on the body of a young man named Chapman, by trade a mason, who died from having his neckcloth tied on in such a way as to prevent respiration. The deceased left home in perfect health in the morning, and was at work whitewashing, when, it is supposed, he must have fallen backwards, and died instantly. Verdict, 'Died by the Visitation of God.' "

14th July 1838

AT OLD STRATFORD

Travellers heading north-west along the Watling Street, cross the border of Buckinghamshire and pass through the first community in the County of Northampton – Old Stratford. Although very small, its situation on the Irish Mail route, and the proximity of the Canal and the railway had made it significant.

"TO BE SOLD BY PRIVATE CONTRACT,
ALL that Freehold, old-established WHARF, situate at OLD STRATFORD . . . comprising a very good DWELLING-HOUSE, with a well-cultivated garden attached, large wharf-yard on the banks of the canal, two capacious warehouses with granaries over, and very extensive arched vaults underneath, built with brick and paved, with stone lime kilns, stabling for three horses, with lofts over, and paddock containing about an acre, more or less, the whole in the occupation of Mr. Edward Johnson.

These premises are well situate, being about one mile from the Grand Junction Canal, on the banks of the branch leading from Cosgrove to Buckingham, and three miles from the Wolverton Station, on the London and Birmingham Railway, close to which the Grand Junction Canal passes. . . .

The property is very desirable to a general merchant, who might, in conjunction with the coal trade, advantageously carry on an extensive Timber and Iron Trade. The cellarage would contain a great number of barrels and is well adapted for the business of a wholesale dealer in Beer and Porter.

There are no outgoings, the property being Land Tax Redeemed. . . ."

(*Northampton Mercury* 14th July 1838, p. 1, col. 2.)

Outside the village lay the ancient forest of Whittlewood. The edge of it was (and is) marked by the keeper's lodge. Two or three hundred yards to the east of this house, Shrob

Lodge, was a busy coaching inn. This was the Black Horse. According to its last innkeeper (John Brown, who was first listed in *Kelly's Directory* in 1910, and who died in 1949) the deer from the forest were loaded onto the London coaches at the inn. Villagers used to go to the keeper at Shrob Lodge to buy snips and humbles (venison offal as in "humble pie") for twopence a pound.[116]

16th July 1838

MORE ROAD ACCIDENTS

"On Monday . . . [16th July], as the Greyhound coach was proceeding on its way to Denbigh Hall [rail terminal for London passengers], . . . between Elton and Warmington, the axle of the hind wheel unfortunately broke, and the coach upset. . . . Only one of the passengers, Mrs. Fleming, of the Red Lion, Oundle, was injured: she received some severe bruises. Great praise is due to the driver, who, finding his coach going over, jumped on the horses, and immediately stopped them. Another coach was procured, the passengers proceeded, and arrived in time for the train.

"On the same day, a van drawn by two horses. . . . [This was the contemporary equivalent of a hired 'bus. It was carrying ten persons from Eye, near Peterborough, to give evidence in a case at the Assizes in Northampton], when descending the hill at the end of Oundle, the reins broke, when the horses, finding themselves under no control, started off, and ran over a large heap of stones, by which the van was overturned. One gentleman . . . had his arm broken in two places. . . . The horses broke away with the pole, and ran beyond Barnwell bar, although several attempts were made to stop them. They ultimately fell in a ditch . . . one upon the other. . . ."

(*Northampton Herald* 21st July 1838, p. 3, col. 5.)

216

17th July 1838

A NORTHAMPTON BREACH OF PROMISE CASE

At the Assizes, the most interesting cases were usually those dealt with in the Criminal Court. Civil cases in the Nisi Prius Court tended to be rather dull disputes over business or debt. On the day that Charles Allen was before the Criminal Court at Northampton Summer Assizes for assaulting the Wellingborough constables (see 8th May), there was splendid entertainment in the Civil Court. A barrister named Waddington was defending in the case of Chubb v. Fenwick, and he put on the performance of a virtuoso.

Mr. Humfrey opened for the plaintiff, and explained the case to his honour Sir John Bernard Bosanquet and a common jury.

Humfrey: I have the honour to appear before you as counsel for the plaintiff, who seeks to recover some compensation in damages for a breach of promise of marriage. The parties are in an humble situation in life, the plaintiff being a servant to a Mrs. Adams in this town, and in whose service she was, several years back. Her mistress's house was nearly opposite the Goat Inn; the defendant having been ostler at the same. He has now retired on his property, having amassed, as persons in his situation frequently do, considerable wealth, being the possessor of several houses in Northampton. Living opposite each other, an intimacy sprang up between them, plaintiff having been in the habit of going over for beer. Her mistress was aware that defendant was courting the plaintiff, and she used to permit her to go and walk with him whenever she had a half holiday. Their acquaintance began in 1832 or 1833, and continued down to the year 1834. He informed her his intentions were honourable: he told her he intended to make her his wife, and that he should shortly relinquish his situation, take up housekeeping, and marry her. The plaintiff was 23 or 24 years of age when their intimacy began. She is now between 27 and 28. The defendant is between three-and-thirty and forty. Unfortunately for the plaintiff, she placed unbounded confidence in his promises that he would marry her, and she became the mother of his child in 1835. I could state nothing stronger in favour of the girl's character than this, nor need I, that a Mrs. Morgan, a lady living in the town, knowing the manner in which the plaintiff had been ruined, took her into her service (and that conduct on such an occasion did her credit) – and plaintiff remained in it several months, until her former mistress, Mrs. Adams, satisfied of her good conduct, save and except when seduced from it by the artifices of the defendant, prevailed on Mrs. Morgan to permit her to return, and there she now is. Unfortunately, ever since the birth of the child, the defendant has refused to contribute anything towards supporting mother or child, and application was made to the magistrates of the town, and by their order, I believe the child was affiliated upon the defendant. You are no doubt aware of the alteration made in the laws, to persons situated as plaintiff is. She receives now, £10 a year wages, and she has been reduced to the greatest destitution, and been obliged to support the defendant's child. I state that because you might say the present action is brought at a late period; but I firmly believe, that if he had done anything towards maintaining the child, the present action would never have been brought at all. As to damages, that is a question for the jury.

Humfrey called three witnesses, a fellow ostler of the defendant to testify as to the promise of marriage; Mrs. Morgan, who employed the plaintiff, after the birth of the child; and the surgeon to prove attending the birth. There is mention of a man named Yeates, employed, evidently to investigate and gather information helpful to the plaintiff's counsel.

Thomas Knight: I know the defendant. He was ostler at the Goat Inn. I was assistant under him. Harriet Chubb was in Mrs. Adams' service. They kept company in 1834. She was in the habit of going out with him whenever she had a holiday. On the 24th of June of that year, I heard Fenwick promise her marriage. He put his hand on her shoulder and said he would not marry any one but her. I have heard him say he would marry her and go to housekeeping. To my knowledge he was courting her for two years, and it was so known to the people around.

Waddington, cross-examining: Did the defendant *write* that he would marry her?

Knight: He cannot write.

Waddington: Have you ever said what you just said, before?

Knight: I cannot recollect saying it until yesterday. If I have, I have forgotten it. I told it to Mr. Yeates. I told it to Harriet Chubb before yesterday. I told it to her last Sunday, and the time when the action was entered. I also told it her at the Dolphin when the writ was wrote out. I did not hear anything said at the Dolphin about Fenwick having paid £28 to the parish. I never saw them together after the child was born.

Mrs. Morgan: I am the wife of Mr. William Fisher Morgan of this town. I recollect hearing of Harriet Chubb having a child, and after her recovery from her confinement, I took her into my service. This was in January 1837, and she remained with me until last Michaelmas. I had known her as a servant to Mrs. Adams for several years, and she returned to her service. I would have engaged her again, from her conduct being so good, but Mrs. Adams being an aged person, wished to have her back.

After the surgeon had given evidence of having attended Harriet Chubb at the birth of the child, Waddington alone became the case for the defendant, calling no witnesses. What followed was a *tour de force.*

Waddington: Gentlemen of the jury, I confess that, when I heard my learned friend's opening, I was very much surprised; and often as I have had occasion to wonder at the gravity and pathos of my learned friend, I was never more astonished than I was in listening to the grandiloquence of his opening just now. Now if he had not been grossly mis-instructed, he could not have misrepresented things in the manner he has to you, and I am satisfied I shall show you that a more gross pretence to extort money out of the pocket of this unfortunate person, who my friend says, has amassed considerable wealth, and is the owner of a great number of houses in Northampton, was never attempted; for if he possessed them, do you think Mr. Yeates, who comes down from London to rake out evidence, would not have found them out – coming down, as he does, to rake out evidence of a transaction that occurred four years ago? I am very much afraid, gentlemen, these houses are houses of *buckram*, as Falstaff's men. But gentlemen, I address you as men of sense, and I ask you, have you ever in your experience in Courts of Justice, heard of an action for a breach of promise of marriage being brought against an individual, four years after the promise had taken place and the acquaintance is said to have ceased? Nor should we in the present case, but for the incursion of Mr. Yeates into Northampton to disturb the peace of this poor retired ostler of the Goat. What do you think of Miss Harriet Chubb, who bears this romantic name, transporting people so much in her favour that she was *pressed* into the service of Mrs. Morgan. But, gentlemen, according to the evidence, that was not until the year 1837, and when my friend said, "No Madam, you are mistaken: it must be '36"; no, it was no mistake, for she confirms her statement by a memorandum made at the time. So much for the feeling excited in favour of the oppressed Chubb. My friend says she don't want him to marry her – no, all she wants is a little money for the child. My friend has not shown the child is even alive. Where is Mrs. Adams, to whom she could have confided her sorrows? Has my friend proved his case at all? Will you countenance women of this description, mothers of natural children, and find a verdict against a man upon such miserable contemptible evidence as that which we have heard today, and which she has kept in her own bosom from the year 1834 till the month of May, 1838? You have heard the account of the under-boots, as to what Fenwick said, when half-drunk, I suppose: "My dearest Chubb, I'll marry nobody but you." It is clear she thought he was joking, because she makes no reply, and a promise to be binding must be reciprocal. There is a very useful statute, called the statute of frauds, which says, "No promise shall be binding unless it is in writing," and though this does not apply to promises of marriage, yet it would have perhaps been as well if it had. But there would be a difficulty — the defendant, we have heard, cannot write; and the plaintiff, I suppose, cannot read. It puts me in mind of an old Irish song, which I would sing at this moment, if I could do it as well as my friend Mr. Serjeant Adams did it yesterday evening, but as I cannot, I will recite a verse. It is about a poor Patlander, who wishes to write to his mistress, and he says —

> "But when I sat down to indite 'em
> Oh by Jesus I found it too bad;
> For I could not come up to the writing,
> And she couldn't have read it if I had."

(Roars of laughter in Court)

My friend talks about this poor ostler amassing money. It is like the rest of the case. Those ostlers don't amass money like my learned friend. They don't make fortunes quite so fast. No, they get their money by twopences and three-pences. But, gentlemen, are you ready to say that, because he happens to slap a girl upon the back, and says he'll marry her, he is to be liable to a breach of a contract of marriage? If so, the proceedings in Courts of Justice are a mere farce. I trust you will find a verdict for the defendant.

They did.

20th July 1838

A GALLANT FORMER ENEMY PASSING THROUGH

"Marshall Soult passed through Weedon yesterday morning on his way to Rugby. Two troops of the 14th Light Dragoons, the Artillery, and the 20th Foot quartered at the Barracks there, received the gallant veteran with military honours."

(*Northampton Mercury* 21st July 1838, p. 3, col. 6.)

Soult had been the principal French commander in the Peninsular War; had fought against Moore, Wellington and Beresford; and at Waterloo, had been Napoleon's Chief of Staff.

21st July 1838

AN INN THAT WAS NEVER BUILT

"TO BREWERS & CAPITALISTS.
TO BE SOLD,
SIX ACRES of BUILDING LAND, most eligibly situated at the Cross Roads, near ROCKINGHAMSHIRE, where the turnpike roads join from Oundle to Leicester and Harborough, and from Melton and Oakham to Kettering and Northampton.

"A most favorable [sic] opportunity is here presented to any moderate capitalist for the erection of a respectable Inn or Public House, as there would be a certainty of several Coaches changing here immediately on erection, with a fair amount of Posting, besides Droves, and horses standing here during the Hunting Season.

"The traffic along both roads is good – towards Leicester from Oundle it is enormous.

"Apply (post paid) to Mr. BAGSHAW, Oakley, Kettering."

(*Northampton Mercury* 21st July 1838, p. 1, col. 3.)

This crossroads is, at the end of the twentieth century, a roundabout on the road from Corby to Cottingham. In 1838 it was almost two miles from Corby village. The south-west and north-west quarters are still unbuilt on.

25th July 1838

THE CONTENTS OF A SHOEMANUFACTURER'S HOUSE IN NORTHAMPTON

"NEAT AND MODERN HOUSEHOLD FURNITURE, BOOKS, &c. &c. TO BE SOLD BY AUCTION,
By Mr. W. WOOD
On Wednesday next, the 25th July, 1838, on the premises,
WOOLMONGER STREET, NORTHAMPTON,
THE whole of the HOUSEHOLD FURNITURE & EFFECTS of Mr. JAMES BUMPUS, Shoe-Manufacturer, deceased; comprising four-post bedsteads, with mahogany carved pillars, in morine and chintz hangings, lined and fringed; tent and crib bedsteads, feather-beds, mattresses, blankets, and counterpanes; mahogany chests of drawers, night commode, dressing tables, chimney and pier glasses, set of six and 2 elbow neat mahogany chairs, mahogany sofa, imitation-rose-wood couch, mahogany loo and dining tables, sideboard, fitted with cellaret and drawers; large bookcase – the lower tier enclosed with doors; two mahogany stools, with hair seats; brussels and Kidderminster carpets, morine window curtains, bedroom and windsor chairs, oak bureau, mahogany swing cot, excellent eight-day clock; a fine-toned violincello, violin and flute; single-barrel gun, fender and fire-irons, china, glass and earthenware; a variety of kitchen articles;

223

oak linen chest; leather-travelling trunk; 50-gallon copper, 10-bushel mash vat, brewing utensils, lead water-cistern, two salting leads, three half-hogshead casks, water butt, iron trough, large iron beam and scales, small ditto; counter, 7½ feet long, with four large drawers; fifteen shoe hampers; several lots of useful wood doors, &c. Also, about 250 VOLUMES OF BOOKS. . . ."

This auction sale was advertised in the *Northampton Mercury* of 21st July 1838, in the third column of page 3. The books included a forty-five volume encyclopaedia, and were mainly religious. Lest there be any misunderstanding a loo table was a table intended for the playing of the card-game, loo.

29th July 1838

JUST ANOTHER SUNDAY FOR CONSTABLE SPENCER

Between two and three o'clock on Sunday afternoon, 29th July, a Northampton currier, William Harrison, saw the opportunity of a free ride up Bridge Street. A private carriage was climbing the hill, and the seat behind was empty. Harrison stealthily climbed up, undetected by the driver and the owner within. The carriage drew level with an old man walking along the footpath. This was John Shuttle of Roade. Finding himself briefly face to face with the owner, he indicated the cheeky uninvited passenger riding behind. The gentleman immediately stopped the carriage and ordered Harrison to get down. The currier did so reluctantly, and decided to vent his rage on the old man. He struck him repeatedly with a stick, causing a severe wound on the lip.

Constable Spencer of the Northampton Police appeared on the scene, and attempted to take Harrison into custody, but he resisted with great violence, and badly bruised the officer.

All this attracted a large crowd, and so much disturbance was made that the service in All Saints' Church was interrupted for several minutes. Eventually Constable Law came to the assistance of Spencer, and at length they jointly succeeded in conveying Harrison to the Station House.

On the evening of the same day, during the next Divine Service, the congregation of All Saints' was disturbed by a sudden ringing of the bells. Constable Spencer proceeded to the belfry, and found an inebriated railway labourer seated on a bench, amusing himself by pulling two of the bell ropes. He was taken to the Station House.

These events were reported in the *Northampton Mercury* of 4th August 1838 (p. 3, col. 5). On the following morning, Harrison was committed by the Magistrates to the County Gaol for one month. The same Court fined the bell-ringing railway labourer five shillings; and two other labourers from the railroad who had been drunk and disorderly during the time of the Sunday morning service, were also fined five shillings.

30th July 1838

CHARTISTS IN NORTHAMPTON

The first great Chartist meeting in Northampton was held on 30th July 1838. R. G. Gammage, the historian of the Chartist movement, was himself a Northampton man, and an eyewitness. His version of the events has often been used by later historians. But can we rely on him? He has told us that this Northampton rally took place on 1st August – a date specially chosen because it was the anniversary of the emancipation of the slaves in the British Empire. Not true! Monday 30th July was selected because the Northampton shoemakers did not work on Mondays and would therefore be likely to attend in large numbers. Why did Gammage put the wrong day in his record? Either he allowed his romantic feeling for the movement to get the better of him, and considered a couple of days' difference not to matter; or he genuinely forgot, when he was writing, twenty years later. Whatever the reason for the misinformation, it means that Gammage must be treated as unreliable. The two other Northampton eye-witnesses, the reporters of the *Herald* and the *Mercury*, could be regarded as hostile and therefore unreliable. The best we can do is to consult all three versions.

The Chartist organisation was based on the London Working Man's Association, which had published the People's Charter in May 1838. The six democratic demands on the Charter were intended to give working men parliamentary representation. All but one of these demands eventually became very ordinary elements of our constitution — a strong refutation of the contemporary accusations of outrageous revolutionary sedition. Promotion of the Charter coincided with other protest movements such as those against the Poor Law, bad working conditions, and newspaper tax; so affiliations and mass-meetings during 1838 gave it a national following.[117]

In 1854, Gammage wrote about the first Chartist meeting in Northampton.[118]

"The men of Northampton . . . had resolved to shew their sympathy with the movement by holding an open-air meeting to which they invited Henry Vincent. . . . Placards couched in forcible and eloquent terms announced that a procession would leave the Market Square at three o'clock, and, at that hour, the Square and the avenues leading thereto presented a very animated appearance. A number of flags, made for the occasion, and bearing devices emblematic of the liberal principles, waved gracefully in the summer breeze. The members of the association appeared with tri-coloured rosettes at their breasts, and having formed into procession, the band struck up a lively air, to which the people marched forward with almost military regularity. The procession traversed the principal streets, gathering numbers as it advanced, until it reached the racecourse, the grand-stand of which had been secured as the most eligible position from which the speakers could address the meeting."

The principal speaker, Henry Vincent, was one of the London Working Men's Association touring orators. Gammage tells us that the chair was taken by a Northampton journeyman shoemaker, Joseph Wright. Two nonconformist clergymen made speeches. The Rev. John Jenkinson, of Kettering, "took as his text the motto on the Kettering flag, 'justice to all' ". He was the leading propagandist and lecturer of the Kettering Radical Association which had been in existence since 1836.[119] The Rev. J. C. Meeke, Unitarian Minister, made a "bold and manly declaration".[118] A farmer, named Burdett, spoke with "racy old English humour".

When the sky darkened and it began to rain, Henry Vincent urged the crowd to "Stand to your duty my friends. Never mind a little rain." Gammage said that "the heaving mass implicitly followed his injunction . . .". A resolution in favour of the Charter was unanimously carried.

The *Northampton Mercury* account was placed on page 3 of the issue of 4th August 1838 (col. 5).

"On Monday afternoon a public meeting was held in this town, to take into consideration the propriety of petitioning parliament for universal suffrage, vote by ballot, annual parliaments, no property qualification, and wages for Members. A procession was formed in the market Square, which, preceded by a band of music and banners, arrived at the Race Cource [sic], the place announced for the meeting, about a quarter before four. The chair was taken by Mr. Wright, an operative of the town; and Mr. Vincent from London, who attended as a deputation at the request of the Working Men's Association, addressed the assembly in a speech of an hour and a half's duration. The Rev. J. Meeke of the town, and the Rev. J. Jenkinson, of Kettering, Mr. Burdett, of Naseby, and others, also spoke on the occasion. Resolutions in favour of the objects of the meeting were unanimously adopted. The meeting was attended almost exclusively by the operative classes, and owing perhaps to the unfavourable state of the weather, was much smaller than had been anticipated. The numbers present at any one time did not appear to us to exceed 1000. A similar meeting was held at Welling-borough, on Wednesday when a resolution was passed that steps should be taken to form a society upon the principles of the London Working Men's Association. On Thursday a meeting was held at Long Buckby. On Tuesday night, Mr. Vincent delivered a lecture in this town, on the objects and advantages of working men's associations."

The *Northampton Herald* also published its account of the rally on 4th August 1838 (p. 3, cols. 2-3), with a great deal of editorial comment, presumably from the pen of the Rev. Francis Litchfield.

"A meeting of what is termed the 'WORKING MEN'S ASSOCIATION' was held on Monday last on our Race Course, for the purpose of unfurling the banner of democracy, and as a necessary accompaniment, abusing the aristocracy. Great pains were taken to get a grand 'public demonstration' – Saint Monday was fixed upon [the ironic term used by the shoemen for the weekday upon which they did not work] – a band of music with banners paraded the town – Wellingborough, Kettering, Long Buckby and other places were canvassed to swell the number of *patriots* – and, above all, 'Mr. Vincent from London' came specially to 'demand with a voice of thunder the political and natural rights of the working classes'. But, notwithstanding all this, the incorruptible honesty and sound sense of the great majority of the working men evinced itself in their abstaining very generally from taking any part in the proceedings, and refusing to neglect their work for the purpose of being gulled by the revolutionary trash of Mr. Vincent and 'other *friends*'. The Democrat, therefore, had but a very thin attendance, and the elements being impropitious, put a complete *damper* upon the few ardent spirits present who had 'enlisted under the banner of radicalism'. Vincent, to do him justice, is a dangerous character, possessing as he does great volubility of speech and considerable tact; and this must be our excuse for noticing this contemptible 'demonstration' at all: for, however weak a man's arguments may be, if he possesses power to do mischief to any class of the Community, it is the duty of the public journalist to put that class on their guard. As may be expected, nearly the whole of Mr. Vincent's harangue was addressed to the passions and not to the reason of his audience, and all he said was calculated to set neighbour against neighbour, the poor against the rich, the servant against the master; in fact to make the miserable still more deplorable, and to place even the starving man and the beggar in a still less enviable condition. He first recounted the amount of poverty, oppression and degradation that prevailed amongst the working classes, attributing all to the corrupt institutions of the country, taking care to interlard his remarks with hollow compliments to their intelligence, industry and respectability. He assured them that there was not a more unenlightened and stupid body of men in the kingdom than the present house of Commons, and, assuming the prophetic character, predicted that their places would soon be occupied by respectable tradesmen and journey-men mechanics!"

The report concluded on the theme of Christian authority, suggesting that workers would be reluctant to stray from their duty as ordered in the Bible, and prompting upper class readers to remind labourers that their estate was "ordered".

4th August 1838

SHOEMAKING AT ROADE

Why was there suddenly a need for shoemakers at Roade? Had the railway brought unexpected trade? Or had the railway taken away the workers?

"WANTED immediately, Two JOURNEYMEN SHOE-MAKERS, for Strong and Light work. None need apply but good workmen and men whose characters will bear investigation.

229

Apply (if by letter, post paid) to JOSEPH KILSBY, Boot and Shoemaker, Roade."

(*Northampton Mercury* 4th August 1838, p. 3, col. 1.)

5th August 1838

SAINT SEPULCHRE WOULD HAVE BEEN PLEASED!

The Church of the Holy Sepulchre, in Northampton, was known as "Saint Seplchre's Church" (and still is). In 1838, it was subject to restoration, inside and out. It reopened on Sunday 5th August, and the previous day's *Northampton Mercury* carried an interesting description of the improvements (p. 3, col. 5):

"The Church of St. Sepulchre . . . has long attracted the attention of the antiquary. . . . Unhappily, however, it has only been to antiquarians that it has held out any attractions, for a more uncomfortable place of worship it would be difficult to devise. Till within these few weeks, there was no boarding to protect the feet of the poorer part of the congregation from the coldness and dampness of a stone floor; the pews were wretchedly arranged, and those who sat in them exposed to a variety of drafts [sic]. The Church-yard too was till lately full of holes, and most inconveniently traversed by needless footpaths. Thanks, however, to the indefatigable exertions of the present Churchwardens . . . [named], both the inside and the outside of St. Sepulchre have assumed a very different appearance. A great part of the interior has been completely re-pewed, and no less than 162 very comfortable additional new sittings obtained. The walls and monuments have been thoroughly cleaned, all the seats have now, boarded floors, and the cold has been excluded by closing the south door, and placing an inner door at the west entrance. An excellent organ made by Gray, a present from a lady of the parish, has been erected on the north side . . . and the pulpit has been brought forward so as to render the preacher visible to the whole of the congregation. The Church-yard has been levelled, and the paths have been reduced in number, and rendered at the same time more convenient. The path across the Church-yard, leading from Newland to Bull-lane, has been planted on both sides with lime-trees, which will, in time, form an agreeable avenue. And all these improvements have been effected entirely by private subscription, there having been no Church-rate in the parish during the last three years.

The Church is to be re-opened tomorrow. . . . We trust that the friends of the Church in this town will be disposed to contribute liberally, especially when they are informed that of the new sittings, by far the larger number are open to the poor."

The collection on that Sunday raised £89. 5s. 11d.

6th August 1838

A SALARY FOR THE MAYOR OF NORTHAMPTON

On the first day of the year, Northampton Town Council had been told that providing funds for the town fire engines was illegal by the terms of the Municipal Corporations Act. Many regarded this as an alarming situation, but it remained a problem without solution until the Quarterly Meeting of the Town Council on Monday 6th August.

T. Sharp: As the proposition I made at our last meeting, on this subject has not been generally understood, and much misrepresentation has got abroad, I shall repeat what I said on that occasion. I have lately visited a corporate city, and found the council there in the same difficult situation as ourselves, respecting the payment of public subscriptions out of the corporate funds; and considering that they ought

231

to be paid, they had agreed to allow the Mayor a salary, for the express purpose, and only purpose, of discharging the same. They had taken the best advice, and were informed that they might do so legally. To this, all parties were, therefore, agreed. I think it is a very good scheme for us to adopt. There is no fund out of which to pay either the expense of the fire engines, or the annual subscription of fifteen guineas to the Infirmary, now due. No objection can be made on the ground of economy, as the town will be saved considerable expense. Mr. Barry has informed me that the fire engines are attended with an expense of about thirty pounds a year. I shall now, therefore, move that the sum of fifty pounds be granted to the Mayor for the current year, leaving it open for the Council to fix whatever salary might be deemed requisite in subsequent years. The Mayor, I am sure, would not think of pocketing any surplus that might remain.

Theophilus Jeyes, Town Clerk: The 92nd clause expressly states that salaries might be granted to the Mayor and the Recorder.

Christopher Markham: This is a jesuitical way of proceeding. . . . Our expenditure will be increased without our having any warrant for what we are doing. I shall consequently object to the payment of bills for which we have no authority.

T. Sharp: The proposition only refers to the present year, to enable us to meet claims actually due. I must remind Mr. Markham that he has invariably objected to all bills relating to the fire engines when they were brought in, as also the subscription to the Infirmary, and divided the Council on them. There is nothing jesuitical in the present proceedings, as everyone knows that the payments ought to be made, and this is the best way of doing so, to enable it to be done legally.

Motion carried.

Two days later, an event proved how important the fire engines were.

8th August 1838

FIRE IN NORTHAMPTON

"About twelve o'clock on Wednesday . . . a fire broke out in the top attic of the house of Mr. John Stanton, in Abington Street. Ball, our active superintendent of police, hearing Mrs. S. call out 'Fire', proceeded immediately to the spot, and found the servant's room in flames. He endeavoured, with the assistance of two or three gentlemen, to extinguish the fire, but finding their efforts unsuccessful, Ball went for the engines, and in about half an hour succeeded in subduing the flames. The whole of the bed and bed furniture, and a part of the servant's wearing apparel, were, however, destroyed. . . . An abundant supply of water was afforded on the spot by the pipes of the Water Company."

(*Northampton Mercury* 11th August 1838, p. 3, col. 5.)

8th August 1838

THE FIRST PATIENTS RECEIVED INTO THE LUNATIC ASYLUM

"NORTHAMPTON GENERAL LUNATIC ASYLUM
"August 8, 1838.
"THE COMMITTEE OF MANAGEMENT beg to announce that the HOUSE being COMPLETE IN ITS SEVERAL DEPARTMENTS IS NOW OPEN for the RECEPTION OF PATIENTS, and that any information relative to their admission will be given upon application to the Officers of the Establishment.

"Strangers will be allowed to visit the Asylum, upon being introduced either personally or in writing by a Director, from Ten till Twelve and from Two till Four on

Mondays, Wednesdays and Saturdays. And in thus giving an opportunity to persons who feel an interest in the welfare of the Institution and may wish to inspect its arrangements, it is distinctly to be understood that this cannot be carried further than is consistent with the personal comfort and privacy of the Patients, which must always be preserved.

EUSTON, Chairman"

With this notice from Lord Euston, published in the *Northampton Mercury* on 18th August 1838 (p. 3, col. 3) the Northampton Lunatic Asylum declared itself open. This was the hospital later to become St. Andrew's. The concern expressed for the "comfort and privacy" of the inmates must have surprised anyone who witnessed the removal of the "insane", chained and manacled, to the new asylum from the old lock-up in Fish Lane, Northampton (later Fish Street). There they had been chained to the floor where they lay on straw.[120]

The fullest factual account of the historical background to the establishment of the Northampton General Lunatic Asylum was compiled over thirty years later, by John Hensman. It includes information not given in later, published histories of the Asylum. Hensman was appointed legal adviser to the Asylum, and having examined the trusts, papers, accounts and books relating to the institution, he presented a report to the Directors and the County and Borough Magistrates, on 4th August 1869.

"In the year 1804, a benefaction of £100 was given to the governors of the Infirmary by an unknown person, the principal to be reserved towards the design of a provision for persons disordered in mind." Hensman said that additional money was donated in 1807 and 1809, with the intention of setting up at the Infirmary a department for treating the insane. This was declared not expedient by the Infirmary Governors on 30th September 1809. "On 3rd May, 1828, Sir W. Wake communicated to the Governors . . . that the subscribers to the Northamptonshire Yeomanry Cavalry Fund had resolved that . . . £6000 be subscribed to the fund for erecting a Lunatic Asylum. . . ." The land was purchased in July 1834 for £2,900. "In August, 1834 the special committee of governors of the Infirmary resolved that a public meeting be held on the 17th October following at the George Hotel, Northampton . . . and stated that it was intended that the establishment should be entirely independent of the General Infirmary. . . ." Architects were invited by press advertisement, to submit plans for an asylum for fifty "pauper patients" and twenty "class patients in indigent circumstances, but above the need of parochial assistance."

This was in April 1835. The 1840 Annual Court of the Asylum stated that it had been built for 52 patients of the 5th class or lowest rate of board, and 30 private "patients of the preceding superior classes".

9th August 1838

A CHARTIST DEALING HIS FROTH

Henry Vincent, the travelling lecturer of the Working Men's Association who had addressed the mass rally on the Race Course, was still in Northampton. R. G. Gammage wrote that an indoor meeting was to have been held in the Saracen's Head on the Market Square, "and bills were posted, but Tory influences caused the keys to the room to be with-held, so Vincent spoke in the Market Square".[118] We have the point of view of his opponents in the *Northampton Herald* report of 11th August 1838 (p. 2, col. 6).

"Our townsfolk were not a little amused on Thursday [9th August] at another attempted display by that conglomeration of knaves and dupes who have taken upon themselves the title of 'The Working Man's Association'. It appears that the tramping printer, who is just now 'bartering his slang for the poor man's pennies', applied at the Saracen's Head Inn, to engage the great room for a lecture(!) and being unknown to Mr. Read, the landlord, an agreement was partly entered into; Mr. Read, however, upon ascertaining the purpose to which his room was to be devoted, and not liking to risk his silver spoons and other moveables to such a company, very unceremoniously refused to permit the pack upon any terms to enter his premises. Not being allowed the use of any other room in the town, a cart was procured and placed upon the Market Hill; but alas! even the 'cart's tail' refused them, for the owner, on missing his property, and ascertaining its whereabouts, sent his horse and walked off with it, and thus saved his cart from pollution.

"The inflated 'Cock Speaker' was however so anxious to deliver himself, that he mounted the pump and holding hard by the rails, he in that position dealt his *froth* to such as would listen, which were few in number, and the very great majority of THEM were persons who were drawn together by accident or curiosity. The fellow commenced his 'hotch potch' by abusing our kind-hearted friend Read, of the Saracen's Head, for unkennelling the pack, and he then, of course, proceeded to praise himself. . . . As Conservatives, we ought to rejoice at the mad ravings of the fellow, which tend to strengthen our ranks, by driving every well-meaning Whig or Radical, who has a shilling to save, or a home to be protected, to them. . . ."

11th August 1838

RUSHDEN: CHURCH CUSTOMS, AND A WINDMILL FOR SALE

John Cole described an unusual funeral custom at Rushden, that was, in 1838, falling into disuse.[99]

". . . When a funeral takes place on a Sunday . . . half the portion of time allotted to chiming [is] devoted to tolling

236

the corpse to the church, when the body of some well-known individual of the parish is, for the last time, 'gathered to the place of prayer', and remains at the entrance during the entire service. This was a practice which was anciently more prevalent than at present, and I can see no objection to its continuance, when the individual has not died of any pestilential disease. . . ."

Mary Ann Smart recalled the Rushden of 1838 in an interview in 1911.[112]

"People used to carry a silk bag to church containing their books. No jackets were worn [by females], always shawls or cloaks. Clergymen wore black gowns, and preached for about twenty minutes." Rushden was not the shoe town that it became later in the century. "There was no shoemaker in Rushden then. There was one in Higham, Owen Parker, and boys used to go to Higham to fetch stabbing (Army boots). Girls used to make lace. Buyers used to come round – one from Bedford, and Mr. Radburn of Rushden used to buy some. They earned about three shillings a week."

There were two windmills in Rushden. The lower half of one of them still stands, having been converted into a dwelling, standing just inside the parish and county boundary on the hill overlooking Wymington. The other, long gone, has its site marked by Windmill Road. That one was part of an estate that came on the market in August 1838.

"RUSHDEN, Northamptonshire.
TO BE SOLD BY PRIVATE CONTRACT,
ALL that messuage or FARMHOUSE, with the BAKEHOUSE, and all necessary and convenient outbuildings thereto belonging, together with an Orchard, containing nearly one acre of land thereto adjoining, situate in Duck Street in Rushden, in the county of Northampton.
    Also a CLOSE of good Arable Land, situate in Rushden aforesaid, containing about Seven Acres and a half, or thereabouts, more or less, all of which premises are now in the occupation of Mr. Samuel Achurch.

"And also all that WINDMILL, with the newly-erected Messuage or TENEMENT thereunto adjoining, also situate at Rushden aforesaid, and now in the tenure or occupation of Mr. Job Knight.

"To view the Estate, apply to Mr. SAMUEL ACHURCH, of Rushden; and for price and further particulars either to him, or at the Office of Mr. BURNHAM, Solicitor, Wellingborough."

(*Northampton Mercury* 11th August 1838, p. 2, col. 5.)

August 1838

A SET OF IDLE FELLOWS

The people of every period of British history have believed that vandalism, criminal damage, and the worst forms of anti-social behaviour, are recent trends, and rarely occurred in the past. One of the 1838 manifestations in the following report: the destruction of a footbridge at the bottom end of Cow Lane; occurred where the west corner of Becket's Park is now. The complaint was printed on page 3 (col. 3) of the *Northampton Herald* of 18th August 1838.

"The town of Northampton contains a set of idle fellows, who nightly infest the streets and outskirts and carry on their mischievous pranks and depredations to a great extent. Scarcely is a wall built up but a portion of it is found thrown down the next morning; lucky is the gardener if his fruit escapes their grasp. The trees and hedges in the New Walk present a disgraceful specimen of these fellows' mischievous folly; the posts and chains by Perkins's nursery are mostly broken and destroyed; indeed scarcely anything escapes. A few nights ago a newly-erected bridge over the ditch from Cow Lane to the Meadow, was wantonly thrown down and otherwise damaged, and this must have been a work of considerable labour. Several must have been concerned. . . . The Town Council have offered a reward of ten pounds for the conviction of the depredators. . . ."

14th August 1838

THRAPSTON IN NEED OF A CURRIER

Currying was the finishing process in the production of soft, supple leather. The tanner produced hard, stiff leather, not suitable for harness, or shoe uppers. By using a selection of oils and greases, and various special tools, the currier produced leather of desired quality, colour, weight and texture. The currier's function was quite separate from that of the tanner, and it was illegal for both trades to be carried on in the same establishment. In the following advertisement, a drying shop is included in the currier's premises. This was necessary because, after dubbing had been brushed on the hides, they spent several weeks slowly drying.

The harness-makers of Thrapston and the surrounding area would have been pleased at the prospect of having the local currying shop in business again.

"TO CURRIERS, LEATHER CUTTERS, Ac.
VALUABLE LEASEHOLD ESTATE, THRAPSTONE,
TO BE SOLD BY AUCTION
By W. SMITH,
"At the George Inn, on Tuesday, August 14th, 1838, between the hours of six and eight in the evening (unless previously disposed of)
ALL that brick and tiled DWELLING HOUSE, selling shop, CURRIER'S SHOP, Drying Shed, Stable, Gig House, and Yard, the property of the late J. J. Stevenson, where a business in the above line was successfully prosecuted many years.

The above is leasehold of the Manor of Thrapstone, and had 93 years of the lease unexpired on the 5th of April last, subject to the annual quit-rent of 1s. [one shilling].

The premises are well adapted to the business, and an opportunity is presented to any person to commence, as there is no currier in the town. . . ."

(*Northampton Mercury* 11th August 1838, p. 1, col. 2.)

August 1838

COMPLAINTS OF THE NORTHAMPTON SHOEMAKERS

During August 1838, an eight-page pamphlet was delivered to each of the Northampton shoe manufacturers. Its title was "An Appeal From the Northampton Society of Operative Cordwainers, to the Boot & Shoe Manufacturers of Northampton, on Behalf of Their Workmen".[121] The slogan "Live, and let live" was its sub-title, and the document tells us a great deal of the working conditions of the shoe workers. It is necessary to have in mind that the trade was not mechanised, and the shoemakers or their wives went to the warehouses to be issued with leather to make up into shoes at home. The factories referred to in the text were workshops organised by the shoemakers themselves. It is clear that the clickers, in addition to their basic function of cutting out the shoe-leather, had the responsibility of giving it out.

In setting out six recommendations (they were certainly not phrased as demands), the "cordwainers" were no doubt inspired by the Chartists, whose recent meetings they had attended in large numbers.

The text, headed "ADDRESS" begins:

"Gentlemen, The Society of Operative Cordwainers respectfully call your attention to the following appeal on behalf of your work-people. We are persuaded that the large manufacturers are not aware of the unjust system on which their business is at present conducted by their clickers, nor the smaller manufacturers of the misery created by their mode of getting up and disposing of their goods; or feeling assured that such a destructive and oppressive system of manufacturing would cease. . . .

"One of the most prominent evils now in operation is the power invested in clickers of distributing that part of the work executed by women and children – such work being given out chiefly to a CHOSEN FEW – consisting of clickers' wives and acquaintances, who have no claim to the trade – while the MANY, consisting of the wives and families of the makers, have so little that it is insufficient to enable parents to train up their children in knowledge and respectability. As soon as their children have sufficient strength to work, in very many cases they become the tools and slaves of clickers and their favorites [sic], want of regular work and fair wages compelling parents to let out their little ones for a few pence towards their maintenance. . . . Gentlemen, the practices of these factories are heart-rending: – Children from five years of age and upwards toil in them from morning till night, with scarcely any intermission for meals or exercise – in many instances taking their scanty supply of bread with them, or nibbling it as they move along the streets to their HARD LABOUR. The natural results of the father's want of regular work and fair remuneration and the child's ill-paid toil are to be seen in the deformity, dwarfishness, paleness, bad clothing, ignorance, and bad habits which prevail in the latter, who grow up burdens and curses instead of blessings to society. . . . Imagine an honest and industrious workman, striving to maintain a family, earning from 12s. to 15s. a week, with which he has to feed, clothe, and shelter himself and family, and educate the latter, frequently six or seven in number. . . ."

As remedies, the Society of Operative Cordwainers, made six recommendations, and supplied a paragraph of justification for each of them. The first was

"A more equalised rate of wages . . . because, under the present system, journeymen shoemakers, unlike all other mechanics, seldom know what they shall receive for their work until they have done it; then they must take what the employers and clickers think fit to give them, which is a very small pittance, and that perhaps less by 2d. or 3d. per pair than the workmen expected; in some instances so much lower than is paid by other employers for the same kind of work. Thus, when trade is slack, and a man is driven by necessity to accept an unfair remuneration for his labour, a precedent for reduction of wages is established. . . . The workman has no encouragement to study the interests of an employer who takes advantage of his necessities."

The second was

"A more equal distribution of that part of the work performed by women and their children . . . because at present, clickers' wives and families . . . monopolise the greatest and best part of the work. . . . Clickers work fewer hours and obtain better wages than the makers, and have no grindery to buy out of their earnings. . . ."

The third was an immediate abolition of the Factory System, so prevalent amongst journeymen.

"The factories of journeymen are alike unhealthy, immoral, cruel and unjust: unhealthy because of the sedentary nature of the occupation, with the number of hours which these youthful slaves are compelled to work in a bad atmosphere – producing bad digestion, deformity, languor, and consumption; immoral because close confinement and hard labour present obstacles to the attainment of knowledge, the mind becomes enfeebled from sympathy with the body, and ignorance and depravity result; cruel because productive of the evils complained of, and subjects them to to the oppression of their proud, selfish and idle task-masters; unjust because a great part of the work is monopolised by a few of these factory holders, to the serious and permanent injury of the hard-working, honest, and single-handed craftsmen, whom they deprive of a comfortable livelihood, as the employment of these infants enables them to do work for lower wages. . . . We humbly hope . . that you will not allow these factories to continue in existence on account of the paltry difference they make in your profits. . . .

"Fourth — An abolition of the present competition system is highly important, as that is the general cause of the reduction of wages, and injurious to manufacturers and workmen. . . . It reduces the amount of profit, and . . . it reduces the rate of wages. Manufacturers . . . calculate upon a reduction of wages and materials, to enable them to compete with others in the market for the sale of their goods, together with improving the workmanship to the highest pitch of elegance and solidity, thereby rendering wages a mere nothing in comparison with the labour. By reducing the wages, manufacturers are worse off in the end, for when one reduces, the others reduce. . . . Therefore, while competition is carried to such extremes amongst themselves, no good can accrue from a reduction of wages. Any advantage which they might expect is lost in their eagerness to underrate each other in their contract for work. Hence the present depressed state of our trade."

The Cordwainers' fifth recommendation was a protest against "truck". That was the practice common among employers, of remunerating their workers with goods rather than cash.

". . . It prevents the workman from making the best of his little earnings. Many of the manufacturers carrying on this principle do not admit that they are actual trucksters, because, say they, we pay our work-people in cash; and if they like to purchase anything of us they may; but . . . they would not long employ a person who did not purchase goods of them, although these goods may not be equal in quality to those they could buy if they could go where they pleased. Generally the goods sold by the masters are of an inferior description according to the price, in bread especially short weight has to be deplored. . . ."

The sixth request was for a general rise of wages.

"The price of provisions is fast *increasing*. The style and beauty of workmanship are fast improving, thus requiring more ingenuity and labour on the part of the workman. . . . Consequently the workmen cannot possibly obtain an honest and comfortable livelihood. Hunger inhabits the cottage of the labourer; his children are starving around him. They are crying for bread. He has none for them. Affection for his children drives him into debt . . . and at length what they sought to avoid comes to them – the necessity of applying to the parish. . . ."

The pamphlet concluded with an appeal to the manufacturers' sense of justice and benevolence; and was "signed on behalf of the Committee" by the Secretary, Joseph Jones, of Bearward Street, Northampton.

There is evidence that the manufacturers themselves were organised (as they had been at a time when it was illegal for their employees to form unions). The *Northampton Mercury* of 22nd September 1838 (p. 3, col. 1) carried an advertisement of a London combination of shoe-manufacturers, issued four days earlier:

"CITY OF LONDON MASTER BOOT AND SHOE-MAKERS' SOCIETY. . . . The Master Boot Makers having found it necessary to resist the unreasonable demands of the men in connection with the Shops' Meetings, they are in WANT of steady and good BOOT-MEN, BOOT-CLOSERS, SHOE-MEN, &c. who have no connection with the Union. Wages the same as before the strike in May last; boots, with stitched rands, or seats from 6s. to 7s. making, and the other branches in proportion. . . ."

17th September 1838

THE LONDON AND BIRMINGHAM RAILWAY

The first train from London to Birmingham on the day of the official opening, carried the directors of the Company, Robert Stephenson the engineer. The Duke of Sussex was also a passenger as far as Rugby. *The Gentleman's Magazine* of October 1838 (p. 437) gave the time of arrival at Birmingham as three minutes past twelve; but it had the date wrong, and the timing it calculated does not seem accurate.

"The directors arrived at Birmingham at three minutes past twelve, having performed the whole journey including stoppages in four hours, forty eight minutes, and exclusive of stoppages in 4 hours and 14 minutes . . . being two hours less than the time occupied by Marshal Soult and attendants a few weeks ago."

In fact, this special train was scheduled to leave Euston at seven, but did so at twenty minutes past.

The *Northampton Mercury* of 22nd September 1838 had some informative remarks (p. 2, col. 1; and p. 3, col. 5). The first public train left London soon after eight o'clock carrying nearly two-hundred passengers. It was made up of nine first-class carriages, two mail, and four gentlemen's carriages. The first train from Birmingham left at seven in the morning. These trains were watched by thousands of Northamp-tonians. Every available horse and conveyance had gone from the town "at an early hour". The weather was fine, and no mishap occurred on this important day.

In Northamptonshire, the line went through the parishes of Hartwell, Ashton, Roade, Blisworth, Gayton, Lower Heyford, Weedon, Dodford, Norton, Long Buckby, Watford and Kilsby, and until the previous Saturday, 15th September, "labourers and artificers" had been hard at work along that stretch to be sure that all was ready. "There is still an immense deal of labour to be performed . . ." said the *Mercury*. "Many of the stations also are yet very incomplete; that at Blisworth consisting of little more than a wooden shed and a tremendous flight of wooden steps."

The Editor of the *Mercury* was "glad to observe that in the useful little table of distances and fares, published by the Company, Blisworth is marked as a First Class Station". In the issue of 6th October, however, editorial complaint was made that Blisworth had been re-classified as Second Class, and Roade had become the nearest First Class Station to Northampton. All trains stopped at the First Class stations. The reason given for this revision was the lack of accommodation for travellers at Blisworth, and no inclination there to improve the road.

There were seven trains a day in each direction, four on Sundays. The times were given in the London and Birmingham Railway's announcement which had been published in the *Northampton Mercury* on 15th September (p. 3, col. 3). The times of the trains conveying the mails, passengers were reminded, were fixed by the Postmaster General, under statutory powers. The Company offered to carry passengers, parcels, private carriages and horses "throughout the whole distance between London and Birmingham". Four modes of travel were advertised: mail carriages, carrying four inside (day-time only); first-class carriages, carrying six inside; second-class carriages, enclosed (night trains only); and second-class carriages with open sides (day-time). Higher fares were charged for night travel.

Francis Coghlan, in one of the several handbooks to the newly-completed railway, provided detailed guidance for the passengers.[122] Visualise those excited first-day passengers at Roade or Weedon station, clutching their tickets (yellow for first-class, blue for second-class), supervising the porters (no gratuities allowed) as their luggage (sixpence extra) was stowed. "The traveller should *see* it placed upon the roof or under the seat of the carriage in which he has taken his place." The second-class passengers were soon to find that the only way to avoid "being chilled by a current of cold air, which passes through these open waggons" and "being nearly blinded by the small cinders which escape through the funnel" was to sit with back towards the engine, "against the boarded part of the waggon". Those travelling in the mails and first-class carriages found that "all the seats are alike comfortably fitted up". Every train was "provided with guards and a conductor, who is responsible for the order and regularity of the journey". Procedures were followed when trains arrived at the stations that would have surprised travellers of a later age. "All persons are requested to get into and alight from the coaches *invariably* as directed by the conductor." Passengers were "desired to be in good time, as the train will leave each station as soon as ready, without reference to the time stated in the printed tables . . .".

What were the locomotives like? An assumption is sometimes expressed that they must have been of Stephenson design. Not so. Edward Bury had the contract for building the L. & B. R. engines.[123] They were all four-wheelers because he believed that the smaller locomotives were cheaper and more reliable; but they lacked power, and most passenger trains needed two or three. Contemporary illustrations show grey boilers and smoke-boxes, large brass domes over the fire boxes, oval brass number-plates on the sides of the boiler, and brass numerals high on the front of the tall chimney.

Mechanical signalling was entirely absent. "Constables are placed at [intervals of about a mile-and-a-quarter] along the entire line. Each man is furnished with two flags, red and white, during the day, and a lamp at night, which is made to show either a white, green or red light. The first announces to the engineer of the approaching train that there is no impediment; the green colour directs him to slacken the speed of the train, and the red to stop it as soon as possible. The flags are used for a similar purpose, except that upon seeing the red flag, the engineers lessen the speed, which renders a green flag unnecessary. . . . Each man, besides being in the employ of the Company, is sworn as a county constable; they receive the same pay, and wear a dress similar to that of the metropolitan police, except in colour, which is green. . . ."[122] One of these policemen was knocked down by a train, and killed, at Roade, on the night of Wednesday 26th September. Whoever submitted the report of this accident to the *Northampton Mercury* (29th September 1838, p. 3, col. 6) believed that the man had "mistaken the line of rails upon which the train was travelling".

The advertisements of the coach firms, coinciding with the opening of the railway through Northamptonshire, demonstrate a steadfast conviction that a demand for coach transport to London would continue, especially if fares were competitive. There was bound to be new business carrying railway passengers to the stations:

"T. SHAW respectfully informs his Friends and the Public that for their accommodation, Coaches will leave his Office to meet every Train for London and Birmingham, both at

Blisworth and Roade, commencing on Monday next. Any information may be obtained at the Angel Hotel, or at Mr. Shaw's Branch Coach Office, adjoining the Railway Company's Station at Roade. N.B. Post Horses Chaises and FLYS, at Roade.

Bridge Street, Sept 14. 1838"

(*Northampton Mercury* 15th September 1838, p. 3, col 3.) And separately:

"THE OLD NORTHAMPTON COACH,
AT REDUCED FARES, TO LONDON.
FIFTEEN SHILLINGS INSIDE.
EIGHT SHILLINGS OUTSIDE.

THE PUBLIC are most respectfully informed, that for their better accommodation, the above Coach will in future leave the ANGEL HOTEL, every Morning (Sundays excepted) at Eight o'clock, through Newport, Woburn, Dunstable and St. Albans and arrive at the George and Blue Boar, Holborn at Three o'clock in the afternoon.

"Leaves the George and Blue Boar at Half past Ten, and the Peacock, Islington, at Eleven o'clock the same morning, and arrives at Northampton at Half past Six o'clock.

Performed by THOS. SHAW, & CO.

"P.S. No change of Coach or Coachman, throughout."

On the following Saturday, the *Mercury* carried an advertisement for an entirely different "Old Northampton Coach" (22nd September, p. 3, col. 1):

"RAM INN, NORTHAMPTON,
OLD NORTHAMPTON COACH OFFICE.

THE Public are respectfully informed that the OLD NORTHAMPTON COACH continues running as usual from the above INN, every Morning (Sundays excepted) at nine o'clock, and from the Bull-and-Mouth Hotel, London, a half-past eleven, through Newport Pagnel, Woburn Dunstable, St. Albans and Barnet.

"Performed by their obedient servants,

SHERMAN & ELWORTHY, & Co

"Fares as low as any other Coach.

"September 21, 1838."

In Wellingborough, Messrs. Horne, Page, Gilbert & Co. issued their notice on 13th September:

"OPENING OF THE LONDON and BIRMINGHAM RAILWAY.

"In consequence of the opening of the London and Birmingham Railway on Monday, the 17th instant, the Public are respectfully informed that a COACH will, on and after that day, leave the White Hart Inn, WELLING-BOROUGH every Morning (Sundays excepted), at Half-Past Seven o'Clock, through Olney and Newport Pagnel, to the Station at Wolverton, without changing Coach or coach-man, and arrive in London at a Quarter-past One.

"The Down Coach will, on the same days, on the arrival of the Two o'Clock Train from London, leave Wolverton for Wellingborough.

"Passengers and Parcels booked at the George, and Blue Boar, Holborn.

"FARES

	s	d
From Wellingborough to Wolverton, Inside	6	0
Ditto Outside	4	0

The OLD WELLINGBOROUGH COACH, to London, every morning, Sundays excepted, at Half-past Seven o'clock.

The Down Coach will continue to leave London at the usual time.

FARES

	s	d
To London, Inside	18	0
Ditto Outside	10	0"

Many Northamptonshire main roads were turnpike roads, administered by trusts which were incorporated as profit-making businesses. Arthur Cossons has shown that the effect of the railway depended on the geographical relationship of the road to the places served by the new trains.[124] The profits of roads leading to stations continued to rise; but roads serving distant towns on the railway, even if the route was remote from the line, fell as the traffic was absorbed by the train service. The 1839 tolls on the Old Stratford to Dunchurch turnpike road were less than half those of 1834. Was the railway company anticipating sabotage?

"LONDON and BIRMINGHAM Railway.
TEN POUNDS REWARD.
The above Reward will be PAID, on conviction, to parties giving information of any Person or Persons OBSTRUCTING or causing obstruction to the PASSAGE of the TRAINS on the London and Birmingham Railway.

"By order,   R. CREED. ⎱
       C. R. MOORSOM ⎰ Secretaries

"September 22, 1838"

(*Northampton Mercury* 29th September 1838, p. 1, col. 2.)

17th September 1838

MARY THE TRANSVESTITE STOPPING THE PETERBOROUGH TRAFFIC

On the day that the railway was officially opened in Northamptonshire, great excitement was caused when Mary Gretham appeared before Peterborough Magistrates, dressed as a man. She was charged with causing an obstruction. The explanation was given in the *Stamford Herald* of 22nd September 1838.

"The unfortunate creature had been discharged from the asylum, and finding that it was impossible to gain employment as a female, she assumed the male dress in which she then appeared" [in court]. During the harvest time, she had earned twelve shillings an acre as a reaper. she had then worked as a rick-maker and thatcher, earning half-a-crown a day "until a few weeks since, when, falling off a rick, she received a severe injury to her hip, when her master and mistress, to their surprise and horror, discovered her sex, which becoming public, she attracted the notice of the idle boys and people of the city, who followed her in crowds on her going to seek some relief. She stated that some money was owing to her for work done for her late master, and she was sent to the workhouse, until inquiry could be made. . . ."

22nd September 1838

A VIOLENT EVENING AT HANNINGTON

A fire started in Hannington, early on Saturday evening, 22nd September. Among those helping to put it out, were some Brixworth men who were evidently led to believe that they would be rewarded with drinks when the job was done. No one told the local publican. Whether or not the misunderstanding was wilful on the part of the fire-fighters, there was a riotous incident in the public house when they were refused beer. As a result, William Cockerill and seven other men were indicted, and appeared before Northamptonshire Quarter Sessions, on its second day: Friday, 19th October 1838, charged with assaulting Nicholas Marsh, Constable, at Hannington. Mr. Waddington, prosecuting, called five witnesses. This is their version of events:

William Coleman: I keep a public house at Hannington. A fire broke out between six and seven o'clock on the night of 22nd September. My house is about two hundred yards from the fire. About ten o'clock, several men came into the house in a very riotous manner. They forced their way into the cellar. I sent for Marsh, the constable, to protect me and my property. They broke the glasses, and stopped me from drawing beer.

Nicholas Marsh: I am a constable, of Hannington. I was assisting at the fire. I went home at ten o'clock, but I was called to Mr. Coleman's house. The cellar was full of people

251

when I arrived there. I said I wished them to leave the cellar. They said they would not – till they had some beer. They did leave the cellar, and then I wished them to go home. Cockerill said he would sooner see the town in flames, and every farmer in it. Mr. Pell was there, and he wished me to charge somebody to assist in getting them out of the house. I produced my staff, and I ordered them to quit the house. Two of them, Tyrrell and Kaber then held my staff, and said, "Let's pull the bloody constable out and do for him." They then dragged me along the passage, and attempted to get my staff from me. Mr. Pell and some others came to my assistance. They then broke the door of the beer-engine.

Mr. Miller, for the defence, cross-examining: If this incident was so serious, why were these men not apprehended without delay? it was a long time before they were taken, was it not?

Marsh: I live five or six miles from Brixworth. The prisoners were taken up six days after the occurrence.

Thomas Pell: I live at Moulton Lodge. I was at Hannington at the time of the fire. Marsh, the constable, was called in to quell a disturbance. I went into the cellar of Coleman's house and found Marsh there. There were a great number of people there. Cockerill was kicking up a great disturbance, and wanted to fight me. I told Marsh he had better get assistance. I was knocked down in the passage, and Cockerill put his fist in my face and said, "Damn your eyes, what have you to do with it?" I had a candle in my hand, which they knocked out, and they threw me down.

Two other witnesses confirmed that the accused men had become violent when beer was refused them. For the defence, Mr. Miller told the jury that "it was a mere scuffle for ale which had been ordered for them . . .". The jury retired for a few minutes, returned and acquitted two of the men, who were discharged. The other six were found guilty. Cockerill was sentenced to nine months in prison with hard labour. The others were sentenced to six months and three months.

25th September 1838

THE STATUTE FAIR AT KETTERING

The Statute Fair could also be called the Hiring Fair, at which prospective servants could offer themselves for employment. William Hircock, who went to live in Kettering in 1838, was interviewed at the age of 93 in March 1904.[93]

> "When was the statute fair? Every Year on Sept. 25th. The servants used to stand on the pavement on the Market-hill for the ladies to look at. Drivers wore a bit of whipcord in their hats, shepherds a piece of wool, thackers a bit of straw, so that those who wanted to engage them would know what they were before they were hired. . . . It was quite a holiday. Young men brought their sweethearts; it was quite a 'rum and water night'."

1st October 1838

POLITE THIEVES

That was the heading over a story in the *Lincolnshire Chronicle* of 6th October 1838.

> "At the Peterborough Fair on Monday [1st October], Mr. Vergette of Marholm, was hustled and robbed of his gold watch, fifteen sovereigns, and a cheque for £60. A few minutes after the robbery, one of the thieves, accosting him with great civility, gave him back the cheque, saying that he feared it would prove useless to his friends, and might be of service to him. The thief most politely thanked Mr. Vergette and darted amongst the crowd."

Is it possible that the victim of this ridiculous incident, is the Robert Vergette, whose 1846 cast-iron grave memorial still stands in Marholm church-yard?

4th October 1838

DRESS SHOEMEN WANTED

"TO DRESS SHOEMEN, &c.

E. COOK, St. John Street, NORTHAMPTON, can give Employment to Superior Dress Workmen at the under Wages.

Dress Button Boots   2s 3d. per pair
Dress Shoes   2s 1d.

Oct 4th, 1838."

(*Northampton Mercury* 6th October 1838, p. 3.)

15th October 1838

KETTERING'S RAIL LINK

"THE RISING SUN COACH
FROM THE GEORGE INN, KETTERING, TO LONDON.

The Public are respectfully informed, that for their better accommodation, on and after Monday next the 15th inst. the above Coach will leave the George Inn, Kettering, every morning (Sundays excepted) at a quarter past eight, through Northampton, to the RAILWAY STATION, at ROADE, arriving in time for the First-class Train at 11 o'clock, which reaches London at two p.m. Leaves London every afternoon at two o'clock, and arrives at Kettering at a quarter before eight in the evening.

Passengers and parcels booked. . . . Performed by CHAPMAN, SHAW, & CO.

Kettering, October 12th, 1838"

(*Northampton Mercury* 13th October 1838, p. 2, col. 6.)

15th October 1838

PROBLEM CHILDREN AT THE SUNDAY SCHOOL

The oldest Teachers' Minutes Book of the Rushden Park Road Baptist Sunday School shows that a meeting took place on the evening of Monday, October 15th, at which difficult children were discussed.[16] The entry states:

> "It is agreed that the scholars behaving bad during service shall be forfeited one ticket. It is further agreed that Mrs. Whittemore shall visit the friends of such children that neglect the School to investigate the cause."

Mrs Whittemore was the wife of the Baptist Minister. There is no clue as to what the tickets were for.

28th October 1838

HE MARRIED HIS GRANDMOTHER

An anonymous letter was printed in *The Times* on Friday 16th November 1838, from "One of the Oundle Board of Guardians".

> ". . . A young man, aged twenty, who was illegitimate, applied lately to the clergyman of his parish (Glapthorne) to be married to a young woman of the same age, the widow of his reputed grandfather. The clergyman having refused to perform the service, the parties applied to the superintendent registrar of the district, Mr. Tibbits, who commenced giving notices as required [by the 1836 Marriage Act] in the Board room. The clergyman upon this, entered a *caveat* against the marriage, on the ground of the affinity of the parties. The superintendent registrar immediately consulted the registrar-general, and was informed in reply that 'however objectionable the marriage . . . may be in a moral point of view, yet the *caveat*

does not contain any grounds on which the marriage can be legally prevented'. Mr. Tibbits . . . felt it to be his duty to proceed, and the parties . . . were actually married by him on 28th [October]."

People were becoming adjusted to changes in marriage customs. The first Registry Office wedding had been solemnized in August 1837, and the first legally-recognized wedding in a Northampton nonconformist church, a month later. Notices such as the following were common in the press at this time:

"[Duty Free] NOTICE is hereby given, That a separate Building named SALEM CHAPEL, situated in Salem Lane, in the Parish of WELLINGBOROUGH, . . . in the District of the Wellingborough Union, being a Building certified according to Law as a Place of Religious Worship, was, on the first day of November, 1838, duly REGISTERED for Solemnizing MARRIAGES therein, pursuant to the Act of 6th and 7th Wm. 4th, Cap. 85.

"Witness my hand this second day of November, 1838
HENRY M. HODSON, Superintendent Registrar."

(*Northampton Mercury* 3rd November 1838, p. 2, col. 5.)

30th October 1838

THE FOXHUNTER REGRETTED THE DEATH OF THE FOX

A fox that had been hiding in an open drain at Whilton, emerged foolishly among the Pytchley hounds. The incident prompted a rather incoherent letter over the pen-name "BRUSH" in the *Northampton Herald* of 3rd November 1838 (p. 3, col. 6).

"Sir – Open drains are general nuisances, and more so to the occupier of the land than to any one else; he has his drain broken up, in several places; his land unnecessarily trampled upon, and his poultry placed in additional jeopardy by the shelter he gives a fox near his yard. But the annoyance does not stop with himself. A whole field is often deprived of sport for the day: either the fox is disabled, by the dampness of the ground, from running, or, as on Tuesday last [30th October 1838], at Whilton, he is sacrificed to the huntsman's cupidity [and is added to] . . . a long list of deaths. Nothing can excuse the start of a fox from a drain among the hounds, but a long series of ill-luck in killing. We had experienced great difficulty in finding, and were therefore, the more surprised at this wanton sacrifice of a good fox. I may venture to say good, for he broke away from Nobottle Wood in gallant style and led us straight away through the open to Whilton, disdaining plantations, hedgerows &c."

30th October 1838

"ACCIDENTALLY BURNT TO DEATH"

That was the jury's verdict at an inquest on Tuesday, 6th November 1838 conducted by George Abbey, Coroner, in Northampton. It was briefly reported in the *Northampton Herald* of 10th November 1838 (p. 3, col. 3). The name of the deceased was not mentioned. It was

"a child of Mr. Lay's, a hatter, of the Market Square. It appeared that the child was left in [the] charge of a little girl, a niece of Mr. Lay's, named Mary Dalorzo, on Tuesday week [30th October], who left it, hearing her brother crying in the street. While she was absent, a brother of the deceased, a little boy about four years old, put a piece of string into the fire and threw it upon her, which ignited her clothes, and occasioned her death . . .".

1st November 1838

A DAVENTRY ADVENTURE MISSED BY THE YOUNG GENTLEMEN

"As an elderly man was walking up the Dog-lane, in Daventry, in the afternoon of Thursday the 1st [November], a very fine hare passed him at moderate pace, making for the High Street, but on her arriving opposite the road leading to Mr. Hewitt's Academy, she was, with some difficulty, turned by a boy into the gateway, followed by him and the man. On her arrival on the playground, the gate was immediately closed, and Mr. Hewitt, who happened to be there, stood to prevent her escape, while the man and the boy chased her round the playground till nearly exhausted, when, after several ineffectual attempts to jump over the brick wall, she at last took refuge in the parlour, and was safely captured by the man, alive and without injury. Unfortunately the young gentlemen were out walking at the time, or no doubt they would have been highly delighted."

(*Northampton Herald* 10th November 1838, p. 3, col. 3.)

2nd November 1838

CLARENCE MEN AND BLUCHER MEN WANTED

(See the entry for 11th May 1838.) A Clarence was an ankle-boot with a gusset in the side. It was the forerunner of the elastic-sided boot, but with a soft leather insert instead of elastic.[125] The following advertisement is dated "November 2d, 1838" (*Northampton Mercury* 3rd November 1838, p. 2, col. 4).

"TO BOOT AND SHOEMAKERS.

GOOD Workmen of the following descriptions may have full employ, good materials, and the best wages, by application to GEORGE MOORE, Horse-Market: Clump Clarence Boots, best sprigged Clarence and Middling Clarence, Clump Bluchers, best sprigged Bluchers, Cloth Boots, &c &c."

Why "Clarence"? Why "Blucher"? Before his accession, King William IV was the Duke of Clarence. Blucher was the commander of the Prussian army that fought on Britain's side against Napoleon at Waterloo.

November 1838

THE CHANGING LANDSCAPE OF KETTERING

Robert Smith's 1826 map of Kettering shows a very large complex of buildings directly to the west of the parish church. It stretched from the very narrow main street opposite the George Inn and George Lane, right up to the tower of the church. The same area in modern Kettering is occupied by the impressive rising approach to the church, the southern half of the market square, and the wide street. A report on the progress of re-arrangement of this area was printed in the *Northampton Mercury* of 3rd November 1838 (p. 3, col. 6):

". . . By the removal of the buildings which formerly obstructed the entrance to the west font of [the] church, a considerable portion of ground has been thrown open, with the kind consent of his Grace the Duke of Buccleuch, by which means the tower and spire, so universally admired . . . are exhibited to public view. Upwards of £200 has already been expended in the removal of the buildings, and the erection of walls to enclose the ground. This expenditure having exhausted the monies already collected, a new subscription is now commenced . . . it being estimated that at least £150 more will be wanted to erect iron palisades, with a gateway in front, steps at the basement of the tower, and to repair the window therein. . . ."

3rd November 1838

RAILWAY CONSIDERATIONS

After six weeks, the railway was no longer a novelty, and had become an accepted feature of Northamptonshire life. Many lives and livelihoods had been affected by it. The prospect of further railway building in the county was not looked upon as good by some people. Their opinions were expressed at length and with regularity in the *Northampton Herald*. Letters from travellers who had experienced discomfort, inconvenience or discourtesy were given prominence in the columns of the *Herald*. The *Railway Times*, organ of the London and Birmingham Company, said:

". . . There is an obscure print published in the county of Northampton, at no great distance from the line, which, for some reason or other (probably none of the purest), has, for a considerable time past, lent its columns to the vilification of this Company – nay, has publicly invited the communications of all who may feel discontented or dissatisfied with their arrangements, pledging itself to give currency to the accusation. . . . So long as the calumny is confined to the pages of the provincial journalist, there is no great harm done . . . but when as not infrequently occurs, the slanders are copied into the *Times*, and other influential papers, the conductors of which may believe them to be well-founded, the public are misled, and the Company wronged to a very serious extent. . . ."

The *Northampton Mercury* of 3rd November carried a strong defence of the railway, and attacked the *Herald*:

". . . The present reduced coach fares from this place to London – reduced solely in consequence of the opening of the railway – are given as though they were the *permanent* fares. if we can travel in the inside of a coach at this moment for 15 shillings instead of 24 shillings and on the outside for 8 shillings instead of 15 shillings, it is to the railway alone that we are indebted for the benefit. . . ." (p. 3, col. 2).

The same issue of the *Mercury* (p. 2, col. 1), reproduced a delightful piece of sarcasm in defence of the railways.

"We are indebted to a correspondent for the following enumeration of the weighty considerations which should induce the inhabitants of this county to petition parliament against the Railways. ANTI-RAILWAY PETITION.

'We beg to recommend to the consideration of those who may be engaged in drawing up this important document, the following cogent reasons for the immediate abolition of all Railways, and the London and Birmingham in particular:

1. That it has thrown out of employ many bargemen, cads, hostlers, and stable boys of high character and great moral worth, who, by reason of the extreme delicacy of their usual occupations, may find a difficulty in turning their hand to anything more laborious than picking pockets or executing thimble-rig.

2. That her Majesty's subjects instead of suffering with Spartan-like heroism the excruciating tortures of a stage coach are now compelled to sit with comparatively luxurious ease and comfort; by which means the hitherto bold and hardy Briton runs a risk of dwindling into the effeminate and feather-bed milk-sop.

3. That the policemen in the employ of this company are of such respectable prepossessing appearance as to unsettle the minds of many cooks and housemaids living near the line: a circumstance which it is to be apprehended may cause a lamentable increase of "sweethearting", to imprudent marriages, and the consequent increase of population in this already over-peopled country.

4. That railways may occasionally become a slight inconvenience to fox-hunters, whose interests in this

commercial country should, of course, be watched with the tenderest solicitude.

5. That the shareholders are now expected to receive an annual dividend of eight or nine percent, as the reward of their spirit and enterprise, an anticipation which has a bad tendency towards engendering envy, jealousy. . . .

6. That since the opening of the line, no less than two band-boxes have been materially damaged, and three or four small people lost all their temper.

7. That the advertisements concerning the arrival and departure of the trains were not sent to the *Northampton Herald* till after the earnest and reiterated applications of the proprietor.

8. That many country gentlemen of good repute and tender consciences, have, in an unguarded moment, been seduced by a love of filthy lucre, to ask and accept about eight times the value of their land; a proceeding which has ruined their peace of mind to a degree which makes them anxious to take back their acres and restore such ill-gotten wealth.

9. That the company having insisted on paying their own servants, take it out of the power of a free-born Englishman to display that generosity which was wont to keep up such a kindly feeling between coachmen, guards and porters on the one hand, and passengers on the other.

10. That sundry porters, constables, labourers and inspectors, having been tormented with silly questions beyond the power of human temper's endurance, have not answered with that alacrity and humiliation which the consequence and mightiness of the interrogators would have approved of.

11. That the valuable time of many people is now taken up in writing frivolous and vexatious complaints, to the great grief of their acquaintances, who fancy that these imaginary sufferers might, without at all compromising their dignity, have shown a little more toleration and indulgance, or even better taste and feeling.

12. That the inhabitants of Northamptonshire having opposed by every means in their power, the designs of the London and Birmingham Railway Company, feel them-

selves extremely ill-used at only having six stations, either in or on the very borders of their county.'

In addition to which, we would recommend to above-mentioned concocters of this petition by no means to omit the old but highly sensible and delectable remark, that 10 miles an hour is quite fast enough! Ha! Ha! Ha! most wise, profound, and far-sighted generation!"

The provision of accommodation for railway travellers was, of course, an expanding industry. Here is the evidence of two "New Inns":

"NEW INN, ROAD.

ROBERT BECKETT, returns his most grateful thanks to his numerous Friends and Customers for past favors [sic], and begs to inform them that his house has undergone a thorough repair, and he should be most happy to accom-modate them or others passing to and from the Railway Station, Road.

WELL-AIRED BEDS
WINE AND SPIRITS OF THE PUREST QUALITY,
Home Brewed Ale, and London Porter,
DUBLIN STOUT, SCOTCH ALE, LEMONADE,
& SODA WATER,
Good Corn, Hay, and Grass Keeping,
STALLED & OTHER STABLING.

The New Inn is situated on the Northampton road, half a mile from the London and Birmingham Railway Station, Road.

Valuations made on Farming Stock, and Crops, as usual."

This notice was published in the *Northampton Mercury* of 3rd November (p. 1, col. 4). It was in fact rather more than half a mile from the station. At some time during the follow-ing ten years this inn was the scene of a curious adventure involving a London detective sergeant, the railway, and a wanted criminal known as "Tally-Ho Thompson". It was recorded by none other than Charles Dickens in *Household Words*.

The other "New Inn" was advertised on the front pages of the two following issues of the *Mercury*, 10th and 17th November:

"NEW INN
AND RAILWAY ACCOMMODATION HOUSE, WEEDON
RALPH HUMPHREY, having made arrangements for the
superior accommodation of RAILWAY PASSENGERS, &c.
begs most respectfully to solicit the support of the Gentry
and the Public in general; and trusts from the advantages of
a suitable locality, and by unremitting attention to the
comforts of his supporters, to realize a liberal share of
public patronage.

Conveyances from the Station for Passengers and Parcels
to the neighbouring Towns and Villages.

Good Stabling, loose Boxes, and lock-up Coach-houses."

A new weekly market was soon to become another
beneficial effect of the railway at Weedon (see 11th
December).

November 1838

THE MYSTERY OF THE DUKE OF BUCCLEUCH'S SILVER PLATE

There is no mention in any of the biographies of the 7th Earl
of Cardigan, of the missing silver plate of the Duke of
Buccleuch. The Dowager Duchess of Buccleuch who died in
1827 was second-cousin of Cardigan, and left a service of
silver plate for the use of his father. Should any Earl of
Cardigan die without male heir, the silver was to be returned
to the possession of the Buccleuch family. When the 7th Earl
returned from India in 1838, he found the silver in the strong
room of the London house. In November, he signed an order:
"Deliver my plate chest to Messrs. Garrod." Garrod was a
London silver smith, and it was believed that the plate in
question was melted down and re-modelled or sold. This
evidence was produced in the Rolls Court, when the Duke of
Buccleuch, after Cardigan's death, claimed the value of the
plate from his estate.

Why should Cardigan want the value of the silver rather than its use? He was a serving army officer, commanding a regiment now at Canterbury, and having inherited a vast estate. In fact, he was spending a large sum on his Northamptonshire home at Deene, which was "undergoing extensive repairs and additions". The *Northampton Herald* reported this on 22nd September 1838 (p. 3, col. 3). The work at Deene must have been considerable, because the Earl and Countess took Hales Place, near Canterbury, for twelve months. At the end of August, the Conservatives of Kettering gave a huge banquet in honour of the Earl of Cardigan, which was reported by the *Northampton Herald* in a special supplement. The *Northampton Mercury* gave it a mention of five lines − treatment which the *Herald* considered outrageous.

George Loy Smith,[126] a soldier serving under Cardigan at this time, described "most severe punishments for trivial offences" resulting in many desertions. "Our greatest trouble" was the white sheepskins that had been cleaned by servants in India. Whatever cleaning agent had been used turned them "a very bad colour". Cardigan was now insisting that they must be pure white. Many extra parades were ordered, sometimes involving the whole regiment. On one occasion, the men were sitting on the grass near the barracks, "beating the chalk out of their sheepskins" and singing *Rule Britannia* (". . . Britons never, never, never, shall be slaves"). Cardigan sent the adjutant to tell them not to make so much noise.

In the Rolls Court in 1870, the order was that the value of the missing silver should be paid out of the Cardigan estate.

November 1838

PROSPECTING FOR COAL AT KINGSTHORPE

There is no coal in Northamptonshire. There have been several attempts to find some.[127] In 1766 exploratory boring at Kettering was abandoned because no rich sponsor could be found. In 1791, Earl Fitzwilliam financed trial bores on his land at Great Harrowden. The Earl of Westmorland financed an exploration at Nassington. Towards the end of the nineteenth century there were searches at Orton (1884), and near the railway at Wellingborough in 1893. The most expensive of these failures was the experiment that began at Kingsthorpe in 1836. The operation went on for several years, public interest being kept alive by fraudulent rumours of actual discoveries of coal. One of these reports was put out in mid-November 1838. It was dismissed lightly by the *Northampton Mercury* of 17th November, but this reaction drew the fury of the *Herald* on 24th November (p. 3, col. 1):

"Search for Coal — The *Mercury* of Saturday last, noticed with a kind of sneer, the report that coal had been discovered at Kingsthorpe. Now whether coal be discovered or not, the question is a very important one as concerns . . . the prosperity of Northampton. Should the search, conducted as it is, at great expense, be rewarded with success, the inhabitants . . . will have reason to thank the triumphant company beyond the power of language to express. . . . Great disgust was felt, and naturally so, by many inhabitants that read the paragraph to which we refer. . . ."

13th November 1838

THE LAST BULL-RUNNING RIOT AT STAMFORD ST. MARTIN'S

13th November was the day of the traditional bull-running in the streets of Stamford. Bull baiting had been made illegal in September 1835. This being a law of the Whig Government, the Stamford Tories encouraged the men of the town to defy it. See under this date in 1837 how the bull-running had been done successfully. In 1838 the Home Secretary, Lord John Russell, was determined that it should not take place. At noon on Saturday 10th November, thirty-five troopers of the 14th Regiment of Light Dragoons arrived from Northampton Barracks, under the command of Captain Harvey. The evening of that day saw the arrival of a dozen police officers of "A" Division of the Metropolitan Police. A year previously, the Stamford Magistrates had sworn in 240 townsmen as special constables, but they had done more harm than good.

The 1838 events were described in the *Stamford Mercury*, whose version was borrowed by the *Northampton Mercury* on 24th November. The Stamford editor was strongly opposed to the bull-running, which was "a scandalous interruption of business, and the violation of the public peace and safety". Some time during Tuesday 13th, a dealer drove nine cows through the town, with a cart containing a bull calf. Was this an innocent journey, or was it planned? They headed south, over the Welland Bridge into the Northamptonshire parish of St. Martin's. All was quiet until they were "opposite a house, for which Mr. Ryde, the steward of the Marquis of Exeter, is assessed". The implication is that what happened next occurred at a building owned by the Tories. Suddenly a gang of men emerged and set upon the cart. They pulled out the young bull and drove him back to the centre of the town "followed by an immense concourse of yelling persons". They were driven back over the river. In St. Martin's again, near the nunnery, Captain Harvey and his Dragoons joined in to assist the police. There was "a very sharp collision" with the mob, in the lane behind the George Inn, "from the river to the Sun public house". The little bull was recaptured, and the police and soldiers were "violently pelted with stones".

26th November 1838

HOW COGENHOE GOT A NEW CHURCH CLOCK

There is an entry in the churchwardens' accounts at Cogenhoe for the year 1838, that states:

"Nov. 26 To Mr. Corby of Castle Ashby for an 8 day clock
for the church with iron movement & dial
as per estimate   £25
fixing same by agreement   £5
Total   £30.0.0."

John Ouless, the incumbent at Cogenhoe in 1974,[128] wrote that the clock was still there, "with the name J. Corby, Castle Ashby, stamped on the inner dial." Corby was the carpenter on the Castle Ashby estate. Although the clock was described as "8 day", said Ouless, "we know to our cost, that as fitted, it will only go for 24 hours per wind".

It is interesting to note how, in 1838, money was made available for this clock. The vestry minutes explain.

"At a Vestry meeting held in Cooknoe on June the 18th, 1838, for the purpose of considering the propriety of having a Church Clock, it was unanimously agreed to offer to Mr. Sharman a lease of the Church Lands for a Term of fourteen years for the sole purpose of defraying the expense of the said clock. And Mr. Sharman having consented to place in the hands of the trustees of the said lands a sum of thirty pounds in consideration of a lease for the above period which lease shall commence on St. Thomas's day next ensuing, it was resolved that a lease be made out accordingly, and the necessary instructions be given for putting up the clock."

27th November 1838

THE VICAR OF FLORE IN THE COURT OF QUEEN'S BENCH

A law of 1746 (Statute 18 Geo II, c.20) stated that no person should be a justice of the peace unless he owned land with an annual value of £100, and that value had to be over and above all expenses and debts. The Vicar of Flore was a justice of the peace. The living of Flore was worth £500 per annum, but the Reverend Mr. Tarpley was in debt. A writ had been issued against his property, but the Sheriff of Northamptonshire had made a return that he had no goods or chattels in his baili-wick. In 1834 a Court had directed a writ to the Bishop of Peterborough, endorsed for the sum of £2,276. The allowance out of the rents and profits of the living at Flore to Mr. Tarpley, and out of which the upkeep of the Church had to come, was only £120.

The case of Pack v. Tarpley, Clerk, heard in the Court of Queen's Bench on Tuesday 27th November 1838, was a peculiar action to recover a penalty of £100. This was a fine ordered by the Vicar in his capacity of magistrate. It was alleged that because of the debt, he was not qualified. The Court had to decide whether or not a sequestration having been issued against the living, which was the defendant's qualification for serving as a justice, caused the living to be no longer a qualification.

The plaintiff's case was that Tarpley's possession was as nominee of the Bishop, at whose pleasure he was remove-able. The defendant's case was that the sequestration did not vest the fee in the bishop, and so the Vicar was qualified.

The Court took time to consider.[129] The ultimate judgment awaits anyone, a Flore historian perhaps, who considers it worth a visit to the Public Record Office.

30th November 1838

WATERPROOF THIGH BOOTS &c

A Northampton boot-maker issued his advertisement on 30th November.

"ROWLAND FISHER,
BOOT MAKER, DRAPERY, NORTHAMPTON
RETURNS his grateful Thanks to the Nobility, Gentry, and the Public in general, for the unexpected patronage already received, and begs to inform them that he manufactures the newly invented WATERPROOF THIGH BOOTS, for Hunters; TOP BOOTS, DRESS WELLINGTONS, &c. &C. and every Article in general wear, equal to any London House.
    Patent Vegetable Boot-Top Powder, and Everett's Blacking. . . ."

(*Northampton Mercury* 1st December 1838, p. 3, col. 2.)

December 1838

COACHES IN THE WINTER

At the time of year when in previous years, coach services would have been restricting themselves to more limited winter schedules, the two Northampton firms were showing no signs of flagging in their competition with the railway and with each other. Thomas Shaw was now calling his version of the Old Northampton Coach the True Old Northampton. William Elworthy, having dropped the name Sherman from the name of the firm, was libellous as ever against his rival Shaw. Both had greatly reduced their London fares.

Thomas Shaw began his new series of advertisements in the *Northampton Mercury* of 1st December 1838 (p. 3, col. 2):

"THE TRUE OLD NORTHAMPTON COACH.
THE PROPRIETORS of this Old Favourite, in offering their best thanks to its extensive circle of friends, beg to assure

them, they are so anxious to preserve a continuance of that patronage and support which they have for many years been favoured with, that they are determined if it be possible, by exertion in superior working, and the REDUCTION of their FARES still to receive that decided preference (The strongest testimony of Public approbation) which has so long been their encouragement and reward.

On Monday next the Fares to and from London will commence at

Inside   12s. only.
Outside   6s. only.

The True Old Northampton leaves the Angel Hotel every morning (except Sunday) at a Quarter before Nine o'clock, and by its usual route, arrives in London, at half past three o'clock in the Afternoon.

Passengers and Parcels are booked at the George and Blue Boar, Holborn, and the Peacock Islington, London; the latter of which it leaves at Eleven o'clock A.M. and arrives at Seven o'clock in the evening, at the Angel Hotel, Northampton.

To those Ladies and Gentlemen who prefer the old-fashioned way of travelling as superior to the new, the True Old Northampton offers in every respect, the safest and best accommodation they can wish for.

THOS. SHAW & Co. Proprietors. . . ."

William Elworthy issued his responding advertisement, including a vitriolic attack on Shaw, from the Ram Inn at Northampton on 14th December (*Northampton Mercury* 15th December 1838 (p. 3, col. 1):

"Are the Inhabitants of Northampton and its Vicinity to have a Coach to and from London or not?

OLD NORTHAMPTON COACH OFFICE.
RAM INN, SHEEP STREET, NORTHAMPTON.
THE Public are respectfully informed that the OLD NORTHAMPTON COACH will, in future leave the above INN at half-past eight o'clock in the Morning, instead of nine; and from the Bull and Mouth, London, at half-past eleven, as usual.

271

FARES – to London, inside, only . . . 12s.!!, outside, only 6s.!!!

The above alteration, in time and fares, is made in consequence of the violent and unworthy opposition of Mr. Shaw to a Coach which he, only a short time since, declined working – gave it up as worthless – and insulted the Town of Northampton generally, by saying he would never work a Northampton Coach again. He, then, *great man*, thought he had all the power in his own hands, and could compel every person to go to London when and how he pleased. A very little experience soon made him feel the mistake he had made, and he is now again supplicating that support he so lately spurned, and boasts that he will carry passengers for nothing, and give them breakfast at starting, but he will ruin the Old Northampton (POOR man, he reckons without his host). But it is evident, his object is, if possible, to run us off the road; and what have the public then to expect from him, but that he will serve them as he has done before – leave them without any Coach-accommodation, and turn them again over to the great Railroad Monopolists!

"The Proprietors of the OLD NORTHAMPTON COACH, Wm. Elworthy & Co . . . beg to assure [the public] that IT SHALL *continue running* for their accommodation, notwithstanding every effort of combination to effect its ruin.

Ram Inn, Northampton, Dec. 14. 1838."

Meanwhile the Wellingborough coach service, with no serious rival, was following normal practice and going into a reduced winter service:

"WELLINGBOROUGH, OLNEY, NEWPORT, AND WOBURN POST COACH

The Public are respectfully informed, that the above Coach will, for the Winter Season, leave the White Hart Inn, Wellingborough, every Monday, Tuesday, Thursday, and Saturday Morning at half-past seven o'clock, to the George and Blue Boar, Holborn, London:

the Down Coach will, on the same Mornings, leave the above Inn at half-past ten; Cross Keys, St. John Street, at a quarter before eleven; and the Peacock, Islington, at eleven o'clock precisely.

Fares from Wellingborough, Inside, 16s., out 9s.
Messrs. HORNE, PAGE, GILBERT & Co. Proprietors.
N.B. The RAILWAY COACH from the above Inn will be DISCONTINUED on WEDNESDAY and FRIDAY for the remainder of the Winter Months, but will continue to run on Monday, Tuesday, Thursday, and Saturday Mornings, leaving Wellingborough at half-past seven o'clock, through Olney and Newport, to meet the Train at Wolverton Station, which arrives at London at fourteen minutes past one. The Down Coach will, on the same days, on the arrival of the two o'clock Train from London, leave Wolverton for Wellingborough at five o'clock. Fares from Wellingborough, Inside, 6s., out 4s.
To commence on Monday the 10th of December, 1838."

(*Northampton Mercury* 8th December 1838, p. 2, col. 6.)

9th December 1838

GOOD MORNING POACHERS

"A notorious gang of about fifteen poachers was observed in the preserves of W. L. W. Samwell, Esq., of Upton Hall, near this town, about two o'clock on Sunday morning."

reported the *Northampton Mercury* of 15th December 1838 (p. 3, col. 6). The observers were Samwell's keeper, George Harrison, and two of his men, who evidently decided that, as they were outnumbered, five to one, there was little that could be done. Harrison called out to the gang: "Good morning." The poachers were most likely expecting a more forceful challenge, but Harrison called out: "We know you, but we wish you to go on. We do not wish to have any piece of work with you." The poachers, however, attacked the keeper and his assistants, with sticks, and guns used as clubs. Harrison's head was severely cut. His two companions were both knocked down several times. Three Harpole men were the ringleaders, two brothers who were shoemakers, and a farm-labourer. On Monday morning, Harrison went to a magistrate and . . . a warrant for their apprehension was issued.

11th December 1838

A NEW MARKET AT WEEDON

An important benefit of the railway, increased opportunities for trade, was realised by producers in the Weedon district. They organised themselves and held the first of their weekly markets on Tuesday 11th December. The success of it was enthusiastically described in their advertisement in the *Northampton Mercury* of 15th December 1838 (p. 3, col. 2).

"WEEDON ROYAL, near Daventry.

On account of the unparalleled facility of access to WEEDON, the Holyhead Road, the Grand Junction Canal, and the London and Birmingham Railway, all passing through the town; Weedon also being a Military Station, and in consequence of the Inhabitants having been particularly requested by the principal Farmers, Graziers, Corn-dealers, Cattle-dealers, and others, of the surrounding neighbourhood, to hold a

WEEKLY MEETING, AT WEEDON.

For the Sale of Corn, Flour, Cattle, Sheep, Pigs, Butchers Meat, Fish, Poultry, Butter, Eggs, Fruit, Vegetables, &c. &c. A Public Meeting was held on the 30th November, at the Red Lion Inn, Weedon . . . to take the subject into further consideration, when it was unanimously agreed to comply with the said requisition.
Weedon, Dec 4th, 1838.

"The Meeting at Weedon . . . took place on Tuesday last the 11th Instant, when the number of Gentlemen who attended, and the quantity of business done, far exceeded the most sanguine expectations.

274

"A Meeting of Gentlemen, Farmers, Graziers, Corn-dealers, Cattle-dealers, and others, formed themselves into a Committee, and appointed to meet at the Globe Inn Weedon, on Tuesday next, the 18th Instant, with a view to further the object . . . and also to make arrangements for four extra meetings, yearly. . . ."
Weedon. Dec. 15th, 1838."

13th December 1838

A MEAL AT THE CROSS GUNS

"A parish constable of Braunston, undertook the other day, for a trifling bet, to eat 2¾lbs of beef, 3lbs of potatoes, and 2lbs of bread, and to drink two quarts of ale, and six glasses of gin and water, in ten minutes. He won his wager at the Cross Guns public house, on Thursday week."
(*Northampton Mercury* 22nd December 1838, p. 3, col. 6.)

LAST WORD ON 1838

During the year, the slaves of Jamaica were finally emancipated. This was the great achievement of the Kettering missionary William Knibb. The law to abolish slavery in the British Empire had been passed five years earlier, but many slaves were still held in a form of compulsory apprenticeship. At the risk of his life, Knibb, the son of a Kettering tailor, caused the reluctant planters to recognise the wage-earning status of the former slaves.[130]

The greatest cause of death in Northamptonshire in 1838 (as elsewhere) was consumption (tuberculosis). There were 762 deaths from that cause, in a total mortality of 2,361.[131]

The Rector of Courteenhall was married to the daughter of Henry Grattan, the Irish politician and orator. The great man's widow died at the rectory in 1838. She has a memorial tablet in the church.

Workmen engaged on structural alterations at Rushton Hall discovered the walled-up door of a hidden closet in the passage leading into the great hall. Inside this hiding place, wrapped up in a large sheet, were the family papers of the Treshams. Francis Tresham, shortly before the Gunpowder Plot of 1605, having associated with the plotters, paid a last visit to the family home at Rushton. He discharged the servants, walled up the Tresham records, shut up Rushton Hall, and took his mother and sisters to London.[132]

In 1838 at Marston Trussell, Stephen Flint was turned off the land he held from the parsonage share of the fields. This church holding was very large (314 acres) and the rules were strict.[133] The minutes of the Easter Vestry at Marston Trussell show that Flint's eviction was for bad husbandry. Instead of ploughing the stubble back into the land, he had cut the straw and taken it for his own use.

Three orphaned Pytchley girls, with their mother and stepfather, emigrated to South Australia. They were Charlotte, Caroline and Emma Dean, aged 13, 11 and 7, and on the "Prince George", they arrived at Port Adelaide in December 1838. Life was very hard in the colony, but all three were still alive in 1920.[134]

In the autumn of 1838, the young Queen Victoria appointed a new Lady in Waiting. She was Lady Sarah Lyttelton, the recently widowed daughter of the second Earl Spencer of Althorp.[135] She was 51 years old. Within months, she was one of the Whig ladies whom the Queen refused to dismiss at the insistence of the Tory leader Sir Robert Peel, in the notorious "Bedchamber" incident.

A five-year-old boy was bending over while his father administered a birching. Let us hope that this painful ritual did not happen too often. When the punishment was over, the boy was asked for his opinion. "It did not hurt much," he said. "There was a brown owl flying by." The boy was Thomas Powys, of Lilford Hall, later 4th Lord Lilford, and the most famous ornithologist of the century.[136]

276

14th January 1839

THE PRIVATE SCHOOLS REOPENING AFTER THE CHRISTMAS HOLIDAY

School attendance was not compulsory, and the only state interest in education was the payment of small annual grants to the schools of the National Society and the British and Foreign Society. There were a few of their schools in Northamptonshire, a few charity schools, and a few private schools. Only 1 in 24 of the population were receiving any schooling.[137] The private schools were before the public eye because they advertised.

> "LADIES BOARDING SCHOOL, MOULTON.
> THE MISSES STANTON BEG to inform their Friends and the Public that the DUTIES of their school will re-commence on Monday, January 14th 1839.
> TERMS: Board and Instruction in English Grammar, History, Geography, Writing, Arithmetic, plain and family Needlework. FIFTEEN GUINEAS per annum."

(*Northampton Mercury* 29th December 1838, p. 1, col. 1.)

> "YOUNG LADIES' BOARDING SCHOOL, GOLD STREET, NORTHAMPTON. MRS. WRIGHT . . . Re-opens on Monday the 14th January, 1839.
> TERMS, from 18 to 20 GUINEAS, according to the age and attainments of the Pupil. Music and Drawing on the usual terms."

(*Northampton Mercury* 29th December 1838, p. 3, col. 3.)

> "BOARDING SCHOOL FOR YOUNG LADIES, IRTHLING-BOROUGH, near Higham Ferrers. MISS BURY, with respect and gratitude for favors [sic] conferred, solicits a continuance of patronage, and announces to her Friends and the Public, her intention to recommence the Duties of her Establishment on Monday the 14th JAN. 1839."

(*Northampton Mercury* 5th January 1839, p. 1, col. 1.)

> "Messrs LATHBURY & JELLEY,
> BEG leave . . . [etc.] intend opening A SCHOOL at

WEEDON, on Monday, January 21st for the reception of Boarders and Day Scholars.

Messrs L. & J. were some years resident Masters at Brackley School, during the time of Mr. Lee, and since . . .

The Terms (which will be moderate) will comprehend instruction in the English, Latin, French and Greek Languages, Writing, Arithmetic, Geography, the Use of the Globes, Book-keeping, Land-Surveying, and other useful branches of the Mathematics . . .

Weedon; Dec. 27th, 1838."

(*Northampton Mercury* 5th January 1839, p. 1, col. 1.)

"MISS RUSSELL . . . her SCHOOL will re-open on the 21st Instant.

Brackley. Jan 1, 1839."

(*Northampton Mercury* 5th January 1839, p. 1, col. 2.)

"LADIES BOARDING SCHOOL, NORTHAMPTON.

Miss Whimple . . . after the Christmas Vacation she will have VACANCIES for TWO young Ladies as BOARDERS, who will be admitted on moderate terms, enjoy domestic comfort, and receive a liberal and useful education.

The DUTIES of the School will RE-COMMENCE on Monday January 21st, 1839."

(*Northampton Mercury* 22nd December 1838, p. 3, col. 1.)

"MISS EDWARDS

BEGS to thank her Friends for their continued Kindness, and informs them that her SCHOOL WILL RE-OPEN January 25th . . .

Wood-street, Northampton, Dec 21st, 1838."

(*Northampton Mercury* 22nd December 1838, p. 3, col. 2.)

29th January 1839

A FUSS ABOUT A PEW IN ALL SAINTS' CHURCH

Many advertisements for the sale of houses in towns at this period entice the prospective purchaser by stating that a pew in the parish church goes with the property. The position of a family pew in relation to the altar, was of social significance.

On Tuesday 29th January, 1839, the case of Becke v. Marshall and Page came before the Arches' Court in London. John Becke was a solicitor whose reputation was growing, but when he moved into Northampton he had been unable to secure a pew to his satisfaction in his parish church of All Saints. For this he blamed the churchwardens, and after five years, he promoted a suit against them in the Consistory Court held in All Saints' Church, on 6th September 1837. On that occasion, the Chancellor of the Diocese of Peterborough, Dr. Butler, found for the churchwardens, and awarded two thirds of the costs to them. The churchwardens' case was based on three points. The first was that Mr. Becke's landlord ought to have seated him. John Becke's answer to that was that the landlord had no pews which were not already occupied. The second defence was that Becke was at one time claiming to be seated in the Vicar's pew; and the third point was that he had been offered a seat which he had refused. John Becke said that upon his application for three vacated seats in the pew called the Vicar's pew, he was told that he might have them if he paid rent for them to Mr. Scriven, who occupied the remainder of the pew. Becke had objected to this because Scriven was not a parishioner, and in any case, a payment for a pew should be made to the Vicar or his churchwarden. Mr. Scriven had subsequently let the pew to friends of his own, without the sanction of the churchwardens, and when Becke commenced this suit, he had got himself rated to the All Saints' poor-rate, although only part of his garden was actually within the parish. No other suitable seats had been offered to Becke, and his proctor (representative) in that 1837 hearing, gave notice of appeal. That is how this matter came before the Arches' Court.[138]

Sir Herbert Jenner delivered the judgment: "This is an

appeal from a decision of the Chancellor of the Diocese of Peterborough, against the churchwardens, Marshall and Page . . . calling on them to show why they have not seated Mr. Becke, a parishioner, in a suitable and convenient seat or pew in the parish church . . . according to his situation and condition in life; Mr. Becke being an Attorney at Law and Solicitor in Her Majesty's Court at Westminster, and occupying a house in the aforesaid parish. Now the learned judge of the court below this . . . was of opinion that the answer of the churchwardens was sufficient; and he dismissed them from the suit. . . . The facts are . . . that Mr. Becke, in the year 1832, became an inhabitant of All Saints' in Northampton; that in 1833 or 1834, he occupied the house in which he now resides, and that in the month of November 1834, he applied to Mr. Phipps and Mr. Page, who were then the churchwardens, for a pew or sittings . . . and the grounds were, that he was a resident, occupying a principal house in the town, for which he paid the sum of £75 a year, and that his family consisted of himself, and at that time, of two sisters and a brother. There was no pew vacant, nor any sitting, but one in a pew at the south-east corner of the church . . . and as Mr. Becke said, it was used as a kind of accommodation pew for occasional attenders. This pew did not appear to be such as Mr. Becke thought his family ought to be seated in. . . . He also refused the offer of a seat in another family's pew because the head of that family wanted to charge a fee. In the year 1836, a further application was made. Mr. Becke says that other pews have become vacant, and have been allotted to other persons. I recommend that the churchwardens investigate pews held by non-parishioners, and by members of faculties, but I believe the previous decision to have been right. I am therefore of the opinion that I must dismiss the appeal; and I condemn Mr. Becke in the costs of the suit."

It is interesting to speculate whether there was a political element in this dispute. John Becke was later to become very prominent in the Whig Party, and election agent to Earl Spencer.

30th January 1839

SECOND CLASS BLISWORTH AND
FIRST CLASS ROADE

The nearest station to Northampton on the London and Birmingham Railway was Blisworth, but the Company was having difficulties with its premises there. The line passed over the main road at a height of fifty feet, and a suitable permanent site had not yet been decided. The nearest first-class station to Northampton was Roade. The trustees of the turnpike road through Blisworth had ideas for a site convenient for horse traffic, but they did not have the approval of the Railway Company. Captain Moorsom of the Company wrote to Mr. Howes of the Trustees:

"Birmingham, January 30th, 1839.

"Dear Sir,

"I have laid before the Directors your letter of 17th inst. with the Resolutions of the Trustees of the Towcester Road.

"After the full explanation given to you by Mr. Stephenson, of the difficulties presented by the height of the embankment, the quantity of material to be moved, and the consequent expense, the Directors regret that the Trustees continue in the opinion that the most eligible spot for a Station at Blisworth is the close called Cliff Hill.

"You must recollect that I also distinctly and more than once explained to the Trustees, that it was so difficult as to amount to an impracticability to make the necessary "siding" for the "up" or Eastern line at the spot in question, and that a Station there would afford only half the accommodation for private carriages which it is desirable to have, and on which the public lay so much stress.

The Resolutions allude to two sites, though naming only one. If the other be the level ground on the North side of the Canal, under Gayton Hill, the Directors are of the opinion a convenient Station may be formed there, and they are prepared to incur the expense of the Buildings providing the road and approaches are made to the satisfaction of the Company's Engineer, as I stated in my letter of 20th December.

The advantages of the level site to the Company are the saving of from £3,000 to £4,000 . . .

"In fact the spot chosen by the Trustees would only afford a very inconvenient Station . . . at more than double the cost of the other . . .

C. R. MOORSOM."

This letter was issued by the London and Birmingham Railway as an advertisement, no doubt, to inform the public, especially in Northampton, of what progress was being made towards the provision of a good station closer to the town than Roade. It appeared in the *Northampton Mercury* of 2nd February 1839 (p. 3, col. 3).

Roade was, at this time, deriving advantages from its established position on the line. This is how it was described in the *Handbook for Travellers Along the London and Birmingham Railway*, 2 shillings. (1839):

"About this spot we leave the county of Buckinghamshire and enter that of Northampton and, passing rapidly over a lofty embankment of about a mile in length, which divides the village of Ashton in two parts, shortly arrive at the Roade Station.

"The little village of Roade, which lies close to the railway, has suddenly been invested with all the bustle and activity of a town; and will, no doubt, enjoy increasing consequence and prosperity from its locality to this great line of communication. This is one of the numerous instances which could be adduced, of the great benefit which a Railway confers upon the towns near which it is formed; and amidst the changes which are thus originated, many places that heretofore have been comparatively unknown will become towns of considerable extent."

9th February 1839

A COMPLAINT FROM THE CHAPLAIN
AT THE INFIRMARY

When the management committee of the Northampton Infirmary met on Saturday, February 9th, there was a complaint by the chaplain, supported by the House Surgeon, about the Matron, Maria Jewel. She had sent for a dissenting minister to attend a patient who had not expressly desired such attendance. It is not clear from the minute of the committee whether the chaplain was the Vicar of St. Giles or the Vicar of Holy Sepulchre: they both shared the chaplaincy and were paid for it. Some research was necessary in order to verify that the Matron had actually violated a rule of the Infirmary. Eventually it was ascertained that there had been a resolution on 23rd December 1826 about attendance by Nonconformist ministers, which itself referred to an earlier decision of the committee. On 22nd July 1809 it was decided that "any patient may be attended privately by any licensed minister of his or her own persuasion, by application to the matron . . . and the name of the patient and the minister . . . must be entered in a book . . . and laid before the next committee".[139] Now, thirty years later, "the Board do . . . request her strictly to conform to the laws there referred to for the regulation of the religious instruction of the inmates of this establishment".

As a matter of interpretation, it is difficult to see how Maria Jewel had broken the 1809 rule, unless it was by sending for the minister without actually waiting for the patient to request it. In any case, the chaplain, the House Surgeon (James Mash), and the committee seem to have forgotten that the Infirmary was inaugurated through the efforts of Anglicans and Nonconformists working together.

February 1839

BREAD

The standard loaf weighed four pounds, five-and-a-quarter ounces. It was known as the quartern loaf. Bakers could charge whatever they could get for bread, but the weight was not supposed to vary.[140] During mid-February, it was reported in the *Northampton Mercury* (23rd February 1839, p. 3, col. 5) that "informations" had been laid before the Mayor and magistrates of Northampton, against several bakers, "for not carrying in their carts and baskets, scales and weights. They were fined a mitigating penalty. We understand that a general examination of scales, weights and measures, is intended to be made throughout the borough immediately."

20th February 1839

KETTERING LYING-IN CHARITY

Young parents of modern times may sometimes wonder how baby-hygiene was arranged before the days of disposable napkins, running hot water and washing machines. A meeting of Kettering ladies, on Wednesday, 20th February, 1839, at the Girls' National School Room took place at the request of the Reverend Henry Corrie "to take into consideration the propriety of adopting some plan for the benefit of poor married women during the period of their confinement".[141] The reason given on an explanatory handbill, was that "instances of great destitution were frequently occurring, for which there already existed no means of affording requisite assistance".

There was a Benevolent Society in the town, but its scope was limited. The Reverend Mr. Corrie's ladies adopted the following resolutions:

"That a Society be formed, to be called *the Kettering Lying-in Society,* for the benefit of poor married women of good character — and that it be under the direction of a Patroness and Committee.

"That every annual Subscriber of six Shillings be a Member of this Society, entitled to attend all Meetings of the Committee, and to recommend, in the Year, one poor married woman of good character to the benefit of this Charity.

"That Subscribers of one Guinea per annum, be entitled to recommend four cases during the Year.

"That each poor person so recommended, and having, previously to her confinement, deposited four Shillings in the hands of the Secretary, shall receive, in addition, a Bonus of four Shillings, together with the use of a Bag of Linen for a Month, and also the gift of a set of baby clothes when the Linen is duly and properly returned.

"That in particular cases, where the baby clothes may not be necessary, the poor woman shall have the money returned to her, which she had prospectively deposited, together with such portion of the above-mentioned Bonus, and such loan of Linen, as the Committee may judge to be proper, under the circumstances."

The latter resolution is a reminder of the high infant mortality rate of that time. Officers of the Society were named in resolutions. Then:

"That Mrs. TOMLIN be requested to cut out the baby linen, and send the same to such of the Subscribers as are at liberty to make it up, which, when so made up, shall be returned to Mrs. TOMLIN, and forwarded to the Rectory for distribution.

"That the Committee meet once every three months, viz. on each of the quarter days, for general purposes connected with the progress of the Society: the Committee Meetings to be held on the Monday, when the quarter day happens to fall on Sunday."

23rd February 1839

AN INCENDIARY AT KETTERING

John Leatherland was out late on Saturday night, 23rd February. As he walked down the High Street, the "town clock" struck eleven.[142] "On reaching the end of the street, I could either have gone home by turning up Gold Street or by taking Tanner's Lane. . . . I took the latter route." There he met a man he knew, coming from another cross road, "the worse for drink". Leatherland caught him by the arm to prevent him falling over.

"Hallo, Harry, where have you been?"

"To the Bantam Cock."

"You appear to have been in the sunshine: I would advise you to go home."

"Go up the street with me. I have something to tell you."

On the morning of that day, a large barley rick belonging to Farmer Roberts had been destroyed by fire. Harry asked Leatherland if he had helped put the fire out. He had.

"I only heard of the fire this afternoon." said Harry, "But I mean to be at more than one before long. . . . There will be another fire in the town before morning."

"You alarm me," said Leatherland. "How do you know what is to happen?"

"O, I could tell you something, but if you split you'll be shot. There's a plan devised among the Chartists, to rise all over England this very night and to burn the ricks down throughout the nation, and one will burst out not far from Mr. [Gotch]."

Leatherland, a silk-weaver, was Secretary of the Kettering Radical Association that had become part of the Chartist Movement. Partly due to the disapproval of his Calvinist step-father, who was also his employer, he was beginning to have doubts about his membership, and arguing against the more violent opinions of his comrades. This accounts for what was said next. Leatherland continued his narrative: "He also told me they intended to shoot me for being a turncoat, and advised me to take care of myself. I replied, "I hope you have nothing to do with it." He assured me he had not, but that he happened to hear of what was about to take place, and knew it to be true. I then made a stand, as if about to turn back and inform somebody [but] he retracted all he had said, and told me there was no truth in it, but that he only meant to alarm me. I have given the conversation as nearly as I can recollect it; but his admissions were made in such a broken way, and so incoherently . . . mixed up with dark inuendoes, and obscure hints . . . I regarded it as a drunken tale, especially as he denied it before leaving me.

"We parted, and I went home to bed, but not to sleep . . . I lay cogitating for about forty minutes, when I thought I heard the cry 'fire!' At first I supposed it was my own fancy, but in another second or two, cry upon cry became awfully distinct. I instantly jumped out of bed, and went to the chamber window, where, in the direction Harry had named, the town was lit up with a lurid blaze, which my disturbed imagination magnified into a dreadful conflagration. . . . Flinging on my clothes, I left the house, and ran down the street in a state of phrensy [sic], fully believing that a civil war had commenced, and fancying that the noises I heard were the reports of firearms. . . . On reaching the scene of the fire, which I found to be a rickyard – the very spot Harry had indicated – I saw two large wheat ricks in a blaze, with thatched houses almost contiguous. The most strenuous efforts were made to prevent the houses taking fire, and I fell in with a line of buckets, and worked as hard as I could to restrain the fury of the conflagration."

When the fire was under control, Leatherland left the bucket chain and went in search of Harry. He found him "working away at an engine, apparently the most active and zealous of any". The two men left the scene together, and Leatherland went home with Harry. "As soon as we got inside the door, he locked it, put the key in his pocket and told me I was in his power, and that unless I would solemnly swear not to divulge anything, he would take my life . . . I was alone, in the hands of a desperate incendiary. His poor wife and children were asleep upstairs, and, being frightened, I made a dreadful vow that I would keep the matter an inviolable secret."

Harry then confessed that the report of a Chartist uprising

was false, and that he alone was the cause of the fire "with a piece of loose cotton, used in the weaving work, which he carried alight from home in his hat". He said that he had been induced to commit the deed by the stirring words of Chartist leaders. He denied starting the previous morning's fire, but it had given him the idea of starting others. He had intended "to fire other rick-yards in different directions", but after the second act of arson had been committed, "he had jumped the brook at the bottom of the hill, and on looking back his conscience smote him, and he returned to the fire by a circuitous route, and worked with all his might at the engine, to prevent its spreading".

He implored Leatherland not to tell. No mercy would be shown to a Chartist and he was sure to be hanged. "For the sake of his wife and seven children, as well as his aged parents, he begged of me to keep the affair a secret. . . . He would lead a new life."

Leatherland's account is not the only evidence of Harry the incendiary. Martha Sanderson eavesdropped on a conversation on that Saturday night. Either Harry issued his threats, in much the same way as he did to Leatherland, while talking to a young woman; or Mrs. Sanderson overheard Harry talking to Leatherland and mistook the latter for a female. The eavesdropper was looking through her front window, and gave a description of Harry, but she did not describe the appearance of the female, who may have been standing out of the line of vision. If Leatherland spoke with a high-pitched voice, or was listening without comment, Martha Sanderson may well have assumed that he was a young woman.

In a letter postmarked "Kettering Feb 27, 1839, Martha wrote to "Mr. J. Gotch, Banker, Kettering."[143] This is her report:

"Sir, I intended to have written you an anonamous letter, but has my Husband as Named the circumstance to you I place full confidence in you that my Name will never be known.

"On Saturday Night at the time of the fire when looking out of the window I heard a Young Man say to a young Woman I will do more of them so striking his fists together

288

saying I will I will I will he said more on head of what he
would do, but of this I was not able to hear any sentence but
only odd words. The Woman who was with him replied to
him but what I cannot say, the young Man swore and said
[Damn] them I should not care I should not care if they
were all set on fire.

"The last word were not so distinct as the others but I feel
so confident of what I have stated, that I feel as though I
dare risk my life upon it. I have not the shadow of a doubt
that were you to employ a Police Officer you would find
this same Young Man to have kindled the fires. The Young
Man is tall & very light made his dress were dark with jacket
and trowsers. I thought his whole dress had the appearance
of blue he had a cap and a toesel hanging down by the side
of cap he appeared about 18 or 20 years of age. I feel as
though I have not discharged my duty if I do not tell you
what I feel possetive in my own Mind I have heard.

                    "Yours very respectfully
                                        Martha Sanderson

    "He has the appearance of a smart young Man at a
distance but his dress looks shabby when near him. I have
seen him once before."

Now return to John Ayre Leatherland's state of mind.[142]

"I was in a dreadful dilemma, which seemed to increase as
days and weeks passed by. . . . It was then capital
punishment, and I felt convinced this would be the
culprit's doom if convicted; and I thought of his poor
children being made orphans . . . and of his aged parents'
grey hairs being brought down with sorrow to the grave –
for he was an only and well-beloved child. His father
worked on the very next loom to me, and extremely bitter
was he toward the unknown incendiary. He should have
liked to see him burnt in the fire, he said. . . . Then, on the
other hand. I asked myself whether it was not an impera-
tive duty I owed to society, to give up the culprit to justice,
and risk all consequences; and whether, by concealing his
guilt, I was not becoming myself an accessory, and an
accomplice . . .

    "The next week after the fire, large placards appeared,

289

offering a reward, first of £300, then £400, finally of £500, from the government, to any one giving information which should lead to a conviction. . . . Not that I thought of taking the money. . . ."

A bundle of papers at the Northamptonshire Record Office,[144] contains draft minutes of an action meeting at Kettering; an application to the Home Secretary for the assistance of a London detective; the expenses of that police officer whilst pursuing inquiries in Kettering (hotel, stabling, turnpike tolls), and the notes he took during interviews with witnesses and suspects.

The investigation was fruitless, and years passed. Towards the end of 1843, John Leatherland was alone in his cottage in Job's Yard, at work at his loom, when "Harry" entered, in a state of agitation. "I want you to go with me to the rector," he said, ". . . and disclose all we know". Leatherland put on his hat and coat and took him to Mr. Gotch, at the bank, ". . . thinking it better to break the matter to him as I was well known to him. Harry waited outside . . . but thinking that he would probably repent of the step when too late, I made some excuse to Mr. Gotch and came out again. . . ." Harry was insistent: "If you will not tell, I will." He beckoned a police-man and gave himself into custody. When Leatherland's pregnant wife came home and found a policeman there with her husband, she was "taken ill, and a miscarriage was the result". The next day, before a magistrate, Harry denied his own confession, even though his statement had been heard by an independent witness. His relatives accused Leatherland of trying to extort money from him. "This was my reward for all I had suffered on his account − for all my perplexity, sorrow, and anxiety!"

At the trial before the next Assizes, Harry pleaded "not guilty", and was defended by counsel who savaged Leatherland, and produced an array of character witnesses. He was convicted, but Judge Baron Gurney sentenced him, with amazing leniency, to twelve months in prison. The judge's words to Leatherland, technically an accessory, were equally amazing: "You have acted the part of a faithful friend to the prisoner. It was doubtless a heavy trouble to you, but you were not bound to reveal the offence, for if everyone were to tell the secrets of their fellows, society would not exist at all." The reluctant witness "sank down and relieved long pent-up feelings by a flood of tears".

For those who desire the full facts, John Leatherland's narrative benefits from the illumination of a little modern research. "Harry" was Thomas Katterns who was 22 years old at the time of the February 1839 incendiariasm. It was 28th December 1843 that he decided to confess. He was unable to see Gotch the banker, as explained by Leatherland, but he gave himself up to Constable Dewdney, who took his statement in the presence of a shopkeeper acting as witness. He was tried at Northamptonshire Lent Assizes, before Baron Gurney, on Wednesday 6th March 1844. Since the offence, it was said by one of his character witnesses, he had become "exceeding penitent, had attended to his religious duties incessantly, and had been a participator in the Lord's Supper". The judge left Katterns to stew overnight before sentencing him on the Thursday morning, to twelve months imprisonment with hard labour. Another Kettering chartist was before the same court, for arson. He was William Cowper, a 30-year-old carpenter, who had fired a wagon hovel at Deanshanger on 15th January 1844. He was sentenced to transportation for life.

20th March 1839

ACRIMONIOUS POLITICAL CHANGES IN PETERBOROUGH

Earl Fitzwilliam had political control of Peterborough. The majority of voters were his tenants, so the two M.P.s were his appointees. 703 acres of land on the north side of the city, an area known as Boroughbury, were held by the Fitzwilliam family on a lease from the Bishop, Dean and chapter of Peterborough. This was about three-quarters of the accommodation land of the outer city, still mainly rural, and it was let to many tenants (and electors).

By some astoundingly careless oversight, this Boroughbury lease was not renewed by Earl Fitzwilliam, as the date of expiry approached; and Bishop Marsh, not likely to have been a political sympathiser with the Earl, allowed a Tory, C. P. Berkeley, to take it. The old lease was due to expire on 25th March, 1839, and Fitzwilliam was obliged to give notice to his tenants who were the occupants of the Boroughbury land.

As might be expected, tenants not approved by Berkeley were required to leave their holdings. One of them was a farmer, J. W. Mewburn, whose departure seemed to deserve special recognition, and Earl Fitzwilliam arranged a dinner in his honour at the Angel Inn at Peterborough. In his speech at the dinner, the Earl made some tactless remarks about the Bishop of Peterborough, suggesting that he should have restrained the new leaseholder, Berkeley, from evicting former tenants. Worse, he blamed the Bishop's wife for using her influence to have a former tenant reinstated. This was the disreputable former landlord of the Angel in which they were dining, William Daniels (see the breach of promise case of February 1838). Fitzwilliam had evicted him, but Berkeley had allowed him to return.

Fitzwilliam's dinner took place on Wednesday, 20th March 1839, and within three days, he received the following letter from C. P. Berkeley:

"Peterborough
23rd March, 1839.

"My Lord,

In the report given in the *Stamford Mercury* of the 22d inst. of the dinner given to Mr. Mewburn . . . it is stated that your Lordship was present and made use of (amongst others) the following expressions:— 'The Bishop of Peterborough should have restrained Mr. Berkeley, when he disclosed to him the course which he meant to take, and not have permitted and encouraged the oppressive and unprincipled proceedings with the tenants.' In addressing your Lordship, I have no intention of alluding to any observations made at the Dinner on my own conduct, but I think it a duty incumbent on me to inform your Lordship, that neither the Bishop of Peterborough, Mrs. Marsh [the Bishop's wife] . . . were directly or indirectly privy to my arrangements in reletting the land belonging to the Boroughbury Lease, and that any and every responsibility attaches and rests solely upon myself.

"I am, My Lord,

"Your Lordship's obedient humble servant. . . ."

"It is my intention to make this letter public."

Earl Fitzwilliam replied:

"Sir, – The report of what I said is not accurate in its phraseology, but I certainly did express an opinion that, if there had been any reason to expect the disapprobation of the lessor, the transaction alluded to would not have taken place. I rejoice to hear that, hitherto, you alone are responsible for it. The necessity which you have felt of relieving other parties from even the suspicion of being previously connected with it, affords a signal proof of the estimation in which you think it likely that the public may hold it – Perhaps even of the estimation in which, upon reflection, you hold it yourself . . .

"I have the honor [sic] to be, Sir

"Your very faithful servant, Fitzwilliam."

As Berkeley had threatened, he handed the correspondence to the press – a Tory newspaper, of course, the *Northampton Herald* – and it was published on 30th March 1839 (p. 3, col. 4). Of all their Whig enemies, Fitzwilliam was the most hated target of the *Herald's* editorial board, and this Peterborough incident set him up for a blistering attack by the Reverend Francis Litchfield (p. 2, col. 7):

"Our readers who recollect the disgraceful behaviour of Lord Milton in 1832" [Earl Fitzwilliam was the same Lord Milton now elevated to the peerage] ". . . will not be surprised to hear of the way in which [he] has been conducting himself in Peterborough. . . . We knew that Lord Fitzwilliam, after having neglected to renew an important lease, was . . . in the ferocity of his fury, not likely to spare even an aged, infirm, and estimable Bishop from attack. . . . We now find ourselves compelled to defend not only the Bishop from a cruel slander, but the Bishop's most amiable and kind-hearted lady, from a most unmanly insult. As to Mr. Berkeley, the attack upon him by Lord Fitzwilliam is the assault of a degraded peer – a dirty quibbler – upon a gentleman whose word, unlike Lord Fitzwilliam's, never was impugned, whose honour, unlike Lord Fitzwilliam's, never was tarnished, and who never had occasion to shed tears, as had Lord Fitzwilliam, upon being convicted of a LIE!" [This was a reference to the 1832 Reform Bill campaign, during which Fitzwilliam, as Lord Milton, arranged for both the South Northamptonshire Parliamentary seats to be contested by the Whigs, instead of just one of them as agreed; denied it at first, and then admitted it with embarrassment.]

Litchfield added the *Herald* version of what had happened in Peterborough (p. 3, col. 1). Berkeley had evicted Farmer Mewburn for agricultural reasons rather than political spite. He had "just sown 100 acres out of 250 with wheat!" leaving only 20 acres of fallow. His eviction would therefore be approved "as wise and warrantable" by "every gentleman acquainted with the nature of the land".

"The dinner," said the *Herald,* "was a failure, notwithstanding the tickets *given* away . . . and though all the tenants and toadies Lord Fitzwilliam could collect were assembled, only about a hundred persons were present. . . . Of the three newspaper reporters that were present, not one, it seems, would degrade himself by publishing Lord Fitzwilliam's entire attack upon Mrs. Marsh." The *Northampton Herald* has no such qualms. First, the words used by the Earl in criticism of the Bishop: "The Bishop of Peterborough should have restrained Mr. Berkeley when he disclosed to him the course which he meant to take, and not have permitted and encouraged the oppressive and unprincipled proceedings with the tenants." The *Herald* demanded: "Was anything ever uttered so base as this by a nobleman of England, and of an aged Bishop, too, before an audience of which, we say with a blush for their cloth, four clergymen formed part? Was anything so monstrous as this charge, every word of which was foul and false from beginning to end, with all its vile assumption, its cowardly scurrility, and those low insinuations, that to our moral sense carry with them no less than the guilt of perjury. . . .?

"But Lord Fitzwilliam was willing to wound still further. . . . He set himself to attack the private character of Mr. Daniels" [the womanising former landlord of the Angel, and defendant in an unsavoury breach of promise action] ". . . and pronounced him . . . to be a man of such immoral conduct as to make him a pollution for every female to approach. And now hear the abominable language of Lord Fitzwilliam, after having thus spoken of Mr. Daniels. . . . 'No sooner did Mr. Daniels turn round, and give a vote in the Tory interest, than he was taken under the petticoats of Mrs. Marsh, and whitewashed!' Shouts of laughter rang through the room at this observation of the noble lord! . . . Mrs. Marsh had known nothing whatever of any of Mr. Berkeley's arrangements in his choice of tenants, and had not even been made aware . . . that Mr. Daniels had been included in the number. . . ."

26th-29th March 1839

CHARTIST SPRING

During the week before Easter, John Collins, the Birmingham Chartist lecturer, visited the county. His speeches (or "harangues" as the *Northampton Herald* described them), and the associated activities, were well-reported in both the Northampton newspapers. On Tuesday, 26th March, Collins was in Northampton, parading the town during the afternoon, with fifes and drums, and a number of little flags. In the evening, he delivered a two-hour speech on the Market Hill. The *Herald* (30th March 1839, p. 3, col. 2) said that the subject

"was such as mobs in all times have been treated with, and we think it not impossible that Collins spoke from the copy of the same old revolutionary speech. He, of course, abused evrybody and evrything above himself in station and respectability. But the most amusing part of his address consisted in his abuse of the Whigs, and the Whig Ministry."

The *Herald* was equally scathing about the Radical Borough Councillor, John Sharp, the hairdresser of Market Hill ("notorious barber that now shaves every flint, as formerly every face, he can get hold of"). He regretted the absence of the Mayor, and told the police that if he had been at home, he would have offered the use of the Town Hall for Collins' lecture. Even more infuriating to the *Herald,* were Sharp's instructions to Joe Ball.

"Mr. Sharp commanded the principal policeman not to interfere with Mr. Collins! When we add that Mr. Sharp is not a magistrate, our readers will smile at the impudence with which the fellow orders the policemen to do this or that in the case of a wretch like Collins to bring his Brummagem notions of government among the ignorant poor."

Collins also spoke in Wellingborough, Kettering and Daventry. The *Herald's* hostile account of the Wellingborough and Kettering visits appeared on 6th April (p. 3, col. 1). On Wednesday, he was on Wellingborough Market Place.

"When Collins . . . finished his spouting in Kettering on Thursday, two of Rose's brushmakers hired a horse and gig and escorted him [back] to Wellingborough, where it is supposed they got drunk (Oh! these steady sober reformers), and in coming back, while they were in the act of exchanging the reins for the other's turn to drive, the horse took fright, turned at right angles and bolted over the hedge, with the seat knocked completely off, and the two brushmakers sprawling in the mud. One had his arm broken, which Mr. Gibbons afterwards set, and the injury to the horse and gig will cost these fellows twenty pounds to repair. . . ."

The next morning was Good Friday. John Collins applied to the bellman of Wellingborough to inform the inhabitants that he intended to speak at the Cross Keys that evening. The bellman "refused to raise the bell on that day". The word was spread, however, and "the lecturer made a long speech on radical reform, universal suffrage, the advantages of establishing a Female Society to assist him in leading the men in the right way, and the necessity of sending out a Dissenting Minister in different parts of the county to plead the cause."

8th April 1839

ROAD AND RAIL

The Victoria Coach was the first attempt on a grand scale to exploit the railway for the purpose of restoring and strengthening a coach service. In simple terms the idea was to get travellers from the North-West off the train at Blisworth and carry them on a new coach through Peterborough and North Norfolk to Norwich.

"WONDERFUL SPEED!
VIA RAILWAY AND COACH,
From LIVERPOOL, MANCHESTER, *and* BIRMINGHAM;
through NORTHAMPTON, to NORWICH.
275 MILES IN ONE DAY.
THE Proprietors most respectfully announce to the Public that on the 8th April, 1839, they commenced running
THE VICTORIA COACH,

Which starts from the Blisworth Station, every morning (except Sunday), at Eleven o'clock, on the arrival of the Train that leaves Liverpool and Manchester at three, and Birmingham at half-past eight, and proceeds through Northampton, Wellingborough, Thrapstone, Oundle, Peterborough, Thorney, Wisbech, Lynn, . . . and arrives at . . . Norwich, at Half-past Eleven in the Evening.

The Victoria leaves Norwich every morning (except Sunday), at Nine o'clock, returns by the same route to the

Blisworth Station, and meets the Mail Train which arrives at Birmingham at a quarter before three . . .
     Performed by T. SHAW, Northampton.
          D. M'PHERSON, Lynn.
          W. DURRANT, Norwich."

(*Northampton Mercury* 13th April 1839, p. 3, col. 2.)

The "Old Northampton Coach" was still leaving the Angel at Northampton on a daily road journey to London for 12 shillings inside, and 6 shillings outside.

On the same Monday that the shiny new Victoria coach first set off from Blisworth station, there was a fatal railway accident there. The *Northampton Herald,* which reported all railway mishaps, including rude porters, with relish, had the story (13th April 1839, p. 2, col. 7).

"T. Fletcher, a guard belonging to one of the luggage-trains on the London and Birmingham Railway met with a severe accident on Monday last. . . . He had crossed over a truck laden with sleepers, to unfasten a wagon of coal, which was to be left at the Blisworth station. Having done this, he gave the signal to the engineer to proceed, when, owing to the sudden jerk occasioned by the starting of the train, he was thrown off the sleepers. He fell across the line, and the wagon loaded with coal passed over him, causing compound fractures of the right thigh and left leg. He was conveyed immediately to the Hospital, but in less than half an hour he expired. The coal was to have been taken to Roade, but he did not know it, otherwise the accident would not have happened."

9th April 1839

GAS AT OUNDLE

On Tuesday, 9th April, rather a special dinner was given at the Swan Inn at Oundle. The corporate host was the Oundle Gas

Company, and it was a public dinner in honour of the contractor, and in celebration of the completion of the project to bring gas lighting to the town. While the guests were waiting for their dinner, they heard "an instructive and entertaining lecture" in the Town Hall.

The contractor was Thomas Sharp, manager of the Northampton Gasworks. The lecturer was James Sharp (not related), his assistant; and while he was instructing and entertaining the guests, he was also supervising the cooking of their dinner – by gas – in gas cookers invented by himself.

"All the joints were done to a turn, and elicited expressions of approval from the company present. . . ."

(*Northampton Mercury* 13th April 1839, p. 3, col. 5.)

10th April 1839

ARSON AT THE FOXHOLES

At Northamptonshire Quarter Sessions, on Thursday 4th July 1839, before Earl Spencer and five other magistrates, William Tuckey was tried on a charge of maliciously setting fire to a wood called Foxholes, growing at Hinton, the property of W. R. Cartwright, Esq., on 10th April. Mr. Miller, prosecuting, called five witnesses.

William Hunt: I am a hawker, and I live at Brackley. Yes, sir, I've seen the prisoner before. Yes, sir, I saw him on Tuesday the 9th of April, the day before the fire. He bought a box of lucifers of me.

Charles Page: I am a victualler at Banbury. On 10th of April, I was going to Brackley, in company with Mr. Horwood, when I observed in the Foxholes cover, a quantity of smoke, and then flames. I saw the prisoner Tuckey in the meadow adjoining. Upon going up to the wood, I saw that it was on fire. Mr. Horwood rode on to give the alarm. I asked Tuckey what was the meaning of the fire. He said he did not know. He said it was burning when he came down. I told him to give the alarm, and then I rode on.

Edmund Bull: I am a mason, at Charlton. I was going from Brackley workhouse when I saw smoke in the direction of Foxholes Wood. Mr. Horwood came up and told me what was the matter. I went to the wood and exerted myself to stop the flames. I then went to Mr. Wilson's. The prisoner Tuckey was there, but Mr. Wilson did not seem to know anything about it. The next day, as I was going to Brackley, I saw Tuckey, and I asked him whether he had seen the fire the day before. He said he did not see it till he got to the Cabins.

Thomas Wilson: I occupy a farm under Mr. W. R. Cartwright. Tuckey was employed on the 10th April in tending some sheep near the Foxholes. Bull, the last witness, told me of the fire. Tuckey had been with me shortly before, but he had said nothing about it. On the same morning, I found a thorn hedge on my farm partly burned. Tuckey left my service the same evening, and I did not see him again till he was in custody.

Miller: Did you ever see him smoke?

Wilson: Never.

William Marriott, police officer, Brackley: I apprehended the prisoner near Buckingham, about seven or eight miles from Brackley, on the 14th of April. As I approached, he jumped through a hedge and ran away, but I found him in a ditch. I told him he was wanted on a charge of setting fire to Foxholes. he stated that he bought some matches and put it to a hedge, and it burnt. He said he put it out as quick as he could, and went towards Foxholes. When he got there, he tried to light his pipe. The pipe would not draw, and he threw it over the hedge. In a few minutes, when he looked behind him, he said he saw the wood in a blaze. I searched every inch of the wood for a pipe, but I could find no trace of it.

The verdict was "Guilty", and Tuckey was sentenced to imprisonment with hard labour for six months, the first and last months to be in solitary confinement.

On a twentieth century map of the area between Hinton-in-the-Hedges and Brackley, there is no "Foxholes" although a large building named The Cabin is likely to be the "Cabins" mentioned by Edmund Bull in his evidence.

13th April 1839

AN UNAUTHORISED DEBT-COLLECTOR WITH PECULIAR EYES

"NORTHAMPTON ASSOCIATION
For the Prosecution of Robbers, Thieves, Swindlers, &c.
FOUR GUINEAS REWARD
WHEREAS ROBERT EVANS, lately employed by Mr. JOHN PERKINS, of the Bedford Road, in this Town of NORTH-AMPTON, Nurseryman (A Member of this Association), ABSCONDED from his Service on Monday last, and afterwards attempted to procure Payment of the Accounts due to the said John Perkins, from Persons residing in the Neighbourhood, by representing that he was sent by the said John Perkins:
NOTICE IS HEREBY GIVEN,
That no Authority has been given to the said Robert Evans for collecting or receiving any Monies on account . . . and that all representations to that effect are false and fraudulent . . .

The said Robert Evans is a stout-built young man, about 27 years of age, and 5ft. 7in. high, brisk walk, rather peculiar eyes, turning upwards, and usually wears a blue coat and thin striped trousers. . . ."

(*Northampton Mercury* 13th April 1839, p. 3, col. 1.)

20th April 1839

A DANGEROUS BROOK

"Sir, – Permit me . . . to warn all persons who may have occasion to travel between the towns of Quinton and Wootton . . . of the intolerable state of the roads, and especially of the great danger of crossing the brook which separates the Parishes. On either side there are holes and quicksands to a great depth, and it is impossible to pass, even at low water and in broad daylight, without great risk. Last Saturday morning [20th April], as Brownsel's van, from Hanslope, containing nine passengers, was passing this brook, the near wheels sunk so deep in the mire as to cause it to turn completely over, and the passengers, of whom I was one, were precipitated in a confused heap, men and women, through the top of the van, into a rapid current of water nearly three feet deep, being at the same time entangled in the broken head of the van. . . . Fortunately the horse proved a very quiet one, and Brownsel, who was driving very slowly and carefully, perceiving that the van must go over, leaped forward, with a passenger who sat in front, and seized the horse by the head, and held him fast till we had time to extricate ourselves from our perilous situation. . . . We escaped with a few cuts and bruises, torn clothes, and a thorough soaking . . .

The very dangerous and impassable state of this brook has been a subject of general complaint for many years, and I understand has more than once been brought under the notice of the magistrates . . . but without effect . . .
Hanslope, 23d April 1839   ONE OF THE PASSENGERS."

(*Northampton Mercury* 27th April 1839, p. 2, col. 5.)

The brook runs along the south of Northampton and joins the Nene at Upton. The original Ordnance Survey map shows it as a ford at Wootton, but a later bridge now crosses it. The reference to magistrates is a reminder of their county government function, sitting in Quarter Sessions.

1st May 1839

DEATH OF A BISHOP

Herbert Marsh, the controversial Bishop of Peterborough, died on May day. It has been noted in these pages, how, only weeks before his death, he had been under attack (and defended by the *Northampton Herald*) for taking up a political position in Peterborough. But that was nothing new: as a new Bishop he had tried to justify the trial of Queen Caroline. His obituary in the *Gentleman's Magazine* referred to his unpopularity:[145]

"His attempts to repress Calvinism in his diocese soon rendered him obnoxious to the evangelical portion of the clergy, and several publications appeared on the subject, which was ultimately brought before the House of Lords, but without material result. . . ."

The funeral was on the 8th May.

"The Bishop's body was deposited in a vault prepared . . . at the back of the altar, in that part of the [cathedral], called the new Building, where rest the ashes of several of his Lordship's predecessors."[145]

The new Bishop was fifty-nine-year-old Reverend Doctor George Davys. He had been private tutor to the young Queen Victoria. When Bishop Marsh died, "there had been some conferences with Lord Melbourne the Prime Minister, and it was settled that the offer should come directly from Her Majesty. A royal servant called at his house in the Old Terrace, Kensington, with a short letter, saying, 'The Queen says you are to be Bishop of Peterborough'. The writer was the Baroness Lehzen. 'Well,' was the reply [from Davys], 'I have not, I hope, disobeyed Her Majesty yet, and I suppose it won't do to begin now'."[146]

20th May 1839

THE "GREAL MORAL DEMONSTRATION"

The Northamptonshire Chartists intended this to be a rally of great significance. It was not. R. G. Gammage, the Chartist historian, who was there, got the date wrong (again). He did remember that its purpose was to elect a delegate to represent the county at the National Assembly.[147]

The Chartists' own handbill, under the title: "Great Moral Demonstration"; explained.

"At a meeting of delegates from various towns in the county of Northampton, held at Northampton, on Wednesday May 8th, it was unanimously resolved to convene a county meeting, to be held on Whit-Monday, May 20th, 1839 at Three o'Clock, on the Race Course, Northampton, for the purpose of electing a delegate, to represent the interests of this county in the General Convention of the Working Classes; and to take into consideration the most effective measures for causing the People's Charter to become the law of the land. . . ."

The impetus seems to have come from the Kettering Radical Association, which produced a pamphlet on 10th May, entitled "Our Rights; or The Just Claims of the Working Classes . . ." (Price fourpence).[148] The introduction explained that the subject-matter was correspondence with the Rev. Thomas Madge, Curate of Kettering.

"In consequence of the occurrence of two incendiary fires in this town, on the 23rd of February last, the Kettering Radical Association published a handbill, for the purpose of vindicating its members from the aspersion which their opponents had thought proper to cast upon them; and entreating the gentlemen of Kettering and its vicinity to consider 'whether their general hostility to the just claims of the Working-Classes, was not assisting to sever the ligaments of society, and thereby originating a state of things which it is fearful to contemplate'. On the reception of a copy of this handbill, Mr. Madge addressed a note to our chairman, enquiring what were 'the just claims' to which we had adverted. In answer to this enquiry the letter now in the hand of the reader was written. We intended that this Introduction should contain a copy of Mr. M's note; but after it was in type he forbade our printing it; although he had previously granted what we understood to be full liberty of doing so. He has also sent us a long reply to the following statement of our claims. That, in our opinion, his production is a failure, may be inferred from the fact that we offered to publish it at our own cost, provided Mr. M. would take one hundred and fifty copies. This offer he has declined."

The text is of philosophical and political interest, and undoubtedly illuminates national Chartism; but it does not answer questions about those Kettering Radicals. It is respectfully signed "G. T. GREEN, Brushmaker, Chairman" and "J. A. LEATHERLAND, Silkweaver, Secretary". Now, Leatherland has told us (See 23rd February 1839, above) that he knew on the day of the fires, that a member of his Association was responsible for one of them.[142] By his account, he was already turning away from Chartism, when he became involved with the arsonist, Katterns. In this publication of two and a half months later, endorsed with his name, is a denial of involvement in fire-raising, and a well-argued statement of Chartist aims. The historian R. L. Greenall[119] has offered evidence that the pamphlet was actually the work of the Radical Baptist, the Rev. John Jenkinson, but Leatherland allowed it to go out over his own name. The Chartist Hymnbook carries a rousing song by this faint-hearted Leatherland:

> Base oppressors leave your slumbers,
> Listen to a nation's cry;
> Hark! United countless numbers
> Swell the peal of agony!
> Lo! for Britain's sons and daughters,
> In the depths of misery,
> Like the sound of many waters
> Comes the cry, "We will be free!"

(Try singing it to the tune "Deutschland Uber Alles".)

305

Who moved the first resolution at the "Great Moral Demonstration" on 20th May?

"That this meeting views with indignation the miserable and degraded condition of the working classes, which it considers to arise to a great extent from the present exclusive system of legislation."

You guessed it – the deeply disapproving Leatherland.

(*Northampton Mercury* 25th May 1839, p. 2, col. 1).

After several stirring speeches, John Collins of Birmingham, who had visited the county in March, was elected Delegate for Northamptonshire. J. A. Leatherland gave the vote of thanks. In doing so, he alluded to a threat which the Editor of the *Northampton Herald* had alleged had been made to pull down its office and murder him. Leatherland said that the *Herald* office still stood. "The Chartists will not defile their fingers by touching a stone of the place."

The *Herald* had comparatively little to report on these proceedings (25th May 1839, p. 2, col. 7).

The meeting of the Chartists . . . was held in the Market Place. . . . The muster was extremely small, owing partly to the returning good sense of the persons originally pledged to Chartism, and partly to the preparations made by the Mayor to prevent outrage." Home Office instructions had been issued during the month that drilling and marching by workmen were to be prevented. "On the previous Friday [17th May] the Mayor issued about 400 notices" [to men selected for duty as special constables]. "Care was taken to select persons who were likely not to claim for their day's expenses. Among those that complied was the notorious barber Sharp, so familiar with blood-shedding for many years till electioneering had enriched him." (See 26th March 1839 above.) "He bearded the Mayor in the most consequential and impudent manner, demanding to know upon what authority he was proceeding. The Mayor simply replied that the magistrates had sufficient evidence to warrant and indeed to require precautionary measures, but refused to disclose what had come to his knowledge.

Sharp then declined being sworn, and called on his followers to do the like. . . ." Argument took place. "The Mayor requested those persons that were unwilling or afraid to assist in keeping the peace to retire. This was done after Sharp had made another attempt at intimidation by threatening to get every bill of expenses disallowed by the Common Council. The vulgar swaggerer then placed himself on the steps of the Hall, trying to keep all persons from going up. . . . Instead of 300, only about 150 were sworn. . . . With this force of special constables, aided by the regular police, but little was to be apprehended. . . . At three o'clock about 150 fellows were seen to be walking about and abreast, accompanied by the usual assembly of holiday boys and girls. They then came to a standstill in the market-place, and a carpenter's bench placed, from which the speakers might declaim. . . . Two men, Collins and Jones, delegates to the Convention, spoke, and the former was elected to represent Northampton. . . . The language on the whole was carefully guarded. . . . The mob gradually dwindled off. Mr. Sharp did not venture to make his appearance, and so little interest did his ragamuffins excite, that although several clubs were holding their meetings in the adjoining public houses [the traditional Whit Monday functions] none of them thought it worth while to attend . . ."

24th May 1839

THE REGENT COACH

"A NEW COACH
THE REGENT.

THE Public are respectfully informed the above COACH leaves the Angel Hotel, NORTHAMPTON, every Morning, except Sundays, at Ten o'clock, through Market Harborough, to . . . LEICESTER; returns in the afternoon at Four o'clock, by the same route, and arrives at the Angel Hotel, Northampton, at Eight o'clock.

T. SHAW & Co. Proprietors."

This announcement, dated 24th May, appeared in the *Mercury* of 1st June 1839 (p. 3, col. 2). It was probably more than another road link between Northampton and urban south Leicestershire. It would have been a very convenient connection, for London-bound passengers, with the trains at Blisworth.

30th May 1839

THE ANGRY CHURCHWARDENS
OF HOLY SEPULCHRE

The historians of the Northampton "round Church"[149] quote the minutes of an inflamed vestry meeting held on May 30th, at which a vote of censure was passed on the parish clerk, George Haddon,

"for his disrespectful conduct to the parish. He was accused of having refused to account to the churchwardens for their fees . . . received by him (the clerk), and that he persists in collecting such fees although he has been discharged from doing so by the churchwardens, and re-taining the same: and it also appearing that he has in various instances been guilty of extortion in collecting fees not payable, a Requisition be presented to the Vicar . . . respect-fully requesting him to dismiss the said George Haddon from the office to which he was appointed by the Vicar."

The Vicar refused, and when his letter, declining to comply with their wishes, was read at the vestry of 20th June, it was decided to appeal to the Bishop. The problem ended at the meeting of April 1840:

"George Haddon, the officiating clerk, having attended this

meeting and expressed his contrition for his improper conduct in retaining certain of the churchwardens' and sexton's fees received by him, and in demanding and receiving fees not authorised by the Table; and having promised immediately to account for, and pay over to the churchwardens the fees so improperly received and retained, and to conduct himself in all cases in compliance with the Table of fees, and to forward the views of the churchwardens for the future, Resolved:— That for the present no further proceedings be taken relative to his conduct."

1st June 1839

BONE DUST MANURE; BUILDING STONE; AND A PERIPATETIC DENTIST AT THE INN

Among the advertisements in the *Northampton Mercury* of 1st June 1839:

"SHIPLEY WHARF, NORTHAMPTON.

JOHN SMITH begs most respectfully to inform his friends and the public, that he has erected a Mill to grind BONES for MANURE, and that he has now plenty for sale, Coarse Dust at 3s. per bushel, and Fine Dust, at 3s. 3d. per bushel, at Northampton; 1d½. [sic] per bushel returned for ready money. Should any one gentleman, or more, think well to send an order for a quantity of five or six hundred bushels to be delivered down the river Nen between Northampton and his Wharf at Stanwick, he will forward it at 3s. per bushel for Coarse Dust, and 3s. 3d. per bushel for Fine Dust; and on the same terms at any wharf on the New and Old Union Canals, between Northampton and Leicester. Dress land in middling condition with 14 bushels per acre of Coarse Dust, or 12 bushels of Fine Dust — land in poor condition with 18 bushels of Fine Dust, or 20 bushels of

Coarse Dust – and on a fair trial, Bone Manure will be found to produce the best crops, and to be the cheapest compost in use.

"A quantity of MANURE SALT on sale, at Wellingborough Wharf, at 35s. per ton, and at Irthlingborough Wharf, at 36s. per ton.

"All orders punctually attended to, and delivered on the shortest notice."

(P. 3, col. 2, repeated on 8th June 1839.)

"BLISWORTH STONE WORKS AND QUARRY.

THE Public are respectfully informed, that LIME and BUILDING STONES are always in readiness to be forwarded by canal or otherwise, at 1s. 8d. per ton; and LIME, fresh from the kiln, at 2s. 3d. per quarter.

Chimney Pieces, Paving, Steps, Landings, Window Heads, Window Sills, Coping, Sink Stones, Pier Caps, Straddle Stones, &c. executed to order.

N.B. The capability of these stones for ashler, Tooled, Rusticated, and other descriptions of Plain and Ornamental Masonry Work, may be seen at the Buildings erected at the Quarry, and near the Railway Station, Blisworth."

(P. 1, col. 5.)

"MR. STYER,
SURGEON DENTIST,

BEGS respectfully to acquaint his Patrons and Friends, that he has REMOVED to more eligible and convenient Apartments, at Mr. GRAY'S, ST. GILES'S SQUARE, NORTH-AMPTON, where he may be consulted on MONDAY the 3d, FRIDAY the 7th, & SATURDAY the 8th of JUNE.

Mr. STYER will attend professionally at the HIND INN, WELLINGBOROUGH, on Tuesday next, June 4, from nine till two; . . . at the WHITE HORSE, TOWCESTER, on Thursday, JUNE 6, from nine till twelve; and at the WHEATSHEAF, DAVENTRY, the same afternoon, from 2 till 6.

Families desiring Mr. Styer's attendance at their own residences, will oblige him by leaving a note to that effect at

the bars of the respective Inns, early in the mornings of his
attendance.

N.B. Mr. Styer begs to acquaint his patients and patrons in
general, that he has private apartments for their reception at
all the Inns at which he is in the habit of attending.

Mr. S. will visit Thrapston, Oundle, Kettering, and
Harborough, the week after next . . .
St. Giles's-square, May 31, 1839."

(P. 3, col. 1.)

1st June 1839

A DANGEROUS GAME

The report of an inquest on an unnamed child, under three
years old, appeared in the *Northampton Herald* of 8th June
(p. 3, col. 3). The inquest had been held on the previous
Saturday, 1st June, at the Union Workhouse at Daventry. The
child

"while playing with something in the privy belonging to
the women's yard, fell through the seat and was suffocated.
It was immediately got out, and medical aid procured, but
life was quite extinct".

3rd June 1839

"BURGLARY AND SUICIDE AT DAVENTRY"

That was the heading over an unusual story in the *Northampton Mercury* of 8th June 1839 (p. 3, col. 5). The circumstances of the burglary suggest that the reporter was mistaken

over the time of day. The time of discovery of the crime is given as three o'clock in the afternoon. Complete disorder downstairs, while the family was upstairs, and their having to be "aroused", suggests that they were in bed. On the other hand, three o'clock seems rather early in the morning for calling the servant, although there could have been a family emergency; or the sounds of the burglary may have been heard.

Early on Monday afternoon (3rd June 1839] the house of Mr. Sheppard, at Daventry, was broken into, and several articles of plate, linen, silk handkerchiefs, several bottles of champagne, brandy, sherry &c. were stolen. The robbery was first discovered by Mrs. Sheppard, who rose soon after three o'clock for the purpose of calling the servant, and who, on arriving at the bottom of the stairs, found the door fastened on the outside. Suspecting all was not right, she immediately aroused the rest of the family, who, after some difficulty, succeeded in forcing open the door, when their suspicions were confirmed by the disordered state of everything in the lower part of the house. Information of the robbery was very shortly after forwarded by the down coaches to Dunchurch, and it was soon ascertained that a person of very suspicious appearance had been seen to pass through that place towards Coventry. The constable of Dunchurch immediately went in pursuit and overtook him, and succeeded, after a desparate resistance, in taking him into custody, when the stolen property was found upon him, and he was, without delay, conveyed back to Daventry, and lodged in the gaol. During his confinement his conduct was most outrageous; he refused his allowance of food, and on Thursday morning, soon after ten o'clock, it was discovered that he had put a period to his miserable life by hanging himself with a silk handkerchief, fastened to the bars of the grating over the doors of his cell. He was immediately cut down, but life was quite extinct, although he had not been left many minutes when the discovery was made. It is said that he had effected his escape from Aylesbury gaol."

4th June 1839

RINGSTEAD ENCLOSURE

On this day the modernisation of Northamptonshire agriculture took another small step forward, when the Ringstead Enclosure Act was given the Royal Assent. It named John West as Commissioner, and he began his task almost immediately, by setting out seven "public carriage roads and highways" leading out of the centre of the village "through and over the lands intended to be divided and allotted". By 8th August, they were staked and marked out, and mapped. The Enclosure Award followed on 27th February 1841.

8th June 1839

FOOTPADS

We have three mutually contradictory accounts of a highway robbery at Northampton on Saturday night, 8th June. Both the Northampton papers carried reports, on their third pages, on 15th June 1839. They can be compared with the evidence given by the victim at the trial of the culprits.

Owen Wallis was travelling out of Northampton along the Kettering road, going home to Overstone Lodge. "A little beyond" (*Herald*), "a quarter of a mile beyond" (*Mercury*) the toll-gate, at half past seven (*H*), at eleven o'clock (*M*), he was dragged from his horse by footpads, beaten and kicked in a savage manner about the head and face (*M*), his pockets "ransacked" (*H*). He was robbed of ten pounds in gold and silver. Upon being left by the robbers (*M*), at the corner of the race course (*H*), Wallis "walked back immediately to Northampton, and meeting with Ball" (Superintendent of Police at Northampton) "and two others of the night-police" (*M*), "Ball went with him to look for his horse, which they found at the top of Abington Street" (*H*). "They went round by the Mounts towards North End" (*M*). "They then proceeded in search of the thieves. Ball having some suspicion of the parties, and where they were likely to be found, shaped his course in the direction of the Mounts" (*H*). "When near the Bull, Ball observed three men proceeding from the direction of the race-ground towards the Bee's Wing in Todd's Lane, which they entered. Ball ran forward and reached the door before they had time to secure it from the inside, and got into the house. The captain of the gang, seeing Mr. Wallis, escaped upstairs, and search was made for him at the [time] without effect. The other two had evidently been running, and their shoes were wet and grassy. They were of course, taken into custody, and two night-police were left in the house, one of whom, upon going upstairs shortly after, found Brown, the captain of the gang, in bed. The two others gave their names as James Thompson and William Johnson" (*M*). "Two of the party were captured at a house in Todd's Lane, called the Bee's Wing. The Third escaped but was taken in bed an hour or two afterwards" (*H*). "Thompson has since been identified by the police superintendent of Derby, as a man for whom he was on the look-out for a highway robbery ... Brown made his escape from Lincoln Gaol about May last and since he has been in custody in this town [Northampton he has made two other attempts at escape, once from the town, and once from the county gaol. He has been identified by Mr. Wallis as one of the men who robbed him, and the whole of them by the toll-gate keeper as the men who went through the gate a short time before Mr. Wallis . . ." (*M*) "Brown *alias* Hanson, while confined in our town gaol attempted to escape, and nearly succeeded in removing some of the stones above the door of his cell. Since his removal to the county gaol, he made another attempt to escape by getting down the privy, but was prevented by an iron grating. . . He is now closely confined in irons. Brown has made his escape from Lincoln gaol . . . and is wanted by the police there. Application has also been made from Derby for James Thompson, *alias* Rocker, *alias* Eaton" (*H*).

In twentieth-century Northampton, Todd's Lane is Grafton Street. The Bee's Wing stood at the end, close to Regent

Square. The robbers approached it from the race-course at the north-east. The police came over the Mounts to Bull Lane (now Campbell Street). From the Bull Inn, there, they would have been able to see the door of the Bee's Wing.

William Brown *alias* Wiliam Hanan, William Johnson and James Thompson pleaded Not Guilty before Lord Abinger at Northampton Summer Assizes on 10th July 1839. Owen Wallis gave evidence:

"I am a farmer at Overstone. On the 8th of June last, I was returning from Northampton Market, when a little beyond the toll-gate on the Kettering Road, I saw a man, who whistled as soon as I had passed him. That man was the prisoner Brown. There were four or five other men ahead. They surrounded my horse and seized the bridle as soon as I came up to them. They pulled me backwards off my horse, and threw me with my face down upon the ground. Some of them held me down, while others rifled my pockets. I called out 'Murder' as loud as I could, and one of them put his hand over my mouth. But I turned my mouth away and knocked the man down, and called out again: 'Murder'. During this time the other men were rifling my pockets. When they found they could not stop my mouth, they beat me on the head, and then tried to tighten my neckerchief. The last four or five blows were done with a bludgeon. After I was hit with the bludgeon, I lay quiet, till the men left me. Then I got up and looked down the road, but I could see nothing of them." [Bludgeon produced] "Yes, I found that when I got up from the ground. My hat was broken to pieces. I then went back to the toll-gate and called the keeper up. He went to Northampton with me. We went to the station house and saw Ball. He went with us to a house called the Bee's Wing. As we approached the house, there were three or four men going in. We went straight in after them. One man – Brown it was – got out of the bedroom window or the back door. There were two other men in the house. On looking at them, we could see the hair on their heads was wet, as if by perspiration. Their shoes were also wet, and some pieces of grass and daisies were sticking to them. I saw the prisoner Brown in the town gaol next day, and I recognised him as the man I saw first."

Superintendent Joe Ball's evidence added little to that of Owen Wallis; nor did the words of John Forster, keeper of the Bee's Wing, and Joseph Quemby, toll-gate keeper; but a female witness was helpful.

Anne Robinson: "I am servant at the Bee's Wing. On 7th June, six men, a boy and three women came. I saw the men go in and out several times on Saturday. They left at nine o'clock in the evening and returned about twelve. The policemen came in directly after, and Brown went out by the door leading to the yard and staircase. The outer door was locked. I saw him again when Ball brought him downstairs. Brown wore a black hat covered with oilskin, on Friday."

The verdict was "Guilty"; and the sentence was transportation for 15 years. When he heard the sentence, Brown made a remark. The two newspapers had quite different versions of it. *Mercury:*

"Brown looked satisfied, and said in a loud clear voice: 'Ball, I'll have my clothes and pipe, now'."

Herald:

"Thank you, my Lord. Ball, give me my cap and boots."

Take your pick.

10th June 1839

MANSLAUGHTER AT IRTHLINGBOROUGH

In another Court at Northampton Summer Assizes, before His Honour Sir Joseph Littledale, John Keach stood charged with killing and slaying John Smith. In evidence, Jane Smith delivered her eye-witness account:

"I am the widow of John Smith, and I lived with him at Irthlingborough. On 10th of last month, I was at supper with my husband and son. John Keach came into the house and shut the door. He asked for the boy. He accused him of having said something about his wife. He said we harboured the boy in it. We said we did not, and my husband got up to turn him out. He said: 'I'm going to put you out,' and he went to catch hold of him; but Keach kicked the table over. My husband stooped to pick it up, and Keach seized hold of him and they fell. My husband was underneath. He was saying: 'He'll throttle me. He'll throttle me.' I felt round his neck to see whether the neckerchief was tight, but it wasn't. But Keach had his hand under the neckerchief on my husband's throat. My boy hit Keach on the back with a hoe. The men got up, and when he was hit, Keach said: 'Damn you. If I knew who it was I'd kill him.' My husband went to the door and called Bridgeland, our neighbour. He came into the yard where the two men were, now. He threw Keach down. Bridgeland said: 'Don't hit him now, John. He's down.' My husband said: 'No, I won't, but he's hit me pretty well.' Keach got up and came up to my husband who was standing by the doorway, and challenged him to fight; but my husband refused. Suddenly he dropped down, and just died."

A surgeon gave evidence that he had died from the rupture of blood vessels in the lungs. Keach, who did not give evidence, was found guilty and sentenced to imprisonment for six months.

16th June 1839

A TOLL-GATE ON SUNDAY

Joseph Mee was a draper, of Market Street, Wellingborough. He stopped his horse and gig at the toll-gate at the beginning of the Finedon Turnpike road. The gate-keeper indicated that he required payment of toll before opening the gate. The draper demurred: he said that he was on his way to his regular place of worship, and therefore was exempt from toll. The gate-keeper was insistent, and Joseph Mee paid up; but both parties agreed to let the Wellingborough magistrates settle the issue.

The next morning, 17th June 1839, the two disputants went before the Wellingborough Petty Sessions to state their case. Two Anglican clergymen, the Rev. William Stockdale, and the Rev. S. W. Paul, were sitting with Thomas Williams. On this point, their learned clerk would need to be consulted, so any sectarian bias they might have had would not matter. The case of Levis v. Hammond was found to be a deciding precedent. The exemption from toll for persons going to, and returning from a place of religious worship, had been decided not to extend to churches and chapel out of the parish. The General Turnpike Act had been passed since that case, but contained nothing to vary that principle. The magistrates were therefore of the opinion that Joseph Mee was liable to pay toll.

On 15th July, the Wellingborough Petty Sessions found the same case again before the Bench. The legislation (chapter and verse quoted in a written submission) could be interpreted as excluding dissenting places of worship. The magistrates reversed their original decision.

The original dispute was reported in the *Northampton Herald* on 22nd June 1839 (p. 3, col. 5).

17th June 1839

"SEVERAL VERY UNPLEASANT THINGS"

There is reason to believe that the following letter from "A Passing Rambler" which was printed in the *Northampton Herald* of 22nd June 1839 (p. 4, col. 1), describes experiences of Monday 17th June.

"I saw several very unpleasant things during my ramble a day or two ago in the neighbourhood of Northampton. On going out of town I overtook a young lad, about fifteen years of age, conducting a drunken father to his home! I next saw seventy sheep cropping the young shoots of a hedge on the turnpike road, the said hedge not belonging to the owner of the sheep, but to another person! I afterwards saw a labouring man at three o'clock in the afternoon, robbing his employer by sleeping in a field where he was supposed to be working! I then went through the village of Duston, belonging to Lord Melbourne, the Prime Minister of England, and found my nose offended by the stench of open drains, such as, in my opinion, it is disgraceful in any friend to the poor to permit! Lastly, at about five o'clock in the afternoon, I met a tramping woman, half drunk, holding her husband, entirely drunk, by the arm, both the man and the woman having been first seen by me in the morning in the act of begging and of being relieved at a farmer's house. As it may do good to expose such matters . . . I should be glad if you would insert them in your excellent journal."

A cynic might ask: was this writer the farmer who owned the hedge eaten by marauding sheep; who employed the sleeping labourer; who gave to the begging couple money which they spent on drink; and who, as a *Herald* reader would have been a political opponent of the Whig Prime Minister who owned Duston?

20th June 1839

THE STOCK IN TRADE OF A
NORTHAMPTON SHOE MANUFACTURER

Penn & Penn, Boot and Shoe Manufacturers, were bankrupt. The receivers arranged the auction of property and stock-in-trade, on Thursday, 20th June 1839, at six o'clock, at the Goat Inn, Northampton.

The remaining lease of the house and premises, in the occupation of John Denston Penn, "about the centre of Gold Street, Northampton", was for sale. The thirty-year lease had been taken at a rental of twenty pounds per annum from 25th March 1825.

The stock-in-trade, listed in the auctioneer's advertisement (*Northampton Mercury* 15th June 1839, p. 3, col. 3), comprised

"50 dozen of closed and unclosed upper-leathers and quarters, quantity of calf skins, goat ditto, basils, roans, in various colours; enamelled and spotted skivers and skins, binders, linings, sole leather, &c.; a considerable number of patent brass and horn heels, brass and iron tips, copper points, a general assortment of lasts and boot blocks, eight cutting boards, large and small beam and scales, seven 56lb. and smaller weights, desks, and shop fittings . . ."

28th June 1839

THE SCHOOL WITH FAMOUS ALE AND WINE

"DESIRABLE INVESTMENT,
BYFIELD, near Daventry, Northamptonshire,
TO BE SOLD BY AUCTION,
By J. M. Payn,
(unless previously disposed of by Private Contract)
On Friday the 28th of June, 1839, at the Rose and Crown Inn, Byfield, at Three o'clock in the afternoon, THAT capital Freehold HOUSE, now in the occupation of the Misses WYON, situated in the most pleasant part of Byfield aforesaid, having been for nearly forty years established as a first-rate Ladies' Boarding School. The House and Buildings are in a good state of repair, and consist of a capital dining

and breakfast room, two school rooms one of which is 16½ feet by 21, and the other 17 by 17; large kitchen and scullery, famous ale and wine cellars, dairy, pantry, wash-house, laundry, &c.; also, six full-sized bed rooms on the first floor, and five attics above with convenient closets; also a pasture land adjoining, containing nearly two acres; with a good stable, cow-shed, and all other requisite outbuildings.

The above may be viewed any day within a week previous to the sale.

For further particulars, apply to the Auctioneer, Daventry."

(*Northampton Mercury* 15th June 1839, p. 2, col. 4.)

2nd July 1839

A HEAD-ON RAIL COLLISION

Is it possible to detect glee in the *Northampton Herald's* account of a crash on the London and Birmingham line? (6th July 1839, p. 3, col. 3). The *Mercury* did not mention it.

"On Tuesday as the down train was coming near Roade, it met a ballast-train, which by shameful neglect, was on the same line of rails. The engines meeting were both smashed, and we regret to add that by the concussion, the face of a young man came in contact with the forehead of a lady opposite to him, and all his front teeth were knocked out. The whole of the passengers were thrown from their seats and more or less injured. The cost of repairing the engines, it is said, will exceed one hundred pounds."

4th July 1839

A NEW GAOL FOR PETERBOROUGH

The Royal Assent was given on 4th July 1839, to an Act of Parliament providing for a new prison at Peterborough, to be erected in Thorpe Road. This was to replace the ancient gaol in the King's lodging at the main entrance to the Minster Precincts. A year earlier, a prisoner had made an audacious escape from the old gaol by scraping his way up through the pavement of the Minster yard. (*See* 20th June 1838.) It is likely that this was a consideration when the new gaol was decided upon. Certainly Andrew Percival thought so.[31] He was a new arrival in Peterborough at that time. There were two gaols, he tells us. "The other stood upon the site of Cumbergate Almshouses." He mentions a family named Rogers. "They were the black sheep of the place. The head of the family was . . . Jimmy Rogers, and he took it into his head to dine one day upon sheep's head and pluck, which he stole from a butcher's shop. He was ordered to be put into the Feoffees' Gaol. He picked his way out, and this thief of the district and his family disappeared and never came back again. It was thought to be time we had a gaol, and the present building on the Thorpe Road was erected."

W. T. Mellows wrote a brief history of the King's Lodging Gaol in 1933.[150] There had recently been some restoration following the exposure of the bases of three bays of the ancient building in 1927 when the site of the National Provincial Bank was excavated. "The larger room was a gloomy vault in which a great wooden cage was made to secure the prisoners, and the cage was divided by a partition into two cells. Between these and the Gateway was the Gaol Room or condemned cell which, as its 12th century window had been blocked up, had only an iron grated aperture ten inches by seven in the door for . . . light and air." The door had been preserved since the old gaol closed, and it was now restored to its original position, bearing a brass plate with the inscription: "This door was preserved for many years by the Peterborough Natural History and Archaeological Society in its Museum, and was in the year 1930 given by the Society to be re-hung here, its original position, and here remain."

7th July 1839

A VIOLENT STORM AND THE END OF A WINDMILL

The whole county was affected by a tremendous storm on Sunday evening, 7th July. The *Northampton Mercury's* account (13th July 1839, p. 3, col. 5) began with the storm over its home town. It was

"the grandest in effect and the longest in duration within the memory of man. At an early part of the evening the intense purple of the sky in the south and south-east, from which occasional flashes of vivid lightning were emitted, gave token of its approach. Towards ten o'clock it broke over the neighbourhood in awful magnificence. . . . The lightning struck the roof of an old house in Bridge Street, penetrating to the room beneath, tearing up the window sill, passing through another floor, and making its exit by a latticed window which it shattered considerably. The poor woman who occupies the house was in bed with her children in one of the rooms, but although greatly alarmed, none were injured. The chimney of the chapel in Commercial Street was likewise struck, and some bricks displaced. At Rothersthorpe two valuable beasts . . . were killed. . . . At Titchmarsh, an ox . . . was killed; and another . . . at Winwick. . . . A barn in the parish of Upton [Soke] near Stamford, containing about sixteen quarters of wheat was set on fire, and . . . entirely destroyed. . . . The storm commenced at Peterborough about seven, and continued till between one and two . . ."

In a separate report on the same page (col. 6):

"During the tremendous and long-continued storm . . . a windmill, the property of Mrs. Brookes, and in the occupation of Mr. Cox, both of Great Oxenden, was shattered almost to pices. The main post was split in several places, and will have to be removed. Two of the sails were destroyed, besides much other damage . . ."

The original Ordnance Survey map shows only the site of the windmill at Great Oxenden ("Oxenden Magna").

9th July 1839

WAS THE WILL GENUINE?

An altercation between a Northampton solicitor, Henry Becke, and a barrister, Sergeant Goulburn, took place during a case at the Northamptonshire Assizes concerning a Glapthorne will. Becke did not like the way the *Northampton Herald* reported the case, and wrote a letter of protest, which the Editor did not publish, although he did suggest that Becke had a tendency to be hot-headed about his cases.

Let us look at the conduct of the case before the Nisi Prius Court at the Summer Assizes in Northampton, on Tuesday, 9th July 1839. It was listed as *Doe Dem.* Charity and others v Bell, and Mr. Justice Littledale and a Common Jury heard it. Mr. Sergeant Goulburn, for the plaintiffs, explained: This is an action of ejectment to recover the possession of three houses at Glapthorne. The action is brought by the lessors of the plaintiff, Elizabeth Ann Charity, William Blackshaw, and Elizabeth his wife, formerly Elizabeth Charity, the heirs. The defendant, Bell, married one of the daughters of Charity senior, and was allowed to occupy one of the houses in question. I shall show that the elder Charity was in possession of all the houses, and that the lessors of the plaintiff were his heirs-at-law.

Mary Sopps: I am 68 years of age . . . I knew old Charity. he made a will, and I attested it. He died the day after he had made it. My father was parish clerk, and he wrote the will.

On looking at it, there is not so much as there was. Some part is cut off, and some words put in. The will was on a whole sheet. It has been cut at the bottom. It was examined by Mr. Gregory, one of Mr. Becke's clerks. I did not tell him it was in the same state as when I signed it. Yes I did read the will at the time I signed it. There are none of the Charitys' names in it now. They *were* in it.

Mr. Hill, for the defendant, called the defending solicitor himself to give evidence.

Henry Becke: I questioned Maria Sopps this morning. [yes, he got her first name wrong]. She did not say a single syllable as to the will being tampered with. The first time I ever heard of this was a few minutes ago. [in her evidence].

It is obvious that Becke arranged at very short notice, for himself and his clerk to give evidence; and Goulburn is likely to have been greatly displeased.

Septimus Gregory: I am clerk to Mr. Becke. I examined the witness Mary Sopps respecting this will, on Sunday afternoon last. I asked her if it was in the same state as when the testator signed the will, and she said it was. [In reply to Sergeant Goulburn:] The Rev. Mr. Wheelwright said he thought a part appeared to be cut off in a zig-zag manner. . . . On looking at it, I do not think there is any proof of a piece being cut off. It does not appear to be paper at all, but parchment . . . I understand the deceased was a tailor. He might have cut it to measure with shears before using it to write his will upon it.

Mr. Sergeant Goulburn addressed the jury, using derogatory terms about Henry Becke. The jury found for the plaintiffs on two of the houses (those not occupied by Bell).
Henry Becke wrote his letter to the *Herald* on 19th July. He probably knew that it would not be published, and he took the precaution of providing a copy for the rival *Mercury*. It was printed in that paper the very next day (p. 3, col. 6):

"Sir, – I am most reluctant . . . to again draw your attention to the fact (which is a matter of notoriety to the legal profession on this circuit) that Sergeant Goulburn and myself are on terms of strong personal enmity towards each other, and that he takes every opportunity of maligning me in every case where he may be acting as counsel against my client, and when the rules of a Court of Justice and regard to the interest of the client, prevent the solicitor who is the subject of the counsel's abuse from vindicating himself publicly in Court; and although I have, on three different occasions, when thus attacked by Sergeant Goulburn, departed from this rule, and addressed the Judge, in terms of remonstrance, on the unwarrantable conduct of Sergt. Goulburn, and on one of those occasions, the Chief Baron (my Lord Lyndhurst) and the three other learned Judges of the Court of Exchequer, all strongly condemned Sergt. Goulburn's attack on me, and in the most gracious and considerate language, completely exonerated me from his imputations, yet nevertheless I feel reluctant, and indeed am advised, not again to obtrude myself on the indulgence of the Court, as it would cause an unseemly interruption to the proceedings, and perhaps prejudice the cause of my client.

"In the present case, the report of his trial, in the *Herald* of Saturday last, conveys a most partial impression in favour of the plaintiff, of the facts as disclosed in the trial, besides the insertion of that part of Sergt. Goulburn's speech accusing the defendant of 'fraud', and also 'reprehending Mr. Becke for the manner in which the defence had been conducted'. The latter passage is quite true, but I think you should have included in your report that part of the evidence, on behalf of the defendant, which went directly to the fact that the witness Sopps admitted, on her cross-examination, that she had concealed from my clerks and myself the facts she subsequently swore to, as to the alleged interpolation and cutting of the will nearly twenty years ago; and what is more important still, that Mr. Charles Hall, of Uppingham, the plaintiff's attorney, on 18th February last (being the eve of the last Lent Assizes, and when this cause was expected to be tried, but the *plaintiff then withdrew* his notice of trial), wrote me a letter (which was duly proved and read in evidence) wherein he *actually admits the execution of the will* which his counsel now alleges to be a fabricated document, and that my client was entitled to a life interest in one of the houses, and which the result of the trial has at present deprived him of. I am therefore at a loss to conceive why I should be censured in the discharge of an important duty to my client, for conducting the case as if the will were genuine (and which I fully believe it is); and I only attribute the abuse I received to the inimical feeling entertained by the plaintiff's counsel, Sergt. Goulburn, towards myself . . .

"Sergt. Goulburn certainly did throw the imputation on my client [of altering the will], but the dates of the transaction given in evidence showed that this charge was both groundless and absurd, inasmuch as at the time the will was alleged by Sergt. Goulburn to be altered by my client, *it was actually in the office of the registrar,* at Peterborough, where it has ever since remained until it was produced by the Registrar himself at the assizes. I need scarcely say that my client intends moving the Court above, next Term, to set aside the verdict, in the above, and other grounds which will be then disclosed.

"I am, Sir, your obedient servant . . ."

Any reader of Henry Becke's letter is surely inclined to ask why he struggled with hostile witnesses to try to prove the will genuine, if he only needed to call the Registrar to testify that no would-be forger had access to it.

17th July 1839

NORTHAMPTON BAPTISTS

"Mount Zion Chapel, Northampton. The opening of this place of worship took place on Wednesday the 17th, on which occasion three sermons were preached. . . . The place was generally much crowded, so that more than 1,000 persons are believed to have been on several occasions . . . and many were unable to gain admission at all. The chapel is 58 feet by 6 by 44, and there is a large schoolroom underneath for the accommodation of 3 or 4 hundred children . . ."

(*Northampton Mercury* 27th July 1839, p. 3, col. 5.)

This chapel stood in Grey Friars' Street, Newland, to the north east of Northampton Market Square. It cost £2,000 including £500 for the land and a piece at the back for interments.

17th to 24th July 1839

SHOEMAKERS ON STRIKE

The operative shoemakers of Northampton began a general stoppage of work on Wednesday 17th July. Their demands were increases in the payment for categories of work: sixpence per dozen on blocking; threepence a dozen on shoe-closing, lining and binding; a penny a pair on Wellington boot closing and on Clarence closing; threepence a pair on Wellington boot making, twopence on Clarence making; twopence a pair on shoe and pump making; a penny per pair for making youths' shoes and pumps, and on slippers. The manufacturers called their own meeting the next evening, Thursday, and formulated an offer: twopence per pair extra on Clarence and cloth-boot making and a penny per pair on making Bluchers and all shoes. This was rejected. Details of the demands and of the offer were printed in the *Mercury* (p. 3, col. 4).

The Daventry shoemakers, who were also on strike, produced an impressive handbill, composed in an elegant prose style that could well serve as a model for trade-union "spokesmen" of a century and a half later.

"TO THE GENTRY AND INHABITANTS GENERALLY OF DAVENTRY AND ITS VICINITY.
"GENTLEMEN AND FELLOW TOWNSMEN.
"THE grateful recollection of past favors [sic] received

from you on similar occasions, induces us to believe, that this our present necessary and *honest appeal,* will meet with your compliance; trusting it would be superfluous in us to arouse to action your manly feelings, or stimulate your generous sympathies on our behalf by a lengthened detail of our *degraded position,* or by depicting that huge *mass of misery* which so generally pervades our dwellings.

"Be assured Gentlemen, we ask not your assistance for the furtherance of any base, mean, or ignoble purpose, but enlist your sympathies in the meritorious nature of our design, viz. − a small advance of wages. You know Gentlemen, that the accomplishment of a project requires means to its attainment, such necessary means, the journeymen Boot and Shoe-makers do not possess: we therefore crave the protection of our more wealthy fellow-townsmen, hoping that they will patronise our laudable intentions *by their pecuniary donations.*

"We advocate not Gentlemen, the principle of STRIKES, believing them to be often founded in imprudence, and unsuccessful in their ultimate results. We therefore resort to this as a necessary evil, arising from the want of a more close *union* between the apparent conflicting but identical interests of the Employers and the Employed.

"The advance we require is, 3d. per pair on Boots, and 2d. per pair on Shoes, which we do for the following reasons:−

"1st. Because we believe our present wages are far below those of almost any other Mechanics, and quite inadequate for our comfortable support, − bearing no proportion to the high price of provisions, − nor in any way regulated by the demands for the articles we assist in manufacturing.

"2nd. Because the advance if acceded to would not injure our respected Employers, as they would be quite as able to obtain (while there is a brisk demand) 2d. per pair on their Shoes, as the Farmer does very often 1s. per bushel on his corn, as the Butcher an advance on his meat, the Clothier on his cloth, the Tailor on his garments, the Grocer on his sugar, and the Baker on his half-quartern loaf, on Thursday morning.

"Yours Respectfully, The Journeymen Boot and Shoe-makers.

"Daventry, July 22nd, 1839.

"N.B. Persons duly authorised to received Donations, will wait upon the Inhabitants."

The strike lasted from Wednesday to Wednesday. Northampton

"was daily paraded by a vast body of operatives, inspirited by a band of music, and banner bearing the inscription 'No Surrender' and 'Sink or Swim' . . ."

(*Northampton Mercury* 27th July 1839, p. 3, col. 5).

On Wednesday 24th July, the operatives accepted the offer of the manufacturers.

"A great deal of privation will be the consequence of the strike,"

stated the *Mercury*, explaining that it would take a long time for the small gain to compensate for the loss of eight days' work. On the other hand, did none of them consider working on the next eight Mondays?

18th July 1839

LONDON BY HALF PAST NINE IN THE MORNING

"An important alteration has been made in the trains on the London and Birmingham Railway. . . . The earliest train to London . . . was, up to Thursday week [18th July], that which leaves Blisworth at half-past eight. But a train now starts from Roade at the early hour of half-past six, so that the traveller from Northampton may reach London by half-past nine in the morning. We believe we owe this important advantage to the exertions of Mr. Shaw of the Angel Hotel, who has altered the time of the Commercial, hitherto a night coach running to the mail train, accordingly . . ."

(*Northampton Mercury* 27th July 1839, p. 3, col. 5.)

31st July 1839

FLOOD

". . . The rains which had fallen almost incessantly during the whole of July fell more heavily and with fewer intervals . . . as the month drew to its close, and so recently as Wednesday [31st july] the meadows were flooded to an extent rarely observable even [in] winter."

(*Northampton Mercury* 3rd August 1839, p. 3, col. 5.)

". . . In consequence of the almost unintermitting and heavy rain, the meadows . . . have been deluged with a more extensive flood than we can recollect . . . for many years."

(*Northampton Herald,* same date, p. 3, col. 1).

Both papers described St. James's End at Northampton.

"The high road was flooded to the depth of several feet, the water forcing its way through the houses with the fury of a torrent."

(*Mercury.*)

"The water overflowed the banks of the river Nen and flooded the whole of St. James's End, so that the residents there could not gain access to the town for several hours . . ."

(*Herald.*)

"A great quantity of hay has been spoiled; much has been fairly floated off, and . . . must have found its way, ere this, to Peterborough . . ."

(*Mercury.*)

"We have heard of several instances of the hay being entirely swept from the meadows, and the operations of Bugbrook and other mills were effectually stopped, the hay having been forced into the works."

(*Herald*.)

1st August 1839

"THE MAYOR OF SCARLETWELL"

Public attention was briefly focused on a place of forgotten civic prominence in Northampton, at the beginning of August 1839.

"A small but substantial brick building of a classic form, has just been placed over Scarlet Well, in this town. The pediment is inscribed – 'Scarlet Well. Erected by Mrs. Kerr. 1839.' The spring is of very ancient repute."

This was a brief notice in the *Northampton Mercury* of 3rd August (p. 3, col. 5).

Centuries earlier, the well gave red water used for dyeing. That district of the medieval town, near the north-west wall, close to the castle, was important enough to have the Town Hall there.[151] In the words of the seventeenth-century Town Clerk, Henry Lee,

"the old Town Hall was in a little close adjoining the last houses on the right hand in ye lane going from ye Mayorhold to Scarletwell, wch well was much esteemed in those times, there is a mark of stone work circular upon y^3 west end of ye little house that adjoyned to ye old Hall."

All through the Victorian period the inhabitants of this district maintained the custom of electing their own independent "Mayor of Scarletwell". This probably originated when the civic centre moved away to the modern town centre.[152]

332

Although lacking official status, this popular representative of the district known as "the Boroughs" sometimes uttered pronouncements on civic affairs. The custom ended in 1909 when the last "Mayor of Scarletwell" died in office.

2nd August 1839

TWO MILLS FOR SALE

A Rushden windmill was offered for sale by auction on August 2nd. At this time, one of the Northampton water mills was also on offer. Both were advertised in the *Northampton Mercury* of 20th July 1839 (p. 2, col. 6; and p. 3, col. 1).

Samuel Achurch had tried to sell his post windmill at Rushden when it became vacant exactly a year earlier (see 11th August 1838). He moved into it himself, and spent the last year of his life there. Now that Samuel was dead, William Achurch was selling "a close of superior Turnip Land, containing by estimation seven Acres, with the TENEMENTS and POST WINDMILL standing thereon . . . adjoining the Turnpike Road from Wellingborough to Bedford . . ."

The Northampton mill on offer was the "WATER CORN MILL , known by the name of SAINT ANDREW'S MILL . . . and about Twelve Acres of excellent MEADOW GROUND adjoining, in the occupation of Mr. Perry." This mill, usually known as Perry's Mill, had been through many changes during the preceding century, from corn to cotton; from water power to steam and back to water. The building no longer exists, but its site, where Gas Street approaches its former mill stream, may still be found.

5th August 1839

SHOEMAKING AT THE COUNTY GAOL

When Northampton Town Council met on Monday 5th August, plans for the enlargement of the Borough Gaol were ready for the Councillors. On the motion of Mr. H. Marshall, it was resolved that they be forwarded to the Secretary of State for Home Affairs for his sanction.

The minutes of this meeting show that prisoners were not held in the Borough Gaol. Instead, they were interned in the County Gaol, and the County Magistrates had to be paid for their subsistence. A glance at the Borough Fund Account for the year ending 31st August 1839 shows various expenses for the Town-maintained gaol: "Gaoler's salary, and allowance in lieu of fees," £63; repairs, £5 14 shillings and elevenpence; taxes, poor rate, highway rate, church rate, £5 11 shillings and $8\frac{1}{2}$ pence; removing convicts to the hulks (that is prisoners for transportation), £27 12 shillings.

The figures that must have caused those Town Councillors much concern were "subsistence of prisoners in town gaol", 4 shillings and sevenpence; "subsistence of town prisoners in county gaol during five quarters", £376 13 shillings. The above-mentioned Councillor H. Marshall pointed out that considerable savings could be achieved by "undertaking the support of our own prisoners instead of turning them over to the county", but that was not all: shoemakers committed to hard labour in the county gaol "were put upon their seats and made to earn from 8 shillings to 10 shillings a week" making shoes. Marshall himself was in the shoe trade: "I have myself paid six or seven pounds a week for shoes made in the gaol . . . I have paid as much as £30 at a time to Mr. Grant, county gaoler, for work of the same kind. From all this the town has derived not a halfpenny advantage . . ."

When the Town Council met next month, Monday 2nd September 1839, discussion of the future organisation of the Borough Gaol continued. Councillors who wished to put prisoners to work making shoes, were against adapting the building "to the classification system" in which the prisoners were kept in separate groups according to the seriousness of their crimes. Mr. Hallam (also a shoemaker, of Belle Alliance Cottage, Northampton, employing "Clarence, Blucher, and Gaiter shoe-men") believed that discipline was more effective in the County Gaol than in the Borough Gaol. Mr. W. Percival thought so too, and mentioned the case of a man who had often been in the Borough Gaol, where he was unmanageable; but having been placed under the care of Mr. Grant at the County Gaol, for poaching [a county offence, of course], he had become thoroughly tractable, and had worked on the treadwheel as kindly as the rest.

H. Marshall: I don't see much classification in the County Gaol. All the shoemakers there work together in one long room.

Mr. Mercer: Have you seen that, Mr. Marshall?

Marshall: I have.

Hallam: You have seen several working together as if in their shop?

Marshall: Yes, and they do there as they do in their own shop – kick you for something to drink. (Laughter.)

Hallam: But that is not punishment at all.

5th August 1839

LORD CARDIGAN DRAWING ANOTHER ATTACK UPON HIMSELF

The Earl of Cardigan was still at Canterbury, commanding the 11th Hussars. On this day, six of his officers, not on duty, galloped over private land, recklessly trampling down crops awaiting harvest. They were intercepted by the father of the landowner, a magistrate, and also a Radical Whig. The officers were offensive, arrogant, insulting and violent. They bundled him out of their way, and refused to give their names. He followed them to barracks, but they gave orders that he was not to be admitted. Cardigan refused to see him and ignored his letters. He wrote to the Commander-in-Chief, who twice refused to intervene. Meanwhile the Whig press, especially the *Morning Post,* seized on this story, and turned it to political advantage (Cardigan's officers were all Tories).

The *Northampton Mercury* carried a very comprehensive account, over several weeks, reprinting all correspondence in full. Modern readers may turn to accounts to suit their political inclinations. Joan Wake's story is brief, repeating the Tory version from contemporary military books such as *Our Heroes of the Crimea.*[153] Cecil Woodham-Smith's account is hostile to Cardigan.[154] Donald Thomas's version is very fair.[155]

19th August 1839

A RAILWAY ACCIDENT AND A
DISPUTED INQUEST VERDICT

The Coroner, George Abbey, held an inquest at Northampton Infirmary on Monday 2nd September 1839, on view of the body of a Welshman, Thomas Davis, who had died in there two weeks after sustaining injuries in an accident at Blisworth station. Two railway porters gave evidence.

Benjamin Hawkins: I am a porter at the Blisworth station. On Monday week, that was 19th August, the deceased, who was a Welsh salesman, was there, in company with another person. They were both strangers. While they were standing there, the train started, and the deceased and his companion ran after it, with the intention of getting into the carriages. They both failed in the attempt. The deceased was thrown down by the train, and the wheels passed over his feet. One of them was severely lacerated. Another man, and I immediately went to him. He was unable to walk, but I was not able to see the extent of the injury till his shoes were taken off. A surgeon was sent for and came quickly. After examining and dressing the wound, he recommended removing him to the Infirmary. I went with him. I did not hear him complain much. Since the accident, I have been told that he has had fits of insanity. There was no person to blame. We did try to prevent him trying to get on the train.

John Bott, porter, corroborated.

Corbett Whitton: I am a pupil at the Northampton Infirmary. The deceased was brought to the house about nine o'clock on the evening of Monday, 19th August. On examination, I found him to be suffering from a severe laceration of the under part of the right foot, and a compound fracture of the little toe of the left foot. I observed symptoms of insanity in the deceased from the day after his arrival in the house, till he died. I attended him the whole time, and I have no doubt that his death was occasioned by the mortification of the right foot. He died on Sunday morning, yesterday, about 11 o'clock.

The verdict was "Accidental Death, with a deodand of one shilling on the carriage". (The carriage caused the accident so the owner of it must pay one shilling.)

There was a witness of the accident, who did not give evidence at the inquest. This was Francis Tebbutt, of Welton Vicarage. He did not know that Thomas Davis had died until he read an account of the inquest in the *Northampton Herald*. On 17th September he wrote to the Editor of the *Herald* a letter that was printed on 21st September 1839 (p. 3, col. 4).

"Sir, – I regret that circumstances have prevented my earlier attention to your report of an inquest held on the body of an unfortunate Welch [sic] salesman, whose death was occasioned by an accident on the railway at Blisworth station. The evidence of the two railway porters before the coroner was totally at variance with the facts of the transaction. I was a passenger in the train, and a sorrowful spectator of the melancholy occurrence from first to last. Therefore I am enabled most positively to contradict the testimony alluded to. It is false that the poor fellow strove to enter the carriage in opposition to the expressed desire of the porters, or any one else employed by the Company. The deceased and another man were anxious to go, and in consequence, one of the guards gave a signal to the engineman to stop the train. He was not attended to, however, and the velocity gradually increased. I need hardly observe that if the guard had acted humanely, or even discreetly, at that moment, he would have discountenanced the man's attempt to gain the train, but unfortunately, regardless apparently of all danger, he took the poor fellow by the hand, rashly dragged him along over the sleepers, and other impediments, on that huge embankment, close by the side of the train, threw open a carriage door, directed him to seize hold of the handle and spring in. His first attempt failed, and he was nearly killed; in the second, he was felled to the earth, and his bones crushed, and *then* the train stopped! I beg to add that I should certainly have attended the coroner's inquest and stated the above facts, had I known of the poor fellow's death. On this occasion, I think it may be acceptable to the Railway Company to state also that one of the guards in attendance at the time referred to, a short man, whose number, If I remember rightly, was 125, contrary to the rules advertised, smoked a cigar.

"Your obedient servant . . ."

28th August 1839

"FATHER OF ENGLISH GEOLOGY"

There is a white marble monument surmounted by a bust, in St. Peter's Church, Northampton, for William Smith, L.L.D., an eminent geologist. As a mineral surveyor and civil engineer, the inscription tells us, he surveyed for canals and collieries, and published an important "Geological Map of England and Wales". By specialising in that one branch of science, he earned the title "Father of English Geology". The epitaph concludes: "He died in this Town at the house of his Friend, George Baker, the Historian of Northamptonshire, 28th of August, 1839."

Baker's house, a few yards from St. Peter's, was the famous Hazelrigg Mansion, 33 Marefair. Dr. Smith was staying there to break his journey to Birmingham where he was to attend a meeting of the British Association for the Advancement of Science. Baker and Smith made several excursions into the Northamptonshire countryside, and on one of them, the geologist caught a chill.[156]. An obituary notice in the *Gentleman's Magazine* (January 1840, vol. 13, p. 100) says:

> "Dr. Smith came to Northampton from London on Tuesday 20th August. . . . On the Friday following he was suddenly attacked with a bilious diarrhoea, which immediately prostrated his strength, and his death ensued on Wednesday the 28th." He was 70. "His body was attended to the grave . . . by his nephew, Professor Phillips, and his afflicted friend, Mr. Baker, on the Monday after his decease."

29th August 1839

BRIDGE-BUILDING ALONG THE RIVER

> "RIVER NEN NAVIGATION
> To BUILDERS AND OTHERS.
> TENDERS are required for BUILDING a HORSE BRIDGE at Cogenhoe Mill, 60 feet long, set upon piles 20 feet long, to be driven into the bottom of the river six feet, or more if required, the whole to be of prime English Oak, and will require about 245 cubic feet.
> "Also for BUILDING a HORSE BRIDGE at Billing Mill, 60 feet long, set upon piles 17 feet long, to be driven into the bottom of the river six feet, or more if required, the whole to be of prime English Oak, and will require about 217 cubic feet.
> "Plans and specifications of the same to be seen at Mr. Bevan's office, Wellingborough, on the 11th and 18th days of September next, and Tenders to be sent to Mr. Bevan, on or before the 16th day of October next, directed "Tenders for the River Nen."
> "29th August, 1839."

(*Northampton Mercury* 31st August 1839, p. 2, col. 5.)

31st August 1839

CURIOUS ITEMS FROM NORTHAMPTON
BOROUGH FUND ACCOUNT

The Northampton Town accounts for the year ending 31st August 1839 were published at the end of the calendar year, in December. Items from them have been used on an earlier page to illustrate the Council's discussion on the prisons (see 5th August 1839). Here we have the police expenditure. It will be seen that the police station was assessed for rates as the gaol was.

"To the superintendent (Joseph Ball) day and night constables, for salary and service, including constables'

	£	s	d
yearly account	£641	8s	2d
To clothing for constables	40	5	6
To rent of station-house (1½ years)	24	0	0
To repairs for same		9	6
To poor's-rate, 18s, and church-rate, 2s 6d, for same	1	0	6
To coals and candles for same	8	1	6
To the superintendent (Wm Hollis) and special constables	27	14	6"

Some of the items on the "MISCELLANEOUS" list invite speculation:

	£	s	d
"To George Abbey, Coroner, expenses for taking inquests	£52	3s	8d
William Hull, surveyor	68	19	0
John Armitt, for iron chests	52	1	6
Wm Hull, for fencing for close occupied by John Perkins, and for dividing of meadows adjoining the Houghton road	47	16	9
Thomas Cooper for fencing, and dividing meadows	18	8	9
John Perkins, for planting trees and repairing quick	6	4	9

Thomas Watts, for making good the ground adjoining the Waterworks	4	0	0
Marmaduke Newby, for coals for the Town Hall	2	11	3
Atkins & Sons, for mourning at the death of the late King, and for repairs at the Town Hall	7	2	7
Relieving and removing vagrants, £36 16s 11d, & maintenance of a pauper lunatic £28 3s 2d.	65	0	1
Conveyance of Baggage	0	6	0
Excise-officer for keeping account of brisk earth	0	9	0
John Ward, for crying down fire-works	0	4	0"

4th September 1839

INFANTS' CORDIAL

Henry Jackman's travelling theatrical company arrived in Northampton during August 1839, and opened at the Mare-fair Theatre on 19th. Jackman's son-in-law, George Partleton, was a member of the company. His daughter, Frances Partleton, usually performed, but a new baby had been born to the Partletons a few weeks earlier at Uxbridge. Their Northampton lodgings were in Wellington Street.[157]

A contemporary poster shows that "This Evening MONDAY Sept. 2nd. 1839 Will be Presented the Popular New Comic DRAMA, never acted here, call'd THE *White Horse of the Peppers*, . . ." Partleton played the part of Looney.

On the evening of Wednesday, 4th September, baby Helen was "restless". Her mother sent the servant, Matilda Branston, to Bridge Street to fetch a pennyworth of "Infants' Cordial". After being given a teaspoonful, the baby fell asleep so heavily that Matilda became alarmed. She carried the baby to the druggist's shop to make sure that the cordial was correct. Mrs. Harris, the druggist's wife, reassured the servant that all was correct, and the baby was carried back to the lodgings and placed in her cradle. Soon, however, she was found to have died. These events were, of course, related as evidence at the inquest. A doctor who had been called, and who had tried to revive the child, said that death had been caused by the poisonous effects of the sedative. The druggist, Harris, said that he made up "Infants' Cordial" as an imitation of Godfrey's Cordial, a proprietary medicine which contained laudanum. He sold over a gallon of it every week.

The Coroner, George Abbey, happened to be one of the proprietors of the theatre.[157]

7th September 1839

INDECENT ADVERTISEMENT

During August 1839, there was editorial protest in the *Northampton Mercury* against a regular advertisement in the *Northampton Herald,* identified in the former by page and column, but never by the name of firm. The objectionable advertisement was a long announcement by a Northampton chemist, part of which offered a treatment for syphilis.

The *Mercury* of 7th September (p. 3, col. 6) had the following reproof:

"In spite of our advice, our Contemporary it seems is determined to persevere in pocketing his weekly gains and inserting the indecent advertisement. Looking at his determination as opponents, we cannot regret it. We are mistaken in our opinion of many of his Conservative subscribers, if they will be content to see the filthy announcements which are disfiguring the walls of all our towns and villages transferred to the columns of this weekly paper, and thus placed within the view of their servants and children. . . . We shall take the liberty to inquire whether Sir C. Knightley is content with the use which is made of the pages of *his* journal?"

12th September 1839

THE FURNITURE OF A GENTEEL HOUSEHOLD

Miss Harpur was "changing her residence" at Broad Green in Wellingborough, and for a reason not given, decided to sell her furniture by auction on the premises on Thursday 12th September 1839. The detailed list in her advertisement in the *Northampton Mercury* (7th September, p. 2, col. 3), gives us an interesting impression of "genteel and useful household furniture" of the period.

It is necessary to be aware of the following definitions. Dimity was broad striped; moreen was stout woollen material; loo was a card game; zebra wood had alternate black and pale strips; bell-pulls were ropes or lengths of material, which, when pulled, activated wire pulleys to ring bells in the servants' quarters.

A footnote said that "many of the goods are nearly new", so we may assume that they were fashionable: ". . . one mahogany four-post bedstead with dimity furniture, window curtains, one tent bedstead with scarlet moreen furniture, servant's bedstead and furniture, feather and flock beds, wool and other mattresses, four pairs of blankets, marseilles quilt, cotton counterpanes, two sets of drawers, painted dressing tables, six chamber chairs, basins and ewers, swing-glasses, bedside carpeting, eight handsome solid zebra wood chairs, mahogany dining table with loose leaf and cover to ditto, mahogany circular drawing room table with triangular block, square mahogany loo table, sofa with horse-hair cover, Venetian carpet, 15 feet by 12, pair of bell-pulls, moreen window curtains, parlour fender and fire-irons, excellent eight-day clock, mahogany side-board, folding and other tables, six black chairs, twenty four superior knives and forks and carver with ivory hafts, twelve common ditto, cut fender and fire irons, warming pan, japanned and other trays, press bedsteads, tubs, trays, pails, and a variety of articles too numerous to particularize."

September 1839

EXTRAORDINARY MUSHROOM

". . . A mushroom of unusual size was lately taken from a field belonging to Mr. Cowley of Kilsby Lodge. . . . It was three feet nine inches in circumference and one foot three inches wide. It produced nearly a quart of ketchup."

(*Northampton Mercury* 14th September 1839, p. 3, col. 6.)

10th October 1839

PROCESSION IN THE RAIN

St. Katherine's Church in Northampton existed for a century and a decade. It was consecrated on Thursday 10th October 1839 by the new Bishop of Peterborough, and demolished in 1950. It had been arranged that those participating should move in procession along Gold Street and the Horsemarket to the ceremony of Consecration, starting punctually at a quarter to eleven. It rained continuously all morning, and the Bishop and civic dignitaries waited apprehensively in the George Hotel. At the appointed time, the rain eased off, and the formation moved away on its route. Constables led, formed the flanks and brought up the rear. After the leading constables, was the band, followed by the boys of Mr. Dryden's School and the Blue School. Next were the girls of Sargeant and Beckett's School, and then "Gentry", three abreast, followed by the Mayor and the Town Council. Clergy, three abreast, preceded the Vicar of All Saints, and "Minister" of St. Katherine's Church. Why did the new incumbent have the title "Minister"? Was it because his church was not yet consecrated, and he not ordained?

The Lord Bishop of Peterborough followed his Registrar, and preceded the Chancellor of the Diocese. Finally, just before the following constables, were the churchwardens of the town, with wands. The morning's proceedings were described in the *Northampton Mercury* of 12th October 1839 (p. 3, col. 4).

Exactly a fortnight later, on Thursday 24th October, the Bishop of Peterborough had another unusual engagement in his own cathedral. He officiated at the marriage of his own youngest daughter, Margaret Julia, to his Domestic Chaplain, the Rev. Marsham Argles, M.A.[158]

15th October 1839

"I HOPE YOU WILL NEVER BE TUMBLED OUT OF A CART YOURSELVES"

The case of Marriott v Stanley could be made into an entertaining comedy for the cinema. The plaintiff, Marriott, was a carpenter and keeper of the Ship Inn at Peterborough; the defendant, Stanley, was a Peterborough ironmonger.

On 15th October, 1839, Marriott's pony and cart were standing at his door, when a dog flew at the pony and startled it, so that it ran away. He ran after it and caught it, but the cart came into contact with some ploughs lying on the street, over the gutter. Marriott was dragged over them and seriously injured. The ploughs were outside Stanley's shop, but he refused to accept responsibility for Marriott's injuries. When the case came before the Lent Assizes at Northampton in March 1840, the jury were unable to reach a verdict. Marriott decided to persist with his claim, and at the Summer Assizes, it came up again, on the Nisi Prius side, before His Honour Sir Joseph Littledale, on Wednesday 22nd July 1840.

The defendant's case was that it was normal practice to lay out goods for sale in the streets of Peterborough. The pony was a restive animal, and earlier the same day, it had run away and broken to pieces another cart.

Mr. Sergeant Goulburn for the plaintiff, explained to the jury that although the previous jury had remained out all night without reaching a verdict, he intended to continue to press the case to recover compensation for the defendant's negligence. He called his first witness.

Thomas Thompson: I am a labourer, and I live at Peter-borough. I know the plaintiff, Marriott. I was on the long Causeway on 15th Of October last, about six in the evening. It was getting dark. I saw Marriott at his door with a pony and cart. He was going to fetch potatoes. The pony's head was towards Lincoln, but Marriott turned it round towards Thorpe Lane. There was a load of straw there, and a dog lying on top of it. The dog flew at the pony's nose. The pony started off at a trot, the dog running before it, barking. Marriott had hold of the pony's head and kept it until he came to the premises of Mr. Stanley, who keeps a very large ironmonger's shop. Marriott was on the near side. In front of the shop were some ploughs and other articles. They were on the carriageway side of the gutter. The plaintiff was thrown over them, and the pony went on down Bridge Street. If the ploughs had not been there, he might have stopped the pony. I also ran after it, and I had got up to it when the accident happened.

(Cross-examined by Mr. Hill for the defence): The straw was for Mr. Marriott. I have heard that the pony afterwards knocked down a child and broke its arm.

(Re-examined by Mr. Humphrey for the plaintiff): Marriott has no carriageway to his premises. The straw had just been shot down and was in the course of being taken away. I was

346

helping. Marriott had had the pony eighteen months. During that time it had pulled the cart frequently. Whenever I saw it, it went quietly.

William Groom: I am a coachmaker, of Peterborough. I saw the accident. . . . No accident would have happened if the ploughs had not been there. After the accident, the pony ran as far as Mr. Whitfield's, the harness maker's, where I stopped it. On going to the White Hart, a house next to Stanley's, I found Marriott on the sofa, fainted away. His wife was with him, crying and begging that he might be taken home. I helped to carry him home in a chair, and Mr. Southam, the surgeon, was sent for.

Robert Crofts: I was Mr. Stanley's servant at the time. I was in the shop, near the door. I heard a noise and saw Marriott rolling off the plough. A plough was broken by the impact. There were ploughs, a hamper, a small boiler, a box, and many other things, nearly all extending over the gutter.

(Cross-examined by Mr. Hill): Yes I was discharged from Stanley's, but not for getting drunk. I was at the Odd Fellow's Ball, but I was not drunk. I belong to the Odd Fellows, and I think it right to uphold the Order. (Laughter.) I went to a situation at Stamford, and I left that with a view of bettering myself.

Hill: Where are you now? Have you bettered yourself?

Crofts: I am here now, but I don't know that I have bettered myself by coming here. (Laughter.)

Thomas Southam, surgeon, of Peterborough, objected to being sworn until he had been paid his expenses for this and the last Assizes. "According to Gray's 'Practice' I am entitled to two guineas a day." The Judge referred this to Mr. Holditch, Attorney, who directed him to be paid thirteen guineas. Southam objected that he ought to have sixteen guineas, because he had been absent from home three days. Holditch told him: "You need not have left home till Tuesday, but you chose to travel in your own gig, bringing Mrs. Southam with you, and sleeping a night on the road. It is not reasonable that you should be paid for that."

347

Judge Littledale: Swear the witness.

Southam: The injuries were serious. If he had been a man of intemperate habits, or unhealthy, he would have lost his life. He kept to his bed three months, and was delirious for some time. My bill was £22 10 shillings. I am quite sure he had not been drinking . . .

Finally, the plaintiff's representatives produced an exhibit: the local act of Peterborough, prohibiting under penalties, the exposure for sale, of goods on the Long Causeway.

Defence witnesses testified that Marriott had been drunk; and that ironmongery had not been encroaching the road space; that Mrs. Marriott had chided her husband for using his pony, and that Marriott had admitted that Stanley was not at fault.

The jury consulted together for some time, and then expressed a wish to retire. They returned after an hour, and delivered a verdict "for the defendant". There was more conferring among the jurymen, and then the Foreman corrected himself: "We find for the plaintiff."

Judge: Gentlemen, are you agreed? You do not seem to know what your verdict is. Do you find for the plaintiff, Marriott, or for the defendant, Stanley?

A juror: Yes, for the plaintiff.

Judge: Well, what damages?

Juror: Damages, one shilling.

Mr. Sergeant Goulburn: One shilling! Why the plaintiff paid twenty-two pounds ten shillings for a surgeon's bill!

Judge: Have you considered whether the horse was a proper animal to put in the cart a second time?

Juror: Yes, My Lord.

Judge: Well, are you agreed?

Juror: Yes. We think we should have done the same thing ourselves.

Sergeant Goulburn: A shilling! This is trial by jury! I never heard such a verdict. Well, gentlemen, I hope you will never be tumbled out of a cart yourselves.

21st October 1839

SAVED BY THE BONE IN HER STAYS

An inexplicable case of attempted murder and suicide occurred at Newnham on Monday 21st October. Samuel Foster, a tailor, of Dodford shot himself. The inquest was held the next day, at Newnham, before George Abbey, Coroner. The intended murder victim gave evidence, but was unable to give an explanation.

Ann Homan: I live at Newnham. The deceased was 23 years of age. He had paid his addresses to me for about six months. Yesterday he was with me at Dodford in the morning, and in the afternoon we went to Dodford again. After staying there for about three hours, we walked back to Newnham. We were accompanied by a girl named Catherine Hartopp. When we reached the top of the hill, Catherine left us. Samuel wished to accompany me home, and I said he might if he thought well. He then, without saying a word, fired a pistol at me, and the ball struck me on the left breast. Fortunately the bone of my stays protected me, and glanced it off after it had passed through my shawl. He called out, "I have done you," and ran away. I was so terrified that I became insensible. No quarrel had taken place between us. He had not made any offer of marriage. I had not given him any reason to think I had any aversion to him, as indeed I had not. I was not hurt in the slightest degree.

Catherine Hartopp (having confirmed the course of events described by Ann Homan): The deceased and Ann Homan appeared to be good friends while I was with them, and there had been no quarrelling. I went home, and they said they would follow. I had not gone more than twenty yards when I heard a shot and Ann screamed. I ran to meet her, and she said, "I am done. I am done. I think the ball is in my side. He has shot me."

John Hartopp: The deceased asked me, on the turnpike road, whether any young men went after Ann Homan. I

349

replied that there had been one or two, but not lately, at which he smiled, and went on.

William Homan: I am a publican at Newnham. Ann Homan is my daughter. The deceased showed me two pistols, three weeks since. He said he carried them for protection, as he was in the habit of travelling at night.

Mr. Clarke, surgeon: I was called a little after nine o'clock. Foster was then dead. The bullet had penetrated the heart, and lodged just below the shoulder blades, from where I extracted it. It would have caused instant death. In the right pocket of his trousers was a pocket pistol. Another, similar to it, was found near him on the ground.

Jury verdict: The deceased caused his own death while temporarily insane.

22nd October 1839

BREACH OF PROMISE BY A CIVIL SERVANT

The case of Owen v Sharp gives us a glimpse of proceedings in an obsolescent court, soon to be swept out of existence. It was a Northampton case of breach of promise of marriage, heard in the Secondaries Court on Tuesday 22nd October 1839, before Mr. Secondary James. The defendant, Thomas Sharp, was the son of the radical Northampton Borough Councillor Sharp, nicknamed "The barber" by his political opponents. Before leaving for a Government post in London, he had been a close friend of the plaintiff, Catherine Owen.

The case was introduced by the counsel for the plaintiff, William Clarkson, "loud-voiced and swaggering, with one undeviating form of cross-examination".[159]

Clarkson: This is an action brought by the plaintiff, a milliner and dressmaker, living at Northampton, against the defendant, who now holds a situation in the Board of

Control, with a salary of £200 a year; to recover compensation, in damages, for one of the greatest injuries which man can inflict upon a virtuous woman. In this case I shall be able to prove that the injury was as wanton and coldhearted as ever was perpetrated in any civilised society. The plaintiff has neither father nor mother to protect her, and is dependent upon her own exertions for her support. In 1831 the defendant first commenced paying his addresses to her, with the consent of his father and mother, and continued to correspond with her, his letters all breathing the most ardent affection, until August 1838, when he intermarried with a widow lady, Mrs. Winch, who lives at number 112 Park Street, Camden Town; who is reported to have some property and an annuity from her late husband. When the courtship first commenced, the defendant was not in a condition to support a wife; but in 1837, having succeeded in obtaining his present situation, he early communicated to her his good fortune, and stated in the most impassioned language how anxious he continued to be for their immediate union. His first letter to her was dated the 21st of November, 1837, and he continued to write to her with the utmost ardour and apparent affection. But on the 12th of March following, he began to get cool, and writing to her from "The India Board", stated that "ill health has delayed the fairy hopes and castles I have built as to our future happiness". But the ill health was only a hypocritical pretext not to perform his promise of marrying her, although he was well enough in a few short months to marry the widow of Park Street, at whose house he had then been for some time lodging. On the 8th of April, he wrote her again, expressing the pleasure he felt that his father and mother had treated her with so much kindness; but on the 20th of June, all his pretended affection seemed to have completely vanished, and he concluded a short, heartless and unfeeling letter with "Yours &c. &c. Thomas Sharp". This, one would think, was cruel and base enough to a generous and confiding girl; but on the 4th of July following, came the climax of his treachery and cold-heartedness, for he addressed her as "Catherine", and stated that he could not marry her,

351

alleging as his excuse their "repeated quarrels", and her "visible coolness"; yet adding that he would act "honestly" by her. In the same letter, he says: "You may tax me with being a deceiver. Nay, you may even call me a wretch and vagabond — still will I bear them all." Thus was the defendant adding insult to injury. On the 25th of July, he wrote his last letter, dated from 112 Park Street, requesting that his correspondence might be sent to him or destroyed; and so really did the plaintiff imagine that the cause of his not marrying her might have been his ill-health, and the other excuses which he had pleaded, that she requested him to send his portrait to her, which he promised to do, and concluded his letter by subscribing himself as the "once happy man, Thomas S". The result of this cruel treatment, so unprovoked by anything upon the plaintiff's part, was a most distressing illness, from which she had not recovered as to be able to attend to business until the 29th of October; and to this very hour, her sufferings are of a most painful nature. It is not possible that any sum of money which the jury might award in damages could compensate such treatment, but it is all the plaintiff can ask to place her character beyond the reach of malevolence or reproach. As men, however, and as fathers, I have no doubt the jury will do their duty. I have letters to put in as evidence, and three witnesses.

Mrs. Mary Brown: I live at Thrapston. I am a milliner. I know the plaintiff. She assisted me in 1833. During that year, Mr. Sharp visited her as an honourable suitor. Her conduct was unblemished.

C. Jones, cross-examining for the defence: What do you know of the plaintiff's family?

Brown: I was living with her aunt, Mrs. Clarke, when I engaged her. I heard her say her parents lived at Heyford in Sussex. Her father never came to see her while she was with me.

Jones: Is there not some secrecy about her parents? No one ever saw them.

Brown: There is neither secrecy nor mystery about her parents.

Jones: What do you know of the relationship between the plaintiff and the defendant?

Brown: She had a letter every week from him, after he first visited her, and they seemed to be very much attached to each other.

Jones: What is the plaintiff's age?

Brown: She is now about twenty-five years of age.

Jones: Pray Mrs. Brown, was not their acquaintance on the sly?

Brown: On the sly, indeed? Oh, no. By no means. It was no such thing.

Miss Sarah Green: I am a milliner at Northampton. I have known the plaintiff since 1835. From that time she visited me twice a year until 1837, when she entered my employment.

Clarkson: Did the defendant visit her as her admitted suitor during the whole of that time?

Green: He did up to June 1838. His parents knew of the intended match. The defendant's mother has frequently asked my permission for Miss Catherine Owen to visit at her house. I have been present frequently when the young people were together. Their conduct was most becoming.

C. Jones: Is this examination necessary?

The Secondary: I think your examination of the last witness renders it necessary.

Clarkson to Jones: You were casting an imputation upon my client when you asked if the courtship were not "on the sly".

Green (continuing): At Christmas 1837, the defendant, who had been previousy speaking of his wedding, called me out of the room, and expressed a wish that I should come up to London and act as bridesmaid, but it being inconvenient, I agreed to do so in the ensuing spring, as I should then be going up to London on business. The month of April was then fixed upon for the wedding.

Clarkson: What happened when the plaintiff first heard of the defendant's marriage?

Green: Caroline was very ill, and obliged to leave my employment. Her misery and suffering arose from her disappointment.

C. Jones, cross-examining: Did you ever meet the father and mother of the plaintiff?

Green: I never saw either of them.

Jones: Do you know that the defendant's father and mother were known to the plaintiff?

Green: I am satisfied that Mr. Sharp's father was not averse to his son's connection with Miss Owen. She told me, on the contrary, that he treated her very kindly.

Jones: Had they not quarrels, repeated quarrels – which as you know, often end, between lovers, in making them better friends?

Green: I never heard them have any unpleasant words but on the occasion of my sister's wedding, when Mr. Sharp was at Northampton. He seemed to be displeased that Miss Owen went to it at an earlier hour than he did. I never heard her say at any time that she wished him to discontinue his correspondence as it ceased to have any interest for her. That I positively state. After she left me in July, she went on a visit to some friends at Pytchley, and was not able to return until the 29th of October. Her conduct towards the defendant was always affectionate and kind.

Mrs. Margaret Clarke: I am the aunt of the plaintiff. I live at Yelvertoft, near Northampton. I knew the defendant from the year 1831, and in 1833 he first visited me. In July 1838 I brought Caroline from Miss Green's, in a very bad state of health, and suffering from lowness of spirits in consequence of her recent disappointment. In July 1837, I called on Mr. Sharp, the defendant, and he subsequently had an interview with my niece.

Clarkson: Did she ever ask him to discontinue their correspondence as it had ceased to interest her?

Clarke: Never.

C. Jones, for the defence called two witnesses.

Mrs. Charlotte Prideaux: I am sister of the defendant's wife.

Jones: When did you first meet the defendant?

Prideaux: I first saw him early in the summer of 1838, about two months before his marriage to my sister.

Jones: When did he first pay her particular attention?

Prideaux: I cannot say.

Jones: We have heard that the wife of the defendant has property.

Prideaux: She has no property except for a few articles of furniture.

Jones: Is there an annuity from her late husband?

Prideaux: She has no annuity.

Jones: Will you please describe her situation, and the defendant's situation.

Prideaux: She is now about 35 years of age. She has four children, and is now enceinte by Mr. Sharp. He may be about 29 years of age. He has been in very delicate health since his marriage. He has frequently been compelled to have recourse to his father for pecuniary assistance.

Clarkson (cross-examining): Look at this letter, Mrs. Prideaux. It purports to be one written by the defendant to the plaintiff.

Mrs. Prideaux: It is not his handwriting.

Clarkson: Can you swear positively to that?

Prideaux: Yes I can. It is not in his handwriting.

William Burnett Bloxham: I now live at Mitcham. I am a speculator in foreign funds and shares.

Jones: Will you please describe Mrs. Sharp's situation.

Bloxham: I have known Mrs. Winch – now Mrs. Sharp – for

355

some time, and she always was a most distressed woman. Her husband died an insolvent. I lent her half the furniture she now has in her house. In fact the furniture is not worth powder and shot.

Clarkson (cross-examining): Do you know the defendant as well as his wife?

Bloxham: I do.

Clarkson: Have you seen the defendant write?

Bloxham: I have.

Clarkson: Will you look at these several letters and say whether they are in the handwriting of Mr. Sharp. They are the letters referred to as containing promise of marriage.

Bloxham: I am quite sure they are in his handwriting.

Clarkson: That dated July 4th, breaking off the match, is written by the defendant?

Bloxham: It is in his worst hand. [A laugh.]

Clarkson: Were you at the marriage of the defendant to Mrs. Winch?

Bloxham: I acted as father at the marriage, on some day in August 1838, but upon my life, I never kept any account of the day, and I remembered nothing about the matter until I was reminded of it today by my wife.

Mrs. Prideaux and then Mr. Bloxham were both recalled. Neither could state the precise appointment of the defendant; nor if he were receiving an "increasing" salary.

C. Jones addressed the jury at length, complained of the prejudice sought to be excited against his client by the opening speech of his learned friend.

"In not marrying the plaintiff he was not actuated by any sordid motive, for he married a distressed widow with four children. Here I might say that Mr. Sharp is more sinned against than sinning. The jury, I hope, will consider that he has appearances to keep up; that his delicate state of health is the source of increased expense, and that if they award such heavy damages as he could never afford to pay, the effect would be to throw him into a prison, and prove disserviceable to the plaintiff. It is denied that any quarrel had taken place between the parties. If so, why were not the letters of Miss Owen produced in evidence?"

The Secondary: You can produce those letters yourself, as you must have them in your own possession.

C. Jones: The difficulties in the case are quite enough, without this interruption coming from such a quarter.

The Secondary: You were only interrupted, Mr. Jones, because you were irregular.

Jones concluded. The jury brought in a verdict for the plaintiff with damages of £150.

28th October 1839

"A LAD OF COLOUR"

The following case is taken from the list of those dealt with at Northampton Borough Sessions on Monday 28th October 1839, before the Recorder, N. R. Clarke, with eighteen jurymen of the Grand Jury, all named in the *Northampton Mercury* of 2nd November 1839 (p. 1, col. 6).

"CHARLES FOUNDLING, a lad of colour, pleaded guilty to a charge of stealing three pair of worsted shoes, the property of John Wilson his master, and was sentenced to One Month's imprisonment."

29th October 1839

RECRUITING FOR THE COUNTY REGIMENT

James Page, publican, appeared before Wellingborough Petty Sessions on 4th November 1839, to answer an information laid against him by John Robinson, a private in the 48th Regiment of Foot, for having on 29th October, Wellingborough Fair Day, assaulted him in his house.

Robinson (sworn): As I was going up the passage into Page's house, a man came up to me and asked me If I would enlist him. Page came up and knocked me down. He used abusive language, and said, "I'll jump in now".

James Page: The soldier was in the room, and endeavoured to enlist people; and I said, "I'll have nothing of that, here". I have a witness to say that Page struck me on the breast, and pushed me towards the door.

The Magistrates allowed the parties to go out of court to settle the case among themselves, and they did so.

late October 1839

A WOODFORD MAIDSERVANT
SHOP LIFTING IN LONDON

The *Northampton Mercury* of 2nd November 1839 (p. 4, col. 4), had the report of

"a genteel-looking young woman . . . Elizabeth Hodgson . . ., lady's maid to Miss Isham of Woodford, Northamptonshire, at present staying in town . . . charged with stealing a pair of kid gloves from the shop of Mr. Joseph Norbury, mercer, 35 Crawford-street, Marylebone."

Having been placed at the bar, at Marylebone Magistrates' Court, and no person appearing to accuse her, Mr. Cobb, presiding, asked Constable 95D where Mr. Norbury was.

Constable: At home, I believe, sir, and does not wish to prosecute.

Mr. Cobb: Public justice is not to be defeated in this way. He having given the prisoner into custody for felony, is bound to attend here and state his complaint; and I will take care that he does so.

"A summons was then issued and placed in the hands of the constable, who shortly returned, bringing with him, not Mr. Norbury, but Frederick Hanks, his shopman. From the young man's testimony, it appeared that the prisoner entered the shop that morning, and purchased ribbons and other articles, which she paid for, and then went away. Shortly after her departure, he was informed by his fellow shopman that a pair of gloves was missing from the counter near where the prisoner had stood. On learning this, witness pursued the prisoner, and having stopped her, asked if she had not something about her more than she had purchased. She then drew from her bosom the pair of missing kid gloves, and said she had placed them there by mistake for her own, which, however, she happened to have on. She was then handed over to the constable, but nothing more was found except the articles which she had duly paid for.

"The prisoner appeared dreadfully affected at her situation, and as it is supposed to be her first offence, she was remanded, in order that her mistress may be communicated with on the subject."

1st November 1839

NORTHAMPTON BOROUGH COUNCIL ELECTION INSULTS

There was continuous disagreement over political matters in the rival Northampton newspapers. The Whig *Mercury* had encouraged the railway in 1838-39 and the Penny Post 1839-40; the Tory *Herald* the opposite. At the time of the campaign for the Northampton Borough Council election (1st November), the antagonism grew virulent. Dicey, the *Mercury* proprietor, was either "Dosey" in *Herald* columns, or "the Leicestershire Delinquent". As a twin sample of this insulting material, let us note how a piece in the *Herald* of 26th October was treated in the *Mercury* of 2nd November (p. 3, cols. 2-3).

"Whoever took the trouble of reading the letter which was inserted last week, addressed by the Rev. Francis Litchfield in his private capacity, to the Rev. Francis Litchfield in his capacity of Editor of the *Northampton Herald,* cannot fail to have noticed that its *omissions* were far more remarkable than its contents. The charges against our reverend opponent are that being a Clergyman he has not only undertaken the unclerical office of conducting a scurrilous newspaper, but that he discharges that office in a manner utterly disgraceful to him, not merely as a clergyman, but as a gentleman. . . . Alluding to Mr. Litchfield's conversion to Ultra-Toryism from Radicalism, we remarked that 'it was satisfactory to find that the zeal with which he now assails those who formerly were much more moderate reformers than himself, has not injured his worldly fortunes'. Mr. Litchfield tells us that the charge upon which he feels 'somewhat sensitively' is simply this 'that he has gained in his worldly fortunes by the political sentiments he entertains'.

"Mr. Litchfield may strain at the gnat and swallow the camel in this way, if he pleases, but . . . he should prove to demonstration that the preferment which has been showered upon him of late has nothing whatever to do with his conversion . . . Mr. Litchfield has carefully refrained from telling his reader what is the value of his . . . [livings] which he holds in plurality with his living of Farthinghoe . . ."

The *Herald* said:

"We are informed that Mr. Barber Sharp and the Leicester-

shire Delinquent are going about in the streets of Northampton with a swaggering boast that they will publish a
pamphlet showing the entire share they have had in the
several election struggles in this borough."

The *Mercury* replied:

"We need hardly state that the informer as well as the
informed, in this case, are the same person, viz. Mr.
Litchfield himself. Of the accuracy of the information our
readers will be able to judge, when they learn that 'the
Leicestershire Delinquent' as Mr. Litchfield, with the
gentleman-like pleasantry peculiarly his own, is pleased to
term the Proprietor of this *Journal* has not been for the last
five weeks within 150 miles of this town . . ."

2nd November 1839

ESCAPE FROM THE COUNTY GAOL

"During the night of Saturday last [2nd November 1839]
two men confined in the Infirmary ward of our county gaol
effected their escape,"

reported the *Northampton Herald* on 9th November (p. 3,
col. 2). A reward of £10 was offered for their recapture. The
Mercury gave detailed descriptions (p. 3, col. 4).

". . . Richard Parker Gooding, convicted at the Easter
Sessions, 1839, of stealing fowls, and sentenced to two
years imprisonment . . . is 22 years of age, five feet five and a
half inches high, fair complexion, brown hair, oval visage,
round-shouldered, scar on the knuckle of right hand, had
on a pair of cotton cord breaches, flannel waistcoat, fustian
jacket, a pair of blue stockings, striped shirt, low shoes, and
a cap; by trade a labourer, a native of Hannington. . . . He is
supposed to have gone to some of the lines of railway now
in progress, but more especially the Brighton line. The
name of the other one is William Thomas, a seaman,

convicted at the Michaelmas Sessions, 1839, of stealing [a shawl] from a dwelling house, and sentenced to six months imprisonment. He is 19 years of age, five feet, four inches high, sallow complexion, dark hair, grey eyes, round visage, pock-pitted, a heart and dart, and 'B.F.W.T.' marked on the inside of right arm; had on a blue sailor's jacket, a blue waistcoat and trousers, a hat, a pair of striped stockings, striped shirt, and very low shoes; states that he is a native of Newton, Glamorganshire, and is supposed to have gone to some sea-port."

13th November 1839

SARAH PENDERED'S FRIEND'S LITTLE GIRL'S SCALLED HEAD

"JOHN SIMCO
CHEMIST and DRUGGIST,
(Near the Crow & Horse Shoe Inn),
GOLD-STREET, NORTHAMPTON,
Takes this opportunity . . . [etcetera]
The Only Effectual Remedy Yet Known!
SIMCO's PRIMROSE CERATE,
An Unfallible Remedy for Scalled Head, Scabby and Scurfy Head, Ringworm, and Scurvy. Sold in boxes or pots at 13½d. and 2s 9d each. A 2s 9d box or pot equal to three at 13½d.

AN EXTRAORDINARY CURE effected by Simco's Primrose Cerate:—

Mrs. PENDERED, of Bridge-street, Northampton, feels it her duty to lay before the public a real fact. In the year 1837 a little girl belonging to a friend of hers who moved in a respectable sphere of life, had the misfortune to be afflicted with Scalled Head; the disease . . . had assumed an alarming, aggravated form, so as to be offensive both to sight and small . . ., In this dilemma the Hairdresser who occasionally shaved the child's head had endeavoured to recommend a trial of Simco's Primrose Cerate . . . and I assure the public that no child has now a finer head of hair . . .

    – Witness my hand this 13th day of November, 1839, sarah pendered."

This advertisement in the *Northampton Mercury* of 29th February 1840 (p. 2, col. 5), continued with a confirmation from Benjamin Hewitt, Hairdresser, of Bridge-street, Northampton.

20th November 1839

THE WORKHOUSE PORTER WHO HAD TO BE A TEACHER

A new porter took up his duties at the Union Workhouse in Wellingborough on 20th November. The nature of those duties was described in the advertisement which appeared in the *Northampton Mercury* on 2nd November 1839 (p. 1, col. 2):

". . . Salary £18 a year, with Board and Lodging in the House. The Person appointed will be required to assist the Governor and Matron in the general Management of the House, to instruct the boys in some useful trade, and the elder ones (not under the care of the Schoolmistress) in Reading and Writing. All candidates for the above Situation must forward Testimonials of character and competency to the Clerk of the Guardians by Nine o'clock in the Morning of Wednesday the 6th of November . . ."

30th November 1839

NORTHAMPTON COMPLAINTS

"Several complaints have been made to us,"

said the Editor of the *Northampton Mercury* (30th November 1839, p. 3, col. 5),

> "of the state of the high road between Kingsthorpe and this town. . . . The culvert is stopped up, and before the barracks there is and has been for nearly the whole week, an extensive sheet of water, several inches in depth, nearly covering the turnpike road, and a portion of the foot-way. Nearer Kingsthorpe . . . from the half-way house to the toll-gate, there used to be a pleasant, and, on account of the slope, a dry footpath. . . . The scrapings from the road have been heaped directly upon this very path, leaving the pedestrian no alternative but to resort to the high-road. . . . We [understand] that a difference of opinion exists between the Road Trust and the Paving Commissioners, as to the liability to make the necessary repairs in the culvert. . . . A meeting of the Road Trust is announced for the 14th proximo, to 'take into consideration the state of the road between the Bull Inn, in Sheep Street, and the Race Course gate, on the turnpike road leading to Kingsthorpe'."

A correspondent in the *Mercury* of 7th December complained of other turnpikes where the road "scrapings" had been heaped on the footpath. The meeting of 14th December, if it took place, was not reported. The above column of Northampton complaints continued:

> "We cannot but express our deep regret at the destruction of the only ornamented walk of which the town can boast – the new walk at the bottom of Waterloo."

Waterloo was the eastern end of Derngate. It led towards Cow Meadow, later to become Becket's Park.

> "It is some time since the high and beautiful hedge on the north side was almost wholly cut down and destroyed.

Latterly, several of the poplars have been felled, and we observe that the whole are marked for the same fate. . . . If this proposed destruction is carried into effect, it will be a great source of vexation to invalids and ladies who have been accustomed to seek the shade of this walk in summer, and its protection from bleak winds during the [winter]."

This matter was raised at the Northampton Town Council meeting on 2nd December. It was explained that the Estate Committee had ordered the poplars to be felled because they were decayed and unsafe. An expert nurseryman had been consulted.

Another matter under discussion was the fosse. This was the remains of the ancient ditch on the outside of the town walls. Permission was given at this meeting for builders and others to empty rubble into it. There had been protests against the plan. George Baker, described at the meeting as "The King of local antiquarians" had written to say that this was all that remained of the original defences of the town, and that it should be preserved. The work was "respited" for a month, but on 26th December, George Baker wrote to the *Mercury* (28th December 1839, p. 3, col. 5), in outraged phrases:

". . . Impatient of delay, and by what authority I know not, the contractors for the projected new houses in Perkins's garden; have made a road across the upper end of that walk where 'the poplars are felled and adieu to the shade', and are now depositing the soil of the foundations within the fosse. Is this interesting relic of by-gone times to be destroyed, that the contractors may be saved a few pounds in the carting of their rubbish? . . ."

Something of the fosse must have survived for another six years, for it is marked on Law's 1845 Northampton map, along the north of Cow Meadow, and at right-angles to Albion Place.

5th December 1839

A NEW LIVESTOCK MARKET AT OUNDLE

"OUNDLE NEW CATTLE MARKET.
TOLL FREE

THE Commissioners for improving &c. the town of OUNDLE having received a petition, numerously and respectably signed by the graziers and farmers of the neighbourhood, requesting that a STOCK MARKET should be established and held WEEKLY on the present market day, Thursday, and the Commissioners being desirous of complying with such request (they having obtained the Sanction of the Lord of the Manor thereto), Hereby give notice, that on and after Thursday the 5th day of December next, the said market will be held in the following places, viz.

The Beast market, in the New Street.
The Sheep market, at the East End of the Town Hall.
The Horse market, opposite the Dolphin Inn.
The Pig market, in the White Hart Yard as usual . . ."

(*Northampton Mercury* 9th November 1839, p. 2, col. 5.)

10th December 1839

CARRIERS' CARTS AND WAGGONS

There were times when many waggons and carts assembled in parts of central Northampton, on market days in particular. During the winter of 1839, Joe Ball, superintendent of police, had been keeping an eye on a stranger often seen lurking where the waggons were drawn up. The man was in the habit of standing near the market carts, offering to go errands for the carriers.

On Tuesday night, 10th December, at half-past ten, Ball

received information that a number of skins of patent leather had been found lying in Tanner Street. He went to see. Had a robbery been committed? He gave instructions for the leather to be taken to the station house, and ordered the watchmen to look for the suspicious stranger. He himself went off to look in some likely places, and returned at midnight. By then Constable William Coe had apprehended the man and lodged him in the station house. They now looked closely at the skins that had been recovered. The bundle consisted of twenty-four skins of patent leather, directed to Thomas Rowlatt, coach-maker, of Horse-Market, Northampton. It had been stolen from the Birmingham waggon standing in the Woolpack yard. The "direction" had been cut off, and was found the next morning lying in the street.

The arrested man gave his name as John Denton. He was taken before the Magistrates and committed to take his trial at the next Borough Sessions.

The events in the foregoing paragraphs are rearranged from accounts in the Northampton newspapers on 14th December. John Denton went on trial, but the case was stopped by the Recorder when it became clear that there was insufficient evidence. "The prisoner might be indicted again if the prosecutor thinks proper." He was not brought up again.

14th December 1839

GREEN'S NORTON WINDMILL

"WANTED immediately, a JOURNEYMAN MILLER who thoroughly understands the business of a Smock Windmill, and can have a good character.

Apply (if by letter, post paid) to Mr. THOS. GRISBROOK, Miller and Baker, Green's Norton . . ."

(*Northampton Mercury* 14th December 1839, p. 1, col. 1.)

The Penny Post was imminent. Miller Grisbrook would

have to pay for receiving applications, but within a few days pre-paid mail would become the norm, and requests such as his for letters to be paid for by the sender, would no longer be seen in advertisements.

Christmas 1839

THE KINDNESS OF LORD CARDIGAN

"The Earl of Cardigan has given away two fine beasts to the poor of the parish of Corby . . . one each to Deene and Deene Thorpe, Stanion, and Glapthorn, also a suitable quantity of bread and coals; and a quart of ale to each man, a pint to his wife, and a half a pint to each child."

With its own show of good will, the *Northampton Mercury* reported this generosity on 4th January (p. 4, col. 3). The *Herald* missed it.

At Peterborough, Bishop Davys received a present: a book inscribed "The Bishop of Peterborough, with best wishes from his old pupil, Victoria R."[146]

28th December 1839

SHOEMAKERS WANTED

"WANTED, several best SHOE, CLARENCE, and BUTTON-BOOT MEN; also a CLICKER. Apply at LLOYDS, St. George's Street, Northampton."

(*Northampton Mercury* 28th December 1839, p. 3, col. 1.)

31st December 1839

A "FLASHER" AT DELAPRE

"For the last nine or ten months, females walking between Hardingstone and Northampton, through the meadows, have been grossly insulted by a fellow who has come out of the Spinney on the left hand of the path opposite the fish-pond in Mr. Bouverie's park. The attention of Ball, our active and very efficient superintendent of police, was recently called to the circumstance, and on Tuesday week [31st December], he succeeded in apprehending a man named Richard Jones Wright, a shoemaker, living in Bell Barn. He was identified by three females whom he had annoyed, and was committed to the treadmill for three months. The fellow has a wife and family."

(*Northampton Mercury* 11th January 1840, p. 3, col. 5.)

INTO THE 1840s . . .

SOURCES QUOTED

1 "F. A. L." *Drayton House 1880-1926: Recollections of a Grandson. Northamptonshire Past and Present,* Vol. 3, No. 4. 1961. pp. 63, 65.

2 George M. Trevelyan. *English Social History.* 1944. (Longmans Green.) p. 376.

3 Humphrey Wyndham. *The Farming Activities of the Third Earl Spencer. Northamptonshire Past and Present,* Vol. III, No. 2. 1961, p. 47.

4 G. E. Mingay. *Rural Life in Victorian England.* 1976. (Heinemann.)

5 *Kettering Leader* 26th February 1904. (*Kettering Public Library Cuttings Book* 7706 KET 04.)

6 Samuel Smiles. *The Lives of George and Robert Stephenson.* 1857.

7 [F. B. Head.] *Stokers and Pokers.* 1849. (Murray.)

8 *The County Borough of Northampton Police 1836-1966.* 1966.

9 D. E. Roberts and J. H. Frisby. *The Northampton Gas Undertaking 1823-1949.* August 1980. *Leicester: East Midlands Gas,* pp. 6, 9.

10 J. Freeman. *The History of the Town of Northampton . . .* 1841. p. 44.

11 *Northamptonshire Notes and Queries.* Vol. II New Series. No. 106.

12 Thomas Wright. *The Romance of the Shoe.* 1922.

13 Unidentified transcript from the indentures of the *Northampton Herald.* 1832.

14 Herbert Lack. *The Rushden Park Road Baptist Sunday School . . . 1810-1910.* Rushden. December 1910. p. 8.

15 *Ibid.,* p. 9.

16 *Ibid.,* p. 13 quoting the oldest *Teachers' Minute Book.*

17 *Ibid.,* pp. 15-16.

18 London and Birmingham Railway. Extracts from Engineers' Reports. (Typescript 1-192 at Northampton Public Library.)

19 R. Hains. Letter, 26th October 1840. *Northampton Mercury* 31st October 1840. p. 2, col. 2.

20 Roy Palmer. *A Ballad History of England, from 1588 to the Present Day.* 1979. (Batsford.) pp. 112-113 gives as publisher: "Henson, Letter-press and Copper-plate Printer near the South Bridge, Northampton."

21 *Northamptonshire Past and Present,* Vol. VI, No. 6. pp. 325-8.

22 *Northampton Mercury* 18th February 1837. p. 3, col. 5.

23 Guy Paget. *The History of the Althorp and Pytchley Hunt 1634-1920*. 1937. (Collins.) p. 159.

24 "Uncle Scribbler" in *The Huntsman*, Vol. XLIV.

25 Frederick Locker-Lampson. *My Confidences . . .* 1895. (Smith Elder.) p. 331.

26 *Northampton Mercury* 4th March 1837. p. 3, col. 5.

27 *Northamptonshire Notes and Queries*, Vol. II New Series, No. 106.

28 F. F. Waddy. *A History of Northampton General Hospital.* 1974. (Northampton: Guildhall Press.) pp. 34-35.

29 John Cole. *The History and Antiquities of Wellingborough.* 1837. (Wellingborough: C. M. Darby.) pp. 172-3.

30 *Ibid.,* pp. 126-129.

31 Andrew Percival. *Notes on Old Peterborough.* 1905. (Peterborough Archaeological Society.)

32 Thomas Whittaker. *Life's Battles in Temperance Armour.* 3rd. ed. 1888. (Hodder and Stoughton.)

33 *The Shell Book of Firsts.* 1975. (Ebury Press/Michael Joseph.)

34 *Wellingborough News & Northamptonshire Advertiser* 9th October 1953. p. 3.

35 K. J. Allison and others. *The Deserted Villages of Northamptonshire.* 1966. (Leicester University Press.) p. 34.

36 Royal Commission on Historical Monuments. *An Inventory of the Historical Monuments in the County of Northampton*, Vol. I: *Archaeological Sites in North-East Northamptonshire.* 1975. (H.M.S.O.). pp. 76-78.

37 *Lincoln Mercury* 20th May 1837.

38 Royal Commission on Historical Monuments. *An Inventory of the Historical Monuments in the County of Northampton*, Vol. IV: . . . *South-West Northamptonshire.* 1982. (H.M.S.O.). p. 191 and Vol. VI: . . . *North Northamptonshire.* 1934. (H.M.S.O.). p. 131.

39 *Northampton Mercury* 17th June 1837. p. 1, col. 2.

40 William Sharman. *Old Fairs,* in *Bygone Northamptonshire,* ed. by William Andrews. 1891. (Hull: William Andrews & Co.). p. 98.

41 *Northampton Mercury* 3rd June 1837. p. 2, col. 4 and 10th June 1837. p. 2, col. 6.

42 R. M. Serjeantson. *The History of the Church of St. Giles . . .* 1911.

43 *Northamptonshire Notes and Queries*, Vol. 3. 1893. No. 550.

44 Edmund Blunden. *Sketches in the Life of John Clare, Written by Himself.* 1931. (London: Cobden-Sanderson.) pp. 37-38.

45 Henry Goddard. *Memoirs of a Bow Street Runner,* ed. by Patrick Pringle. 1956. (London: Museum Press.) pp. 137 *et seq.*

46 J. M. Lee. *Modern Stamford* in *The Making of Stamford*, ed. by Alan Rogers. 1965. (Leicester University Press.) pp. 94-96.
47 H. O. Nethercote. *The Pytchley Hunt, Past and Present.* 1888. (Sampson Low.) pp. 45-46.
48 V. A. Hatley. *Some Aspects of Northampton's History. Northamptonshire Past and Present,* Vol. 3, No. 6. (1965-66.) p. 248.
49 Lou Warwick. *How Freemasonry Began in the Inns. Northampton Independent,* December 1981.
50 *Northampton Mercury* 12th August 1837.
51 Joan Wake. *The Brudenells of Deene.* 1953. (Cassell.) p. 360.
52 *Ibid.,* pp. 365-7.
53 Donald Thomas. *Charge, Charge Hurrah.* 1974. (RKP.) p. 74.
54 *Hone's Year Book.* 1832.
55 R. M. Serjeantson. *The Grey Friars Excavations. The Journal of the Northamptonshire Natural History Society and Field Club,* Vol. XVI. 1911-12. pp. 8 & 9.
56 *Northampton Mercury,* 23rd September 1837, and 30th September.
57 *Gentleman's Magazine,* November 1837. p. 533. (Obituary.)
58 Joan Wake. *A Northamptonshire Rector.* 1943. (Northampton: Archer & Goodman.)
59 *Northamptonshire Notes and Queries,* Vol. I. 1887. no. 148.
60 W. B. Browne. *A Memoir of the Late Much Lamented Miss Wright of Kettering,* who departed this life 2nd October, 1837, aged thirty-one years; with extracts from her diary. 1838. Kettering. W. Dash. pp. 44-45.
61 H. O. Nethercote. *The Pytchley Hunt, Past and Present.* 1888. p. 137-9.
62 Arthur Cossons. *The Turnpike Roads of Northamptonshire. Northamptonshire Past and Present,* Vol. I, No. 3. 1950. p. 32.
63 Wimersley Bush. *Tales of Whittlebury Forest,* No. 4. *Northamptonshire Past and Present,* Vol. I, No. 5. (1952.) p. 25.
64 J. Taylor. *Antiquarian Memoranda. Kettering Guardian,* 27th November 1891.
65 Joyce and Maurice Palmer. *A History of Wellingborough From Roman Times to the Present Day.* 1972. (Earls Barton: Steepleprint.) p. 155.
66 *Northampton Mercury* 18th November 1837. p. 3, col. 5.
67 Mark Girouard. *The Baiting of Burghley. Country Life,* 31st May 1990. p. 146.
68 *Northampton Herald* 18th November 1837. p. 2, col. 4.
69 George Loy Smith. *A Victorian RSM: From India to the Crimea.* 1987. (Tunbridge Wells: Costello.) pp. 39 and 44. (Original manuscript in Royal Hussars Museum, Winchester.)

70 Hugh Vickers and Caroline McCullough. *Great Country House Disasters.* 1982. (Arthur Barker.) p. 63.

71 Joyce and Maurice Palmer. *A History of Wellingborough . . .* 1972. p. 204.

72 [John M. Ouless.] *Cogenhoe's Heritage: St. Peter's Church.* 1974. pp. 19-20.

73 Northamptonshire Federation of Women's Institutes. *The Northamptonshire Village Book.* 1989. p. 92.

74 *Dictionary of National Biography:* Gordon Goodwin entry on John Hill.

75 Joan Wake. *The Brudenells of Deene.* 1953. (Cassell.) p. 464.

76 Pamela Horn. *Domestic Service in Northamptonshire, 1830-1914. Northamptonshire Past and Present,* Vol. V, No. 3. (1975.) p. 273.

77 *Dictionary of National Biography:* "TFH" entry on Sir Arthur de Capell Brooke.

78 Arthur Cossons. *The Turnpike Roads of Northamptonshire with the Soke of Peterborough. Northamptonshire Past and Present,* Vol. I, No. 3. (1950.)

79 Northamptonshire Record Office: Fisher & Saunders 61/64.

80 *Northampton Mercury,* 26th March 1842. p. 3, col. 4.

81 *The Gentleman in Black. The Pytchley Hounds, Horses, and Men — Past and Present.* Part II. *Bailey's Magazine,* June 1862. p. 340.

82 Thomas Coleman. *Memorials of the Independent Churches in Northamptonshire.* 1853. (London: John Snow.) pp. 220-222.

83 Northamptonshire Record Office: ZA 1253.

84 Henry Goddard. *Memoirs of a Bow Street Runner;* edited by Patrick Pringle. 1956. (London: Museum Press.) pp. 144-147.

85 Victor A. Hatley. *Northampton Re-Vindicated: More Light on why the Main Line Missed the Town. Northamptonshire Past and Present,* Vol. II, No. 6. 1959. pp. 305-309.

86 Northamptonshire Public Libraries: *Northampton Local Studies Collection broadsheets 1-198.*

87 *Dictionary of National Biography:* entry for Edward Vaux [by Sidney Lee].

88 Sally Davis: *Interview with Mr. and Mrs. A. J. Macdonald-Buchanan. Harrowden Hall. Northamptonshire and Bedfordshire Life.* June 1971.

89 *The Complete Peerage . . .* Vol. 6, by GEC. 1982. (Alan Sutton.)

90 David Hall and Ruth Harding. *Rushden, a Duchy of Lancaster Village.* 1985. (Buscott Publications.) p. 182.

91 John Cole. *The History and Antiquities of Higham Ferrers, Rushden and Irthlingborough.* 1838. pp. 201-205.

92 *Northampton Mercury* report, 21st April 1838, p. 4, cols. 2-3, taken from an un-named newspaper of the previous week.
93 Kettering Public Library: cuttings book 1904-5 (interviews in three unidentified newspapers, 18th March 1904, 10th March 1905, 31st March 1905).
94 Margery Fisher, ed. *A Scrapbook of Ashton, 1953.* (Women's Institute 1954.)
95 S. Jackson Coleman. *Lore and Legend of Northamptonshire: Treasury of Folklore 27.* [circa 1962] (Douglas, Isle of Man Folklore Academy).
96 John Cole. *The History and Antiquities of Higham Ferrers* . . . p. 123.
97 *Northampton Mercury* 14th and 21st April 1838.(p. 3, col. 1.)
98 *Northampton Mercury* 19th May 1838. (p. 3. col. 6.)
99 John Cole. *The History and Antiquities of Higham Ferrers, Rushden and Irthlingborough.* 1838. p. 216.
100 John Cole's manuscript diary (extract). *Northamptonshire Notes and Queries,* Vol. 2, no. 370.
101 Alan Blower. *British Railway Tunnels.* 1964. (Ian Allan.) pp. 47-48.
102 A. E. Treen. *The Parish of Kilsby* (MS in Rugby Public Library: M942.55Tr (1925).
103 *Northampton Chronicle and Echo* 13th August 1979.
104 F. F. Waddy. *A History of Northampton General Hospital 1743 to 1948.* 1974. (Northampton: Guildhall Press.) p. 67.
105 *Northampton Mercury* 30th June 1838. p. 3, col. 5.
106 Contemporary press accounts quoted in *Northamptonshire Evening Telegraph* 2nd June 1953.
107 *Northamptonshire County Magazine,* Vol. 4. 1931. p. 102.
108 *Northampton Mercury* 7th July 1838. p. 2, col. 1.
109 *Ibid.,* p. 3, col. 4.
110 *Northampton Mercury* 14th July 1838. p. 8, cols. 2-3.
111 *Northampton Mercury* 21st July 1838, p. 3, col. 6.
112 *Rushden Argus* 8th September 1911: simplified transcript by J. Enos Smith (Book 20). Northamptonshire Record Office 285P/291.
113 C. A. Markham. *Ancient Punishments in Northamptonshire.* 1886. (Northampton Architectural Society.)
114 *Northampton Mercury* 30th June 1838. p. 2, col. 3.
115 Alan Burman. *Northampton Chronicle and Echo* 29th January 1989.
116 Wymersley Bush. *Tales of Whittlebury Forest, 4. Northamptonshire Past and Present,* Vol I, No. 5. (1952.) p. 26.
117 Christopher Thorne. *Chartism.* 1966. (Macmillan: Sources of

History) *and* John L. and Barbara Hammond. The Bleak Age. 1934. 2nd ed. 1947. (Penguin: Pelican.) pp. 177 et *seq.*

118 R. G. Gammage. *History of the Chartist Movement 1837-1854.* 2nd ed. 1894. (Newcastle on Tyne: Browne and Browne.) p. 36.

119 R. L. Greenall. *Baptist as Radical: the Life and Opinions of the Rev John Jenkinson of Kettering (1799-1876). Northamptonshire Past and Present,* Vol. VIII, No. 3. 1991.

120 Lou Warwick, in *Northampton Independent* January 1980.

121 Northampton Public Library Boot and Shoe Collection. 3145.

122 Francis Coghlan. *The Iron Road Book and Railway Companion From London to Birmingham . . . Second Edition.* [1838] (London: A. H. Baily.)

123 J. B. Snell. *Railways: Mechanical Engineering.* 1971. (Longmans.)

124 Arthur Cossons. *The Turnpike Roads of Northamptonshire . . . Northamptonshire Past and Present,* Vol. 1, No. 3. pp. 35-36. (1950.)

125 Information from the Central Museum, Guildhall Road, Northampton, 20th August 1992.

126 George Loy Smith. *A Victorian RSM: From India to the Crimea.* (Royal Hussars Museum, Winchester.) 1987. (Tunbridge Wells: Costello.) pp. 53 and 55.

127 *Northampton County Magazine,* Vol. 4. 1931. pp. 219-221.

128 [John M. Ouless.] *Cogenhoe's Heritage: St. Peter's Church.* 1974. p. 21.

129 *The Times,* 28th November 1838.

130 Philip Wright. *Knibb 'the Notorious', Slaves' Missionary 1803-1845.* 1973. (London: Sidgwick & Jackson.) Chapter 9.

131 Richard Price. *Observations on Reversionary Payments.*

132 Joan Wake. *The Death of Francis Tresham. Northamptonshire Past and Present,* Vol. II, no. 1. 1954. p. 32.

133 James McCloghry. *Our Marston.* 1981. (Privately published.)

134 *Footprints,* Vol. 5, No. 4. July 1984. p. 89. (Northamptonshire Family History Society.)

135 Sarah A. Tooley. *The Queen's Friends. The Woman at Home.* March 1897. Vol. IV. (Hodder and Stoughton.) pp. 571-573.

136 Lord Lilford, F.Z.S.: *a Memoir by his Sister.* 1900.

137 Report of the Select Committee on Education of the Poorer Classes, 1838. p. viii.

138 *Northampton Mercury* 9th September 1837, p. 3, col 5, and information from Mrs. Molly Ward, of Hewitson, Becke and Shaw, Solicitors.

139 F. F. Waddy, *A History of Northampton General Hospital 1743*

to 1948. 1974. (Northampton: Guildhall Press.) p. 150.

140 John Burnett. *A History of the Cost of Living.* 1969. (Penguin: Pelican A1020.) p. 209.

141 Handbill in Northampton Central Library Northamptonshire Collection: "Kettering 164-756".

142 John Ayre Leatherland. *Essays and Poems, with a Brief Autobiographical Memoir.* 1862. (London: W. Tweedie.) pp. 22 *et seq.*

143 Northamptonshire Record Office: GK 178.

144 *Ibid.* GK174-90. (1839.) Kettering Letters.

145 *Gentleman's Magazine* July 1839. pp. 87-88.

146 Alfred T. Story. *The Queen's Tutors. Windsor Magazine,* Vol. I. February 1895. p. 163.

147 R. G. Gammage. *The Chartist Movement.* 1854. (Merlin.)

148 (text reprinted in) Dorothy Thompson. *The Early Chartists.* 1971. (Macmillan.) pp. 94-114.

149 J. C. Cox and R. M. Serjeantson. *The History of the Church of Holy Sepulchre, Northampton.* 1897. (Northampton: Marks.)

150 W. T. Mellows. *The King's Lodging at Peterborough. Annual Report* of Peterborough Natural History Society. 1933.

151 J. Charles Cox. *The Records of the Borough of Northampton,* Vol. II. 1898. pp 170, 256.

152 A. Adcock. *The Boroughs – Northampton. Journal of the Northampton Natural History and Field Club,* Vol. XXI. 1991-2. pp. 162-4.

153 Joan Wake. *The Brudenell's of Deene.* 1953. (Cassell.) pp. 368-9.

154 Cecil Woodham-Smith. *The Reason Why.* 1957. (Constable.) p. 65.

155 Donald Thomas. *Charge! Hurrah! Hurrah! A Life of Cardigan of Balaclava.* 1974. (Routledge & Kegan Paul.) pp. 78-80.

156 *The Northampton County Magazine,* Vol. 3. 1930. p. 103.

157 Lou Warwick. *Theatre Unroyal, or "They Called them Comedians".* 1974.

158 *Gentleman's Magazine,* December 1839, Vol. 12. p. 645.

159 Mr. Serjeant Ballantine. *Some Experiences of a Barrister's Life.* 1882. (London: Richard Bentley.) p. 81.

INDEX